DATE DUE

			PRINTED IN U.S.A.

ENCYCLOPEDIA

OF

Life Sciences

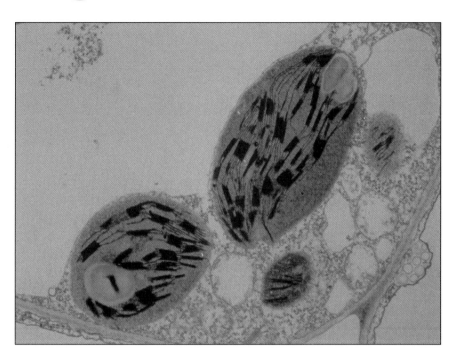

2

Biochemistry – Chemotherapy

Marshall Cavendish
New York • London • Toronto • Sydney

Pittsburgh

Biology education
Kimi Hosoume
Lawrence Hall of Science, University of California, Berkeley

Botany
Dr Nicholas Turland
Department of Botany, Natural History Museum, London

Ecology/Environment
Jefferey Kaufmann, PhD
Irvine Valley College, Irvine, California

Evolution/History of science
Dr James Moore
Open University, Milton Keynes

Immunology
Dr Allison Fryer
Johns Hopkins University, Baltimore

Medicine
David Jacoby, MD
Johns Hopkins University, Baltimore

Microbiology
Professor Rex Kerstetter
Furman University, Greenville, South Carolina

Pharmacology/Biochemistry
Dr Michael Mahalik
Lake Erie College of Osteopathic Medicine, Painesville, Ohio

Zoology
Dr Catherine Allsopp, Michael Amphlett, Dr Elizabeth Bradshaw,
Dr Emilio Herrera, Dr Katrina McCallum,
Dr John Muddeman, Dr Susanne Plesner Jensen,
Dr Claudio Sillero-Zubiri, Dr Kirsten Young
University of Oxford
Adrian Seymour
University of London

Marshall Cavendish Corporation
99 White Plains Road
Tarrytown, New York 10591-9001

© Marshall Cavendish Corporation, 1996

Created by **Brown Packaging Ltd**

Library of Congress Cataloging-in-Publication Data

Encyclopedia of life sciences / Anne O'Daly, editor-in-chief.
     p.   cm.
     Includes bibliographical references and index.
     Summary: An encyclopedia covering the disciplines of
zoology, botany, evolutionary science, medicine, physiology, human
anatomy, cytology, and genetics.
     ISBN 0-7614-0254-3 (set)
     1. Life sciences—Encyclopedias, Juvenile. 2. Biology—
Encyclopedias, Juvenile. [1. Biology—Encyclopedias. 2. Life
sciences—Encyclopedias.] I. O'Daly, Anne, 1966- .
QH302.5.E53   1996
574'.03—dc20   95-18950
                                                         CIP
                                                          AC

Printed in Malaysia
Bound in U.S.A.

PHOTOGRAPHIC CREDITS

Allsport: *241.*
Biophoto Associates: *147, 151, 158, 187, 188, 189 (both), 196, 200,
220, 224 (both), 234, 237, 242, 259, 260, 275, 278, 279, 282.*
C.M. Dixon: *175.*
Frank Lane Picture Agency: *152, 154, 155, 156, 157, 160, 165, 166,
167, 177, 179, 180, 183, 184, 185, 186, 197, 214, 216, 217, 218, 219,
221, 222, 228, 229 (both), 230, 231, 232, 233 (both), 246, 249, 250,
252, 253, 254, 255, 258, 261, 262, 263, 264, 265, 266, 267, 268, 281,
284, 285, 286.*
Mary Evans Picture Library: *201.*
Hulton Deutsch Collection: *192.*
Images Colour Library: *235, 236.*
Natural History Photographic Agency: *153.*
Science Photo Library: *170, 176, 194, 207, 210, 227, 245, 287.*
Telegraph Colour Library: *247.*
University of Utah: *161.*

ARTWORK CREDITS

Bill Botten: *162, 163, 169, 171, 172, 173, 174, 178, 188, 190, 193,
198, 202, 203, 206, 209, 212, 213, 215, 226, 239, 243, 248, 256 (insets
tr & bl), 257, 269, 271, 272, 274, 276, 277.*
Jennie Dooge: *159, 182, 241, 244, 251, 279.*
Marshall Cavendish, London: *199, 204, 205, 211, 256 (main artwork).*

Title page illustration: a typical plant cell seen under the electron
microscope

CONTENTS

Biochemistry	149		Calcium	224
Biological control	152		Calorie	226
Bioluminescence	154		Camouflage and mimicry	228
Biomes and habitats	157		Cancer	234
Bionics	161		Carbohydrates	238
Biorhythms	165		Carbon cycle	243
Biosphere	169		Carbon dioxide	247
Biotechnology	170		Carnivores	248
Birds	177		Carnivorous plants	255
Birds of prey	183		Carotenes	258
Blood	187		Cartilage	259
Bone	197		Cats	261
Botany	200		Cave habitats	265
Brain	202		Cells	269
Bulbs and corms	212		Cellulose	279
Butterflies and moths	214		Centipedes and millipedes	281
Cacti and succulents	219		Chaparral biome	285
Caecilians	222		Chemotherapy	287

BIOCHEMISTRY

Biochemistry is the study of chemical processes within living organisms

Biochemistry is the chemistry of life: the study of the chemical reactions that take place within any living organism – plant or animal – as it grows, moves, reproduces, takes in nutrients, metabolizes them and, in the end, dies. Although these reactions result eventually in an endproduct, they take place stage by stage, and biochemists try to discover the details of each stage. Carbohydrates, for example, do not break down into carbon dioxide and water in a single reaction: their metabolism occurs in a succession of reactions, some rapid and some relatively slow.

One milestone of 20th-century biochemistry was passed in 1937, when the German biochemist Hans Adolph Krebs proposed the eight-stage citric acid (or Krebs) cycle, an essential part of carbohydrate and fat metabolism (see CITRIC ACID CYCLE).

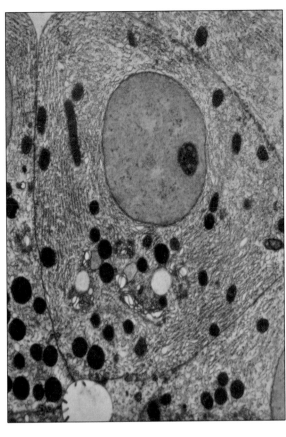

The development of electron microscopy has allowed scientists to discover detailed information on the structure of cells and the sites of biochemical activity enclosed within them. This is an animal cell, from the pancreas of a rat (electron micrograph, x 1875).

CORE FACTS

- Biochemistry is the study of the chemistry of living things.
- Biochemists are concerned to discover the biochemical processes by which energy is stored, transmitted, or consumed by organisms, and to analyze the substances involved.
- Biochemical molecules and processes can be examined by techniques such as ultracentrifuge, chromatography, electrophoresis, radioactive tagging, and x-ray crystallography.

The way biochemists figured out this process is a good example of how they work. Since the cycle was continuous, some way had to be found to interrupt it at each stage, so the product of that stage, and the enzyme involved, could be identified. This was done, either by adding extra quantities of one of the supposed intermediary products, and observing how the rate of the reaction changed, or by adding a substance that would inhibit the action of one enzyme in the cycle, resulting in a buildup of the intermediary product at that point. Biochemists make much use of experimental methods like this.

The biochemist is concerned to discover all the chemical processes by which energy is stored, transmitted, or consumed by organisms. Biochemistry has also been responsible for the development of a wide range of analytical techniques for identifying the substances involved. All living things are built up from water and four basic types of organic molecule: carbohydrates, lipids (derived from fatty acids), amino acids, and nucleotides (of which DNA is composed).

Although much research continues into all branches of the subject, biochemistry has developed most dramatically in the study of proteins or pro-

CONNECTIONS

● The notion of a catalyst in chemical reactions first arose during work on beer **FERMENTATION** in the early 19th century. Biochemists now know that **ENZYMES** are important catalysts in metabolic processes within **CELLS**.

● Chemists once believed that molecules differed between living systems and nonliving systems. However, in the 19th century, scientists recognized that the same laws applied to both. The term organic chemistry describes the study of all compounds that contain carbon and hydrogen.

tein-related substances: enzymes, amino acids, peptides, nucleotides, antigens and antibodies, and genes and gene fragments. Biochemists investigate their physical and chemical structure; how they are involved in the makeup of the surface, or the interior structure, of the living cell; how they can penetrate the cell and affect its metabolism and reproduction; and how metabolic toxins and drugs affect their behavior. They even speculate upon how life began.

Protein engineering

Proteins are made up of one or more chains of amino acids, each linked to the next by what are called peptide bonds, to make polypeptide chains. Some 20 amino acids are found in naturally occurring proteins, and the specific sequence of amino acids in a polypeptide chain is genetically controlled by the cell in which it is synthesized. The size of a protein can range from a molecular weight of only a few thousand (as in hormones such as insulin) to several million in the case of enzyme complexes.

Analysis of proteins can reveal the sequence of amino acids or polypeptide chains of which they are composed, and recent research has turned to the study of how new proteins – modifications of naturally-occurring proteins, or newly designed ones – may be synthesized in the laboratory. These "semisynthetic" enzymes have been produced by attaching other catalyst groups to enzyme molecules, resulting in substances that are up to 200

THE ORIGINS OF LIFE

From earliest times, humans have puzzled over the origin of life. Modern biologists agree that it probably occurred in three stages. First, simple molecules in the Earth's crust and atmosphere reacted together to form complex carbon-containing polymers. Then groups of these polymers began to replicate themselves, and at some point evolved into recognizable living systems. Eventually, biological evolution led to the complexity of the modern living world.

In the 1920s Alexander Oparin, in Russia, and J.B.S. Haldane, in England, suggested – independently of one another – that ultra-violet radiation from the sun, or lightning discharges in the atmosphere, might have brought about the synthesis of life-precursor compounds such as amino acids, nucleic acid bases, and sugars. In 1953, chemists Stanley Miller and Harold Urey from the United States subjected a mixture of water, methane, ammonia, and hydrogen to an electrical discharge for a week, and discovered that significant quantities of amino acids and other organic substances were synthesized.

Further experiments, varying the mixture of gases, have produced many other amino acids. So far, no synthetic substance has the ability to replicate itself. However, following the discovery that nucleic acids can direct the formation of molecules like themselves, it has been suggested that they were the original life forms. Recent research has shown that some species of RNA have catalytic properties like enzymes; current theory is that proteins and DNA were only subsequently formed. The final stage would be the organization of such substances into cells, but how this arose is presently unknown. Biochemists remain hopeful, however, that one day they will discover this mechanism.

A CLOSER LOOK

times as effective as the natural enzyme. In 1984, at Rockefeller University in New York City, the late Emil Kaiser and his colleagues studied calcitonin, a hormone that controls the calcium level in the bloodstream, and produced a molecule that differed from the natural hormone by 60 percent of its polypeptide segments. Natural calcitonin is used in the treatment of Paget's disease, in which the bones are deformed, but it must be given by intravenous injection, because it is destroyed by enzymes in the stomach. The synthetic form was specially designed to resist this enzyme degradation and could be administered orally.

DNA is divided by genetic engineers into segments using so-called restriction enzymes, or nucleases, of which only a limited number are known. Biochemists have been able to develop semisynthetic nucleases that will split DNA at new, specific, points. During the late 1980s, at Genencor, a San Francisco-based joint venture of Genentech and Corning Glass Works, biochemists succeeded in changing the identity of one or more amino acids in a protein molecule by making small changes in the part of DNA holding the genetic code for that protein. In this way any one amino acid can be substituted by any of the other 19 common amino acids.

The research group created nearly 300 variants of the enzyme subtilisin, which is similar to the enzyme used in detergents, and found that several were more resistant to heat, bleach, and strongly alkaline conditions than natural subtilisin. Without a precise knowledge of the function of each amino acid at its point in the chain, however, research of this kind can be "hit or miss." Computer programs have therefore been designed that seek to predict the effect of such amino acid substitutions.

ANALYTICAL TOOLS OF BIOCHEMISTRY

Ultracentrifuge

When biochemists first began to study individual proteins, they found it very difficult to separate them from the material of which they formed a part. A Swede named The Svedberg came up with the answer around 1925. It was known that particles of different masses could be separated by gravitational force (G) in a centrifuge; Svedberg devised the ultracentrifuge, which, rotating at a speed of 45,000 revolutions per minute (rpm), developed a force of 100,000 G. Modern laboratory centrifuges can attain speeds of over 80,000 rpm (developing more than 600,000 G), and experimental models have achieved over one million rpm. These machines can be used to separate mixtures of very large molecules, and they can also be used, by measurement of the rates at which the molecules separate, to calculate their molecular weights.

Chromatography

The second new analytical technique to be developed was chromatography. There are two types: adsorption and ion-exchange chromatography.

The first adsorption form to be developed was paper chromatography. A spot of the mixture to be analyzed is placed near one end of a sheet of filter paper, and a mixture of solvents diffuses through the paper. The rate at which the individual components of the sample move through the paper depends upon their relative solubility in the different solvents, and so they become separated. The paper is then dried and sprayed with an indicator solution that forms a particular color upon reaction with the substance being analyzed.

Another adsorption form is gas chromatography. Here the paper is replaced by an inert powder, something like powdered fire-brick, soaked in a heavy oil, which is packed into a long and narrow column heated to about 392°F (200°C). The sample to be analyzed is flash evaporated into a stream of inert gas such as argon, helium, or nitrogen, and the distance individual components are carried along the tube depends upon their relative solubility in the gas and the oil.

In the ion-exchange technique, the substances to be separated become electrostatically bound to a column of inert material and are then washed out, one by one, by suitable solutions.

Gas chromatography helped researchers from the U.S. Department of Agriculture discover why fire ants carried larvae of the Brazilian wasp *Orasema* back to their nests and looked after them, only to be eaten later by the hatched wasp. Gas chromatography revealed that the chemicals that gave the larvae their particular odor were very sim-

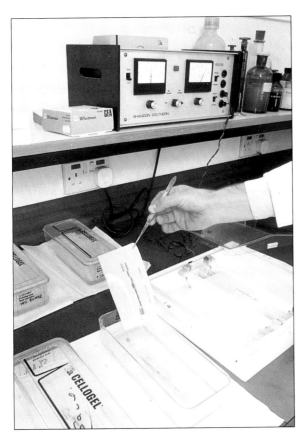

Electrophoresis is used to separate charged molecules in the presence of an electric field. Samples are placed in a slot at one end of an inert porous medium soaked in buffer solution, in this case a pre-cast gel, and an electrical field is produced by direct current (above). Molecules will migrate according to their charge, size, and shape.

ilar to those of the ants themselves, so that the ants did not recognize the larvae as intruders.

Electrophoresis

As it is used today, electrophoresis appears very similar to paper chromatography. A sample is spotted onto a strip of filter paper soaked in liquid, or the surface of a suitable gel – but the difference is that the separation is carried out by a direct current applied across the paper or gel. Each component of the sample moves at a rate dependent upon its electrical charge and molecular size.

Electrophoresis is used to separate the DNA fragments produced by restriction enzymes in the course of DNA typing. The shortest fragments move furthest in the electrical field, and the longest fragments move least. The fragments are transferred from the gel to a nylon membrane; the technique, introduced by Edwin Southern in 1975, is just like drying wet ink with blotting paper, and is therefore known as a "Southern blot."

Radioactive tagging

After Southern blotting, the DNA fragments are "tagged" with a radioactive isotope, so that their positions can be detected by photographic film. This is just one example of the use of isotopes such as tritium (H-3), carbon-14, nitrogen-15, or iodine-125. They can be incorporated into organic molecules, and then traced through complex metabolic pathways. In this way, biochemists have followed the movement of individual carbon atoms in the citric acid cycle.

X-ray crystallography

The photography of crystal structure by means of x-rays was developed by physicists, but is becoming increasingly valuable in biochemistry. For example, confirmation that DNA was a double helix was obtained by x-ray crystallography.

Recent research has aided studies of how aspirin works. It was known that one of aspirin's effects was to inhibit the enzyme prostaglandin H synthase-1, which catalyzes the production of one of the substances that cause inflammation, pain, and fever. Workers at the University of Chicago produced a three-dimensional x-ray crystallograph of the enzyme in 1994, and it was then possible to see how the aspirin molecule fitted into the enzyme molecule and so inhibited prostaglandin synthesis.

Other modern analytical techniques employed by the biochemist include mass spectrometry, which has been used for determining the molecular weight of proteins, and also for investigating the way in which they fold and unfold during chemical reactions; and magnetic resonance imaging, which has been used to observe the effects of therapeutic drugs on the brain.

B. INNES/E. SAREWITZ

See also: AMINO ACIDS; ANALYTICAL TECHNIQUES; CELLS; ENZYMES; FATS AND OILS; PROTEINS.

Further reading:

Gilbert, H. *Basic Concepts in Biochemistry: a Student's Survival Guide.* New York: McGraw Hill, 1992.
Harborne, J.B. *Introduction to Ecological Biochemistry.* 4th edition. San Diego, California: Academic Press, 1993.

HOW IT ALL BEGAN

In Germany, during the 19th century, chemists and medical researchers became very interested in the endproducts of biochemical reactions: substances excreted during metabolism, or that could be isolated from living or dead tissue. This branch of research was called "physiological chemistry," and produced many important breakthroughs. Among these were discovery of the first enzymes, the recognition of proteins, and the purification of many plant and animal products, including a wide range of drugs.

Biochemistry as a separate study began when the physiological chemists started to ask themselves how these endproducts were produced by the living organism, and decided to study the intermediary stages of metabolism. From being almost entirely a German science, biochemistry spread gradually to Britain and the United States. The first American professor of biochemistry was appointed at Yale in 1898, and soon other departments were set up, not only in medical schools but in agricultural colleges.

DISCOVERERS

BIOLOGICAL CONTROL

Biological control is the use of natural biological systems in pest control

The Cottony-cushion scale insect (Icerya purchasi) on a citrus branch.

Almost half the world's agricultural output is destroyed, either before the harvest or during storage, by animal and plant pests. Biological control is a set of agricultural techniques designed to eradicate such pests using biological methods. It is a safer, cheaper alternative to chemical pesticides, the main method for controlling pests since the end of World War II.

In addition to being expensive, the wide use of chemicals has caused many environmental problems. Chemical pesticides are nonspecific: as well as killing pests, they may attack the pests' natural enemies. Without this natural control, the pest population recovers more quickly and so more pesticide is needed. Pests may eventually develop a resistance to a pesticide, so the pesticide is no longer as effective.

Many believe we should return to more traditional methods of pest control, using biological weapons. Some of these methods are based on biological principles and use the pest's natural enemies to control the pest population. These methods are

usually cheaper than chemical control. Unlike chemicals, which must be sprayed year after year to continue to be effective, biological control agents are living organisms that reproduce themselves. Thus, after an initial treatment, the effects of the pest control can continue indefinitely.

If used correctly, biological control causes little harm to the environment. But ecosystems are carefully balanced, and the introduction of a new species can disrupt this balance. Following are the main methods of biological control.

Classical biological control

One of the most common uses of biological control is to combat a pest that has been accidently introduced to a new area. Without its natural enemies, the pest population quickly increases and can cause significant damage to crops.

One of the first pests to be controlled biologically was the Cottony-cushion scale insect (*Icerya purchasi*). In 1887 the citrus fruit industry in California was almost destroyed by this pest. Citrus trees had been imported from Australia in the 1850s and must have come infected with the scale insect, but without any of the insect's natural predators. Entomologist Albert Koebele went to Australia to track down the Cottony-cushion scale's predators. He returned with a ladybug called the Vedalia (*Rodolia cardinalis*), which he identified as the Cottony-cushion scale's natural enemy. In 1889, 129 of these beetles were released onto an infected orange tree near Los Angeles. Within two years the Cottony-cushion scale insect had been eliminated as a pest on citrus trees. The total cost of the project was less than $5000 and the estimated savings ran into millions of dollars per year.

Control by sterilization

Genetic control involves the mass rearing of sexually sterile individuals, which are then released into the pest population. After they mate with wild individuals, the pests either fail to produce offspring, or the resulting offspring are unable to reproduce. This method has been used successfully to control the screwworm, a serious pest of cattle in the southern part of the United States. The screwworm is actually the maggot stage of the fly *Cochliomyia hominivorax*. The female fly mates just once with the male, taking a supply of sperm, which she uses to fertilize all her eggs for the rest of her egg-laying life. Adult males are raised in a factory and sterilized by radiation. When these sterile males mate with wild females, the resulting offspring are unable to breed.

CONNECTIONS

- **AGRICULTURE** developed in Egypt around 17,000 years ago. Since then, many different methods of pest control have been developed. It is only since the end of World War II that chemical **PESTICIDES**, such as **DDT**, have been widely used. These have had a detrimental effect on **ECOSYSTEMS**. The 1970s saw a return to natural methods of pest control.

- Recent technology has made it possible to link biological control with **GENETIC ENGINEERING** techniques. The result is that today, pest management includes methods such as crop rotation, which have been practiced by farmers for thousands of years.

CORE FACTS

- Over 4 billion lb (1.8 billion kg) of chemical pesticides are used each year to control pests.
- Biological control may incorporate the use of the pest's natural enemies.
- Modern techniques use genetic engineering to breed plants resistant to pests.
- Biological control can be combined with selective use of chemicals in a broad approach called integrated pest management.

Pheromonal control

Pheromones are chemical agents used by organisms to control behavior, including movement, mating, and aggregation. As a form of biological control, scientists can isolate pheromones and use them to disrupt mating in pest populations. In Pakistan, pheromones are being used to protect cotton crops from attack by bollworm moths (*Heliothis* spp.). A synthetic pheromone has been produced that mimics the scent released by the females. Plastic twist ties containing the synthetic pheromone are placed around the cotton stems where they "drown out" the natural female scent. This confuses the males, making it more difficult for them to find the females and breed.

Varietal control

Molecular biologists are developing plants that have a built-in resistance to pests. The plants are selectively bred to incorporate physical or chemical features that can protect against pest damage. Scientists found that the Cotton boll weevil (*Anthonomous grandis*) was attracted to cotton because the plants contain a chemical called gossypol. When new cotton strains were selectively bred to contain low levels of gossypol, the weevils ignored the plants. Unfortunately, it became clear that the gossypol had been acting as a repellent to other insects, which then became secondary pests.

Biotechnology and pest control

New methods of biological control include gene splicing, gene cloning, and gene synthesis to breed resistant genes into plants. These techniques are used to breed into plants genes that are resistant to pests. Peruvian scientists are trying to incorporate a gene from the bacteria *Bacillus thuringiensis* into potatoes. This bacteria produces a protein that kills insect pests by dissolving the wall of their gut.

Integrated pest management

Integrated pest management (IPM) takes a broad approach to reducing our dependence on chemical pesticides. It uses a combination of techniques, including disease-resistant crop varieties, biological control, crop rotation, and selective chemical control. If pesticides are used, their application is carefully timed to catch the insect pest when it is most vulnerable or to avoid harming natural predators. There are at present more than 200 successful IPM programs worldwide. Approximately 20 percent of United States cropland is currently under IPM. An IPM program established in 1978 to control cotton pests in the San Joaquin valley in California reduced overall pesticide use by 50 percent. The program included the use of alfalfa as a "trap crop." A cotton pest, the Lygus bug (*Lygus hesperus*), is more attracted to alfalfa than cotton. When strips of alfalfa were planted among the cotton plants, the pest moved away from the cotton and onto the alfalfa.

In parts of India, IPM was introduced after the mosquitoes that carry malaria developed a resistance to the usual insecticides. People were encouraged to clear up the thousands of cesspits, open drains, swamps, and wells where the mosquitoes bred. The wells were stocked with fish that feed on mosquito larvae. In 1986, in Pondicherry, the number of bites had been reduced by 90 percent and the incidence of malaria had also fallen.

The Cane toad, which was imported into Australia to deal with the Grayback cane beetle. Today the toads themselves are considered pests. They have many uses, however. They are often used as laboratory animals in schools and universities, their skin is used to make leather goods, and some are even kept as pets.

Disadvantages of biological control

With all the advantages of biological control, why do farmers continue to use chemical pesticides? One main reason is that biological control is a long-term technique and does not give the fast results of the chemical method. In addition, biological control uses processes that we still do not fully understand, and there is no guarantee of success.

The introduction of the Cane toad (*Bufo marinus*) to Australia is one example of biological control gone wrong. The toad had been introduced to cane fields in Puerto Rico in the 1920s, where it was reported to have eaten large numbers of sugar cane pests. In 1935, 100 toads were imported to Australia from Central and South America to combat the Grayback cane beetle (*Dermolepeida albohirtum*), a pest of sugar cane plants. The toads bred quickly, producing more than 1.5 million eggs, of which 62,000 grew to adult size and were released in selected areas of Queensland. Unfortunately, the toads ignored the cane beetles, preferring to eat the insects' natural predators. As well as failing to deal with the original pest problem, the toads had a high reproductive rate and spread rapidly, soon becoming pests on crops and in gardens.

C. FORMAGGIA

See also: GENETIC ENGINEERING; PESTICIDES.

Further reading:
Gay, K. *Cleaning Nature Naturally.* New York: Walker, 1991.

BIOLUMINESCENCE

Bioluminescence is the production of light by living organisms

Bioluminescence is the production of light by living things, a phenomenon that has fascinated humans since at least the time of Aristotle in the 4th century BC. It occurs in a wide variety of creatures, although it is most common in marine organisms, including some jellyfish, crustaceans, insects, and vertebrates such as deep-sea fishes. There are even several examples of bioluminescent mushrooms. In fact, what interests biologists is not just the ability of living organisms to produce light, but the great number of unrelated species that can do so. Some scientists believe that bioluminescence may have evolved independently over 30 times in the history of the Earth.

The eerie glow produced by most bioluminescent organisms is due to a biochemical reaction that occurs when a substance called luciferin is broken down in the presence of oxygen and the enzyme luciferase. The luciferin and luciferase in one species may be different from those in another, but the chemical reaction is basically the same. This reaction is very efficient in terms of energy. Virtually all the chemical energy is converted into light energy, without emission of heat. For this reason bioluminescence is often referred to as "cold light."

Light sources

Some bacteria, for example those in the genera *Vibrio* and *Photobacterium,* emit light. These bacteria may be free-living, or they may have established a symbiotic relationship with a host organism (see SYMBIOSIS AND COMMENSALISM). For example, some luminous bacteria live in pouches located beneath the eyes of certain species of fish, often known collectively as "lantern eyes." One such fish, *Photoblepharon palpebratus,* lives in shallow waters in the East Indian seas; similar species live in the deep ocean and are often called "flashlight fishes." As long as there is oxygen in the pouches the bacteria glow continuously, but the fish can rotate the light organ, or shut out the light with a black membrane, giving the impression of a blink.

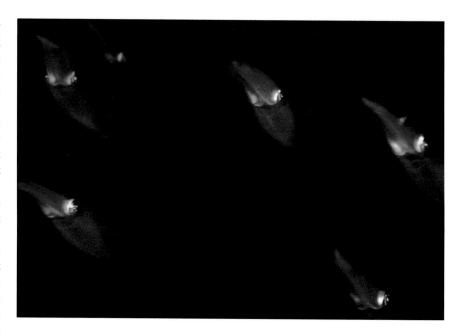

Bioluminescence is particularly common in marine animals such as these Common squid (Loligo vulgaris).

In some other cases, the light is produced by the organism itself, rather than by bacteria, and by means of specialized light-producing cells called photocytes. These cells are usually clumped together, backed by a layer of reflecting cells, and covered by a transparent epidermis, to form luminous organs called photophores.

FUNCTIONS OF BIOLUMINESCENCE

Why has the ability to produce light developed in such a wide variety of organisms?

An aid to vision

A basic function of bioluminescence in large animals is to enable the creature to see clearly in poor light. Some bioluminescent fish forage over coral reefs on dark nights, moving in a school to illuminate their prey. When some species of fish are placed in aquaria that do not contain the bacteria essential for their luminescence, they have difficulty locating food and must be supplied with artificial lighting.

Attraction of prey

Another function of bioluminescence is the attraction of prey. One creature that uses such a tactic is the larva of the New Zealand fungus gnat (*Arachnocampa luminosa*), also known as the glowworm. This tiny creature lives in a tube of mucus, which it suspends from the roof of a cave, the underside of a bridge, or some similar dark location. There it glows continuously, attracting various night-flying insects, which fly close and become entangled in the sticky threads that hang below the transparent tube. Once they can feel the vibration of the struggling prey, the larvae haul them up by the threads and promptly eat them.

CONNECTIONS

● Bioluminescence may be used by animals as an aid to **DEFENSE** or **COURTSHIP,** or simply as a means of **COMMUNICATION** between individuals.

● ATP is the molecule that provides the **ENERGY** needed for the bioluminescent reaction to occur. It is formed in **CELLS** by the breakdown of **CARBOHYDRATES.**

● The components of the photophores in luminescent animals are much like those in a flashlight, which contains a light bulb, backed by a reflector, and covered by a transparent lens.

Identification and courtship

Bioluminescence is also a form of identification in some organisms, allowing members of the same species to recognize each other. To enable organisms to recognize each other more easily, the photophores are sometimes arranged in a complex pattern along the body, and the animal may use a precise sequence of light flashes as a kind of code.

Identification is especially important at mating time. Many creatures, such as tiny marine crustaceans in the genus *Vargula*, use bioluminescence in their courtship rituals. At twilight, the males swim rapidly through the sea, emitting a chain of luminescent pulses. The females are attracted to these displays, and swim toward the males to mate. There is even evidence of a relationship between eyesize and the complexity of display in *Vargula* – those species that use particularly complicated displays usually have large eyes.

Some marine worms also use bioluminescence as a means of communication between males and females. A few nights after a full moon, female Syllid worms (belonging to the genus *Odontsyllis*) swim together in tight circles, giving out a green luminescent cloud. The males are attracted to this display and produce short, intermittent flashes. During this exchange the worms release eggs and sperm into the luminous cloud; zoologists believe the males' flashes may actually trigger the release of eggs from the female.

Defense

Another function of bioluminescence may be to deter potential attackers, who are often startled by the bright flashes in the darkness. The luminescence

also draws attention to the predator and makes it vulnerable to its own enemies.

Many species of bioluminescent echinoderms, such as starfish and sea urchins, use light defensively. The typical pattern of light production in these creatures is 8-10 flashes per second, which travel down each arm, although some of the ophiuroids (brittle stars and basket stars), use more rapid flashing. The luminescence persists even in an arm that has been torn off by a predator, perhaps to give the prey time to escape.

Indeed, experiments have shown that flashing lights do deter predators, particularly in low-light conditions, and some ophiuroids may gather in large

---

BIOLUMINESCENCE AND TECHNOLOGY

In some light-producing organisms the bioluminescent reaction cannot occur until the luciferin is activated. This requires a special biological molecule called ATP, which is involved in the process of carbohydrate breakdown in cells (see ENERGY). The best known example of this is in the firefly. The combination of luciferin, luciferase, and ATP, with the easily detectable product – light – enables the reaction to be used in modern technology. For example, firefly luciferin and luciferase can be added to blood stored in blood banks to test for freshness. If the blood has been kept too long the red cells break down, releasing ATP and initiating the bioluminescent reaction, causing the blood to glow in the dark.

Firefly luciferin and luciferase can also be used to test food for bacterial contamination. The food is treated with an enzyme called apyrase, which breaks down any ATP present in the food but leaves any bacterial ATP intact. If luciferin and luciferase are then added, and the food gives off light, it is clear that it is contaminated. This test can produce results in minutes, whereas more traditional techniques may take days.

SCIENCE AND SOCIETY

FIREFLIES

The best known form of insect bioluminescence is that of the family of night-flying beetles called the Lampyridae, also known as fireflies. These insects have luminescent organs on the tips of their abdomens, which contain light-producing chemicals. Most species of firefly produce a greenish-yellow light, although some produce an orange or red glow.

Many fireflies use their light simply to see where they are flying on dark nights. Others use it for communication. In particular, male fireflies use flashes of light to communicate with females at mating time. There are over 100 different species of firefly in the United States, but each one has a unique pattern of flashes, so that males and females of a species can recognize each other.

Once a female has spotted a male of her species, she responds with a matching sequence of flashes and the male answers her with his original code. The dialogue continues in this way, until the male homes in on the female and they mate.

In North America, the females of some species of firefly, such as those in the genus *Photuris*, are carnivorous; their main food is the males of other firefly species. These females use their light organs to mimic the coded flashes of females of the other species. When the males approach, the females catch, dismember, and eat them.

Despite their name, fireflies are actually beetles in the family Lampyridae. They carry light-producing chemicals in their abdomens.

A CLOSER LOOK

FISHING WITH LIGHT

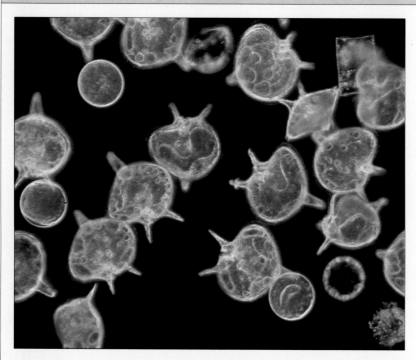

Fishermen have long known that lights flashed on the surface of the water attract fish, and have used this fact to their advantage. However, for many years they have also used the skin of bioluminescent animals, such as squid, as bait. This type of lure is most effective in deep-water fishing, where the bright lights produced by the skin are more likely to attract fish swimming in the dark depths of the ocean. Dinoflagellates (*Peridinium depressum*), shown above, are also used by fishermen when night fishing. The dinoflagellates flash when they are in danger from predators, and in the process reveal the location of schooling fish.

A CLOSER LOOK

numbers to enhance the warning effect. As there are no known photoreceptors (cells that react to light) in ophiuroids, and hence no way in which they "see," it appears that the luminescence is used solely to deter predators, rather than to communicate with each other.

Some mollusks, particularly cephalopods such as squid, eject luminous material into the water to confuse or frighten their enemies. This material is made up of luminescent bacteria that live in special photophores arranged along the squid's body and can be released when the animal is disturbed. The photophores are often arranged in complex patterns and the light may be a variety of colors. A similar defensive tactic is employed by ctenophores, or comb jellies.

Dinoflagellates are a group of one-celled organisms in the kingdom Protista, which dwell mostly in marine environments. These microscopic creatures produce light flashes, each lasting approximately 100 milliseconds. The flashes startle predators, such as tiny crustaceans called copepods, long enough for the dinoflagellates to escape. Another consequence of this defensive flashing is that the dinoflagellates act as a kind of "burglar alarm,"

revealing the presence of the predators, and making them visible to their own predators.

Camouflage

Counter-illumination is another important function of light organs in some fishes, in shrimp species, such as *Sergestes*, and in squid belonging to the genera *Abralia* and *Abraliopsis*. Here, light produced from photophores along the underside reduces shadowing when the animal is lit from above (by sunlight entering the water), making the animal less visible to predators below. The intensity or wavelength of the light produced by the organism can be adjusted according to the surrounding light conditions (see CAMOUFLAGE).

Luminescent bacteria

There are many advantages to bioluminescence: light may aid courtship, attract prey, act as camouflage, deter potential predators, and illuminate dark surroundings. However, light takes a large amount of energy to produce, and it is not so clear what value bioluminescence is to bacteria.

Some scientists think that luminescent bacteria on food may use their light to attract predators, and therefore be transferred to a new nutritious environment – the predator's gut. Others suggest that the light emitted by bacteria, and some fungi, does not serve any real purpose and is simply the by-product of their metabolism.

K. HOSOUME/J. KAUFMANN

See also: BACTERIA; COMMUNICATION; COURTSHIP; DEFENSE; ENERGY; SYMBIOSIS AND COMMENSALISM.

Further reading:

Barkan, J. *Creatures That Glow*. New York: Doubleday, 1991.
Physical Methods for Microorganism Detection. Edited by Wilfred H. Nelson. Boca Raton, Florida: CRC Press, 1991.
Presnall, Judith Janda. *Animals That Glow*. New York: F. Watts, 1993.

EARLY STUDIES IN BIOLUMINESCENCE

Bioluminescence has been a focus of study since the earliest days of scientific thinking. Aristotle, living in the 4th century BC, noted the light-emitting nature of decomposing flesh (due to the presence of luminous bacteria). Over the centuries luminous wood, roots, potatoes, fish, and even cheese have been described (the luminescence here is due to light-emitting fungi). Other ancient cultures would have observed bioluminescence and speculated as to its origins. One of the first known studies of bioluminescence was by Athanasius Kircher (1601-1680), a German Jesuit priest. In 1676, the Dutch lens grinder Antonie van Leeuwenhoek discovered tiny organisms, now known to be bacteria and protozoa, which he called "animalcules." In his book *The Microscope Made Easy*, published in 1743, Henry Baker suggested that it was these tiny organisms that produced the light.

DISCOVERERS

BIOMES AND HABITATS

A biome is a region of the Earth characterized by climate and with distinctive plant and animal life

When you look down from an airplane the Earth seems to be covered with large distinct areas, such as forests, deserts, and oceans, which fit together like an enormous jigsaw. Each of the jigsaw pieces is called a biome. A biome is an extensive region with a distinct combination of animals and plants. There are many different biomes covering the face of the Earth. The boundaries between biomes are distinguished by climate, in particular the average annual temperature and precipitation. The type of vegetation depends on the climate; the vegetation in turn determines the animal life found there.

A biome is made up of different habitats. A habitat is where an organism lives. For example, an earthworm's habitat is the soil, and that of a pine tree includes the soil in which it grows as well as the space above and around the tree. The organisms that live in a habitat form its community.

The biomes of the Earth make up the biosphere, the region of the Earth that supports life.

McKinley Park, Alaska. Although most of the year the tundra is completely covered in ice and snow, in summer the sun melts the surface of the ground, allowing water to collect in ponds, lakes, and marshes.

CORE FACTS

- Terrestrial biomes can be divided up depending on their climates and distinctive plants and animals.
- Aquatic biomes are classified according to the amount of dissolved salts and dissolved oxygen in the water, as well as the amount of light penetration.
- The main terrestrial biomes are: tundra, taiga, temperate forest, temperate shrubland, tropical rainforest, grassland, and desert.

TERRESTRIAL BIOMES

There are various ways of dividing the Earth into biomes. The major land biomes are: tundra, taiga, temperate forest, temperate shrubland, tropical rainforest, grassland, and desert. The polar regions are not usually considered biomes. The extreme polar regions have no real habitats. Wildlife in polar regions is mainly limited to the edges.

Tundra

The tundra is extremely cold and has little precipitation. The average annual temperature ranges from 32 to -13°F (0 to -25°C), while the average annual precipitation is about 5 in (12 cm). The tundra is the furthest north of the terrestrial biomes, stretching between the taiga and the permanent ice and snow of the polar regions. The southern hemisphere has no tundra.

Tundra crosses the northern regions of North America, Asia, Europe, and Greenland. It is covered with snow for up to nine months of the year. The growing season is about two months long. During this period a few inches of the tundra's thin and rocky soil thaw, but a layer of constantly frozen soil, called permafrost, lies just below. The days are very long in the short growing season. Above the Arctic Circle, at midsummer, the sun does not set, while at midwinter, it does not rise.

There are no trees in the tundra. The permafrost prevents the roots of large plants from becoming established. Instead, there are low woody shrubs, such as spruce, pine, and willow, as well as numerous mosses, lichens, grasses, and flowering herbaceous plants.

Few animals live in the tundra all year round: the Snowy owl and Arctic hare are rare exceptions. The birds and mammals of the tundra are homeotherms – animals that can maintain the constant, high body temperature that is essential for their survival in the extremely cold conditions. Caribou, Musk oxen, and Arctic foxes migrate to the tundra in the summer.

Taiga

The taiga, sometimes called the coniferous forest biome, is possibly the largest of all the biomes. It lies just south of the tundra and covers northern portions of North America, Asia, and Europe. Warmer and wetter than the tundra biome, the average annual temperature in the taiga ranges from 14 to 59°F (-10 to 15°C); annual precipitation ranges from 12 to 27 in (30 to 70 cm).

The trees of the taiga are almost all cold-resisting conifers such as pines, spruces, and firs. These trees have adaptations that allow them to survive in soil that is frozen for a large part of the year. Their needle-shaped leaves have a very small surface area, which cuts down water loss. In fact, the taiga is the coldest environment that full-sized trees can tolerate.

The taiga has no permafrost and so the thawing of the soil in summer can lead to swampy con-

---

CONNECTIONS

- The **BIOSPHERE** is the part of the Earth's air, land, soil, and waters that supports life. It is made up of all the different types of biomes, such as **OCEANS, DESERTS, TUNDRA,** and **TROPICAL RAINFORESTS.**

- As the Earth revolves around the sun, the tilt of the Earth's axis changes the way sunlight falls on the Earth. This uneven heating of the Earth's surface produces different climate patterns and, therefore, different biomes.

ditions. The growing season is longer and warmer than in the tundra. There is plenty of animal life. Moose, Black bears, elk, Snowshoe hares, Red squirrels, and porcupines live in the taiga. Birds include nuthatches, chickadees, crossbills, waterfowl, hawks, and eagles.

Temperate forests

There are two types of temperate forest: deciduous and rainforest. In the northern hemisphere the temperate deciduous forest lies just south of the taiga. It crosses most of the United States and parts of Europe and Asia. Originally all of the eastern United States and almost all of Europe and Asia were completely covered by forest. Much of it has been cut down for lumber or cleared for farming. In the southern hemisphere this biome stretches across Tasmania, the eastern coast of Australia, and New Zealand.

There are four well-defined seasons in temperate deciduous forests, with a temperature range of about 27 to 84°F (-3 to 29°C). Average annual rainfall is around 39 in (100 cm). The moderate climate produces a growing season of up to six months. The trees found in this biome are mainly deciduous (they shed their leaves). There are maples, birches, oaks, beeches, and hickorys.

The vegetation supports a tremendous variety of animal life. There are many mammals, including bears, deer, squirrels, mice, shrews, raccoons, and squirrels. Reptiles are represented by turtles, snakes, and lizards. There are also large numbers of amphibians such as frogs, toads, and salamanders.

The temperate rainforest runs along the Pacific Ocean on the northwest coast of North America. It is also found in southeastern Australia and southern South America. High rainfall, thick coastal fog, and wet winds from the ocean give this biome a very high humidity. The humidity, high rainfall, and moderate temperatures produce a rainforest in a temperate zone.

MOUNTAIN ZONES

Climbing a mountain is like traveling north from the equator. The temperature drops as you get higher up the mountain, and the types of plants change with the temperature. Depending upon the location, mountains have a variety of biomes, or zones, in a sequence similar to those from the equator to the poles. The animals and plants inhabiting these zones are ecologically equivalent to species found in the equivalent biomes. The base of a mountain in a temperate region might be covered in deciduous trees. Higher up, the temperature drops, and the vegetation changes to coniferous forest. Higher still, the climate becomes more severe and a kind of tundra occurs. At the top of the mountain there might be permanent ice or snow similar to the polar ice sheets.

Most of the trees are conifers. They include the Western red cedars, Western hemlocks, Douglas firs, Sitka spruce, and Coast redwoods. The forest is a jungle of ferns, branches of vine maples, and hanging masses of moss, which also cover the forest floor like a sponge. Shrubs such as rhododendron, azalea, and blueberry flourish, as do flowers such as trillium, poppies, and lilies. The animal life includes a range of mammals such as squirrels, elk, and other deer, and large numbers of birds and insects.

Temperate shrubland

Temperate shrublands are found in areas with a Mediterranean climate: hot dry summers and mild wet winters. In California the shrubland is known as chaparral, in Australia it is called heath, in Chile it is the matorral, while in the Mediterranean regions it is called maquis. The vegetation looks very similar in all these areas, although individual plant species differ. The landscape is dominated by drought-resisting evergreen shrubs. Natural fires often rage through the shrubland, particularly in late summer and autumn.

Both plants and animals have adaptations that help them to survive drought and fires. Typical animals include rabbits, mule deer, chipmunks, deer mice, and lizards.

Tropical rainforest

Tropical rainforests have the richest variety of plant and animal life of all the terrestrial biomes. It has been estimated that about half of all the known land species are found in this biome. Tropical rainforests are found along the equator: in Equatorial Africa, Southeast Asia, Central and South America, and parts of Australia. The world's largest tropical rainforest is the Amazon Basin in South America.

This biome is characterized by high temperatures and almost daily precipitation. With strong and constant sunlight, the temperature is close to 77°F (25°C) all year. The annual rainfall is between 80 and 180 in (200 and 450 cm).

The plants include over 400 species of trees, vine-like lianas, and epiphytes (plants that usually grow on other plants and obtain moisture from the air and nutrients from rainwater; see EPIPHYTES).

Mature tropical rainforest has at least three distinct stories, or layers, of vegetation. The top story consists of the crowns of the tallest trees. The middle story is made up of the canopy of leaves that block out sunlight, preventing it from reaching the forest floor. The bottom story comprises smaller plants and tree seedlings.

THE WORLD BIOMES

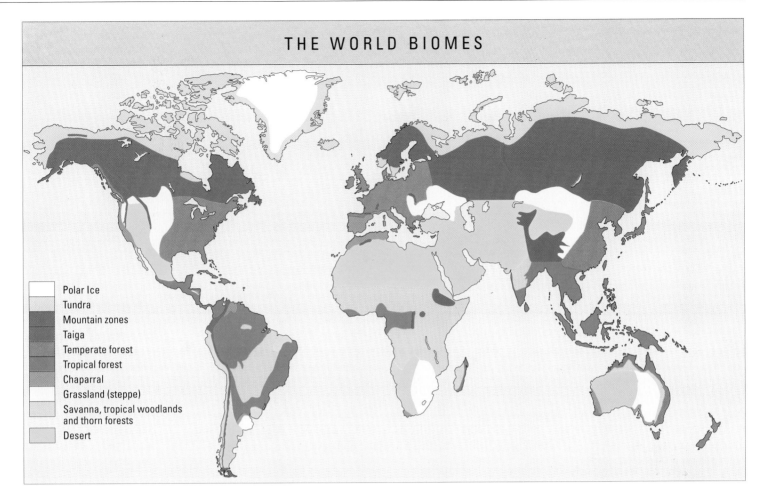

Polar Ice
Tundra
Mountain zones
Taiga
Temperate forest
Tropical forest
Chaparral
Grassland (steppe)
Savanna, tropical woodlands and thorn forests
Desert

There is a diverse range of animal life, especially species that thrive in high humidity, such as leeches, flatworms, giant snails, millipedes, scorpions, and spiders. Reptiles are represented by iguana lizards, anoles, anacondas, and poisonous snakes such as the bushmaster. There are many colorful birds such as parrots, macaws, hummingbirds, and hoatzins. There are mammals such as hutias, capybaras, bats, sloths, spider monkeys, and anteaters. The soil of the tropical rainforests is very poor, and little life exists in the soil itself.

Grassland

Grasslands are known by different names around the world. They are called steppes in Eurasia, veld in South Africa, pampas in Argentina, and savanna in Africa. Grasslands are usually characterized by few trees and many kinds of grasses, although the savanna occasionally sees more rain than other grasslands and can support the growth of scattered trees. Wildlife on grassland includes many insects, and large numbers of herbivorous mammals such as gophers, antelopes, prairie chickens, and jack rabbits. In North America the grasslands are mainly west of the Mississippi River and include prairies (made up of tall grasses) and plains (short grasses).

This biome generally has hot summers and cold winters. The temperature ranges from 32 to 77°F (0 to 25°C) and the annual precipitation is around 30 in (75 cm).

Humans have cut down much of the natural vegetation on grassland and turned the land into agricultural areas. The temperate grasslands are some of the most important agricultural areas on Earth. The rich soil is good for growing grains, such as wheat and corn. For this reason, grasslands in the American midwest and Ukraine have been described as the breadbaskets of the world.

Desert

Deserts cover more than a fifth of the Earth's surface. They all get less than 10 in (25 cm) of rainfall a year, and the evaporation rate is high. Temperatures range from 75 to 91°F (24 to 33°C). Main deserts

This map shows the Earth's major terrestrial biomes. Their distribution depends largely on temperature and precipitation (rain, snow, and sleet).

MIGRATION

Many animals migrate to particular areas for feeding or breeding. Most migrations are local, but in some the animal moves between two completely different biomes. White-tailed and Red deer travel north to the taiga from temperate forests in the summer in search of food. In late spring, porcupines, lynxes, and Red foxes migrate north from the taiga to the tundra. The tundra has only about eight species of birds that live there all year. In the summer well over 100 bird species migrate there from southern regions. In African grasslands large numbers of birds, such as spoonbills, owls, and kestrels, move in from Eurasia and Siberia, seeking winter refuge. After rainfall, many animals migrate to desert biomes looking for food and/or breeding grounds.

Many examples of migration take place in freshwater and marine biomes. Silver trout migrate from the marine biome to the freshwater streams to breed, as do salmon, sturgeons, and lampreys. European eels migrate in the other direction to breed, from rivers to the marine biome. Animals such as seals and sea lions migrate to islands, using these land biomes as places to breed and raise their young, while staying close to food sources in the water (see MIGRATION).

include the Sahara, Gobi, Australian, Arabian, Kalahari, and Great American, which is divided into the Mojave, Sonoran, and Great Basin deserts.

Desert plants and animals survive by adapting to the harsh environment. The plants include grasses and herbaceous plants, which can grow quickly to take advantage of temporary supplies of water. Cacti and other succulents store water in fleshy stems and leaves. Desert animals survive by evading the drought and by cutting down on water loss. Rodents burrow to escape from the intense heat on the surface of the desert. Reptiles' skin is resistant to drying. Reptiles, birds, and small mammals can absorb water from their wastes before excretion.

AQUATIC BIOMES

In the aquatic biomes, the main determinants of plant and animal life are salinity (the concentration of dissolved salts), the amount of dissolved oxygen in the water, and light. Water biomes include marine and estuary biomes, and freshwater biomes, such as lakes, ponds, and rivers.

Aquatic organisms fall into three groups. Plankton are small or microscopic organisms that float on the surface of the water. Nekton are larger organisms and stronger swimmers than the plankton. Benthos live at the bottom, either rooted to one spot or crawling along the floor.

Marine

The marine biome (oceans and seas) covers almost two thirds of the Earth's surface. It has a salt content of between 3 and 3.7 percent. There are far more species and individual organisms in the sea than on land. The most abundant organisms are microscopic crustaceans called copepods, which are members of the plankton group. Marine nekton include fish, squid, and whales, while the benthos group contains starfish, clams, and barnacles.

There are three major marine biome zones, each with its particular population of organisms. The intertidal zone is the shoreline where the land meets the sea. The oceanic zone is the deep open ocean. The neritic zone, containing the most abundant marine life, is the shallow water that lies between the shore and the oceanic zone.

Beneath the oceans lie the coral reef biomes, often likened to the tropical rainforests because of their array of animal and plant life. The reefs are found in warm shallow waters between latitude 30 degrees north and 30 degrees south.

Fresh water

Freshwater biomes can be divided into two groups: standing water biomes, which include lakes, ponds, and swamps, and running water or lotic biomes, which are rivers and streams.

The types of organism in a particular freshwater biome are determined by temperature, turbidity (the amount of suspended particles in the water), amount of dissolved oxygen, amount of dissolved minerals and nutrients, and strength of the current.

Estuaries

Estuaries are found where streams and rivers flow into oceans. They include bays, tidal marsh inlets, and the mouths of rivers. The mixture of salt and fresh water provides an excellent source of nutrients, and the water is usually shallow so that sunlight can penetrate. The combination of nutrients and sunlight is ideal for photosynthesis. Typical organisms include marsh grasses, algae, oysters, barnacles, snails, and phytoplankton.

M. FLEMING

See also: BIOSPHERE; CHAPPARAL BIOME; CONTINENTAL SHELVES; CORAL REEF BIOMES; DESERT BIOMES; GRASSLAND BIOMES; OCEAN HABITATS; POLAR REGIONS; RIVERS AND STREAMS; SAVANNA BIOMES; TAIGA BIOMES; TEMPERATE FOREST BIOMES; TROPICAL RAINFOREST BIOMES; TUNDRA BIOMES.

Further reading:

World Nature Encyclopedia. Texas: Raintree Publishers, 1992.
World Wildlife Habitats. New York: Marshall Cavendish, 1992.

Deserts vary in the amount of rainfall they receive, and this determines what kind of vegetation grows there. Some deserts, such as that in Death Valley in California, are so dry they have almost no vegetation and consist mainly of sand dunes. Others can support some low-growing bushes, as in Monument Valley, Arizona, shown above.

TERRESTRIAL AND AQUATIC INTERACTIONS

The borders shared by land and water biomes are often rich habitats for a wide variety of animals. For example, riverside and pondside habitats are homes to herons, swans, ducks, muskrats, beavers, and many other mammals and birds that feed on aquatic plants and animals. The edges of oceans and seas have tidal zones (also called littoral zones). Some of these are sandy, with populations of sand fleas, clams, crabs, barnacles, algae, tube worms, burrowing urchins, bivalve mollusks, and other organisms that are adapted to survive tidal action, alternate exposure to air and water, temperature changes, and conditions of salinity. Other tidal zones are rocky shores, with inhabitants such as starfish and sea urchins that can cling to rock surfaces.

The interactions between terrestrial and aquatic biomes are not always positive. In South America, as a result of human activity, the Amazon River biome interacts with the rainforest biome in a destructive way. The destruction of the rainforest to provide farmland has led to major annual flooding by the Amazon River, during which the floodwaters penetrate deep into the forests, washing away unprotected soil. This soil ends up filling the riverbeds and choking the river itself.

BIONICS AND BIOMEDICAL ENGINEERING

Bionics is the design and manufacture of artificial body parts, based on the study of how living things work

The human body is a durable machine, capable of repairing itself and running continuously for over a hundred years. But when parts become damaged beyond repair they are very difficult to replace. Bionics is the design and manufacture of artificial body parts, based on the study of how living things work. These body parts include mechanical arms, legs, eyes, ears, and internal organs such as hearts and kidneys.

In bionics, scientists look at the engineering principles by which living things work, such as the construction of an elbow joint or the acoustics of the ear. These must be understood before replacements can be designed. Designing and building the devices is called biomedical engineering, or bio-engineering. The devices are called prosthetic devices or prostheses.

Two of the earliest prosthetic devices can be seen in old pirate movies: wooden pegs to replace lost legs, or hooks for amputated hands. The possible future can be seen in movies such as *The Empire Strikes Back*, where Luke Skywalker's severed hand is replaced with a mechanical hand as good as the original, or *Star Trek, the Next Generation*, in which Captain Jean-Luc Picard of the Starship Enterprise lives with a mechanical heart that seems to require little maintenance.

In the real world, biomedical engineering is still young. Most of today's bionic devices seem crude and unreliable compared to the natural body parts they replace, but that is a normal step in the development of any technology.

CONNECTIONS

● Bionics links engineering principles to an understanding of the human body. Scientists can even design and manufacture complex internal organs such as the **HEART** and **KIDNEYS**.

● The metal titanium is commonly used as a replacement body material because it has an unreactive oxide layer on its surface, which does not provoke a reaction from the **IMMUNE SYSTEM**.

CORE FACTS

■ Bionics is the design and manufacture of artificial body parts, based on the study of how living things work.

■ Artificial body parts include hip replacements, artificial limbs, cardiac pacemakers, and hearing aids.

■ The first artificial heart for a human being was implanted in 1982.

Biomaterials

A major problem for the designers of artificial parts for the human body is finding suitable materials. Human tissues are filled with what amounts to salt water, which will corrode many metals. Plastics and other organic materials are treated by the body as invaders; they are attacked by the immune system or enclosed in scar tissue.

Replacements for bones and joints are often made of titanium, a light, strong metal that resists corrosion. Perhaps the most common prosthetic device today is the titanium ball-and-socket joint to replace a hip joint that has deteriorated due to arthritis. Artificial shoulder, elbow, and knee joints

are becoming more common. Ceramics, plastics, and carbon-fiber materials are also used. A material designed specifically for bone replacement is bioglas, a porous glass that simulates the porous calcium framework of bones. When bioglas is grafted into bone, the body fills the pores with collagen fibers, making a strong resilient bond.

Artificial limbs

The first mechanical hands for amputees came into use after World War I, and the basic principles have not changed much since then. The most common artificial hand is operated by the wearer's own muscles. A strap passes over the shoulder on the side opposite the prosthesis. When the wearer raises the shoulder, the hand opens. The hand may be either a double hook or a simulation of a real hand, in which the thumb and first two fingers may be opened or closed.

Newer artificial arms use an electric motor to open or close the fingers, and sensors that allow the wearer to control the arm by flexing muscles

---

WILLEM JOHAN KOLFF

Moved by the sight of a young man dying of kidney failure, Dr Willem Kolff built the first practical artificial kidney in 1943 in Gröningen, the Netherlands, using cellophane sausage casings to filter the blood. Later he worked on a machine that could pump and oxygenate the blood when a patient's heart was stopped. In 1949 he was the first person to keep an animal alive on the machine.

Dr Kolff emigrated to the United States in 1950 and established the world's first artificial organs program in Cleveland, Ohio. He brought along the idea of the heart-lung machine. The first human patient was treated with the machine in 1955 at the Cleveland Clinic. This was the beginning of open-heart surgery.

In 1967 Dr Kolff helped to develop a pump to be placed in the aorta to assist the heart. This device is used to treat around 300,000 patients each year in the United States. He later moved to the University of Utah and founded the Institute for Biomedical Engineering, now a major center for the development of artificial organs. He is credited with many inventions, but his greatest contributions to bionics may have been as an administrator, getting physicians and engineers to work together.

Dr Kolff retired as director of the Utah Institute in 1986, at the age of 75, but continued to work at the university in his own small laboratory, developing new artificial heart designs.

DISCOVERERS

in the stump. When a muscle contracts it generates a small electric current. Myoelectric sensors (the prefix myo refers to muscles) are placed on the skin above the muscles to detect the current, and a small computer translates the current into a signal to operate the hand. When an arm has been amputated below the elbow, the sensors can be placed over the muscles ordinarily used to open and close the hand. If the arm has been amputated above the elbow the user can learn to control the hand by using muscles in the upper arm, or muscles in the shoulder.

Motor-driven myoelectric arms can also rotate the wrist, and for above-elbow amputees they can move the elbow. Motor-driven hands still use only the thumb and two fingers; there is not enough room in a prosthetic arm for additional motors to operate other fingers, nor is there enough room for the batteries to power them.

There have only been limited experiments with myoelectrically controlled artificial feet and legs. Walking is a very complex operation that requires complicated split-second decisions involving many different muscles. We do it without thinking. Fortunately, most users of ordinary artificial legs get around successfully without high-tech improvements. Research has centered on adding feedback to artificial legs, telling the wearer how hard the leg is pushing against the ground.

Stimulating muscles

Myoelectrically controlled devices have also been used in reverse. A small electric current applied to the skin above a muscle can cause the muscle to contract. This principle has been used to stimulate the leg muscles in people who are paralyzed from the waist down because nerves leading to the muscles have been severed by an accident. The myoelectric stimulators are attached to the inside of a sort of stocking, and are controlled by the wearer through hand switches.

So far, several hundred patients have been fitted with these devices. The movement is jerky, but it is good enough to allow many people to stand and sit, to walk with crutches or a walker, and even to walk up and down stairs. The devices do not replace a wheelchair, however, as most people can only walk a few hundred steps with them. But they do allow enough mobility to enable a person to walk into a building that has no wheelchair ramps, for example.

For people whose arms are paralyzed, similar devices can supply movement to the arms, signaling the hand to open and close. These devices have been fitted to people whose paralysis allows some movement in the upper back and shoulders, so myoelectric sensors attached to the muscles in these areas can be used for control.

Myoelectric stimulators are unreliable: they may slip out of place, and when the patient sweats the electrical conductivity of the skin changes. Some researchers are connecting wires directly to

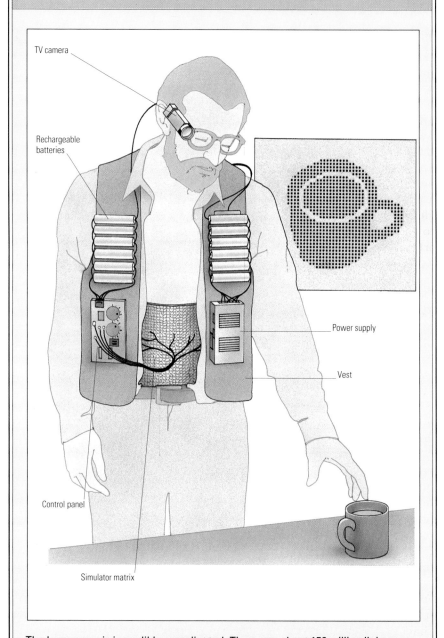

SIGHT FOR THE BLIND?

TV camera
Rechargeable batteries
Power supply
Vest
Control panel
Simulator matrix

The human eye is incredibly complicated. There are about 150 million light-sensitive receptors on the retina (the innermost layer of the eye) connected to a network of microscopic nerve fibers, which relay signals to the visual centers of the brain in ways we still do not completely understand.

But engineers have developed many devices to aid the blind. Some of these convert visual information into touch. The system shown above converts images from a TV camera into a pattern of dots. The pattern is then sent to a receiver, worn on the blind person's stomach or back, that applies pressure to the skin where each dot would be. This creates a pattern of the object on the sensory receiver. Blind people who have tested the device have learned to identify large objects in their path.

Another experimental system uses tiny wires implanted in the visual cortex, the part of the brain that processes signals from the eye. When a current is sent into one of these wires the person "sees" a spot of light, something like the flashes of light you see when you close your eyes and press on the lids. Developers of this system believe that with an array of, for example, 64 by 64 wires, a person could see patterns similar to those on the scoreboards at sporting events.

A CLOSER LOOK

the muscles. Eventually they may be able to implant electrodes completely under the skin, along with a tiny radio receiver that will pick up signals from a transmitter outside the skin.

The mechanical heart

The replacement of a human heart with a heart from someone who has been killed in an accident has become almost routine. But thousands of patients die while waiting for a heart to become available. There are only about 2000 donor hearts each year in the United States, while about ten times that many patients need transplants.

Researchers are trying to perfect a mechanical heart that could be implanted temporarily to keep a patient alive until a real heart can be obtained. However, there will never be enough donor hearts to go around, so the long term goal is a permanent artificial heart.

The first artificial heart for a human being was implanted in Dr Barney Clark, a dentist, on December 2, 1982, at the University of Utah Medical Center. Dr Clark, who was already terminally ill, lived for another 112 days before dying of kidney failure and other problems.

The Jarvik-7 TM heart implanted in Dr Clark consists of two polyurethane plastic chambers. Each chamber is divided by a flexible diaphragm; compressed air is pumped in behind the diaphragm, causing it to expand and push blood out of the chamber through a mechanical valve.

The Jarvik-7 replaces only the right and left ventricles, which do the major work of pumping blood. Compressed air to operate the pumps is brought in through two tubes that enter the patient's lower abdomen. The air compressor is outside the patient's body. A small portable battery-powered compressor allows the patient to move around outside the hospital.

Another type of artificial heart is powered by an electric motor. Power for the motor comes from batteries carried in a belt or shoulder pack, connected to the motor either by wires passing through the skin or from an induction coil outside the body. There is still no power source small enough to fit inside the body that will supply sufficient energy to run an artificial heart. Some researchers have experimented with atomic batteries, which use the energy from a radioactive material to generate electricity.

Many researchers prefer compressed air systems, because an electrical system has many moving parts inside the body for which an operation would be required to make a repair.

The cardiac pacemaker

One of the most widely-used and successful bionic devices is the cardiac pacemaker, which keeps the heart pumping at a steady rate. The pumping of the heart is regulated by a group of cells at the top of the heart called the sinoatrial node, which sends out signals causing the atria and ventricles to con-

tract in the proper sequence. If this signal fails, the heart may beat irregularly or stop. A pacemaker, usually implanted in the upper chest, sends tiny electrical pulses to the heart muscle to keep it beating in time. Modern pacemakers with built-in computers can adjust the heart rate to the body's needs, and even record data on the heart's behavior, which a doctor can read out later.

A variation on the pacemaker is the automatic ventricular defibrillator. Sometimes the heart stops so completely that it needs a sharp jolt (about 100 times as strong as a pacemaker signal) to get it started. The scene in which doctors or paramedics apply such a jolt with two round paddles is common in movies and on television.

For patients whose hearts stop frequently, a device can be implanted that senses the irregularity and applies a pulse of current through wires

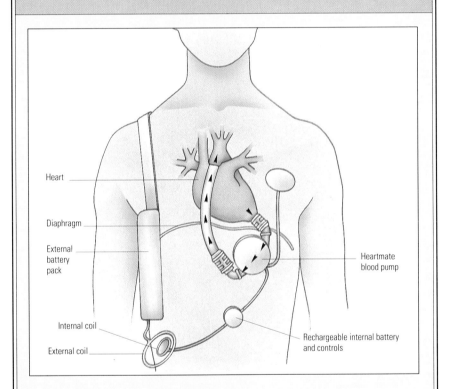

ELECTRIC V.A.D. SYSTEM

Heart
Diaphragm
External battery pack
Internal coil
External coil
Heartmate blood pump
Rechargeable internal battery and controls

The ventricular assist device (V.A.D.) is a pump that assists the heart, rather than replacing it. One type is implanted in the abdomen, just below the diaphragm. A tube attached to the top of the left ventricle draws blood down to the pump, and another tube carries the blood back to the aorta (the major artery leading out of the heart). Blood vessels carrying oxygenated blood are shown in red; vessels carrying deoxygenated blood are shown in blue. Most of the arteries, apart from the pulmonary arteries, carry oxygenated blood.

In the early 1990s ventricular assist devices had been successfully used in several hundred patients as a "bridge" to keep them alive until a transplant became available. Some patients lived very normal lives for almost two years. In some cases the patient's own heart had recovered during its "rest period" so the transplant was unnecessary. Researchers predict that many patients will use these devices as permanent replacements.

A CLOSER LOOK

implanted in the heart muscle. This feels like a sharp blow on the chest, but is preferable to a heart attack. It uses much less current than when defibrillation is done from outside the body.

The artificial kidney

The kidneys serve as filters, removing waste products and excess fluid from the body. When the kidneys are damaged by disease most of the wastes can be removed by an artificial kidney, officially known as a hemodialysis machine (from two Greek words literally meaning "to wash the blood.") About 450,000 Americans with kidney failure remain alive by spending a few hours each week connected to such a machine.

Blood is drawn from an artery in the patient's arm or leg, pumped through the machine, then led back into a nearby vein. In the machine the blood passes through a long tube made of thin plastic, with water circulating outside of it. Blood cells and large protein molecules, such as enzymes and antibodies, cannot pass through the plastic, but small molecules, such as urea (the principal waste product in the blood), can.

The artificial kidney works on the principle of osmosis. In this process, when the concentration of a chemical is high on one side of a membrane and low on the other, water flows through channels in the membrane toward the area of higher concentration to make both sides equal. Fresh water (containing salts in balance with those in the blood) is constantly circulated through the artificial kidney to keep the concentration of waste products low outside the plastic tubes.

Because of the large amount of fluid needed, it is impossible to make an artificial kidney small enough to implant in the body, but small machines are now available that patients can use at home.

Liver and pancreas

Other organs in the body are not so easy to duplicate. The liver is a complex chemical factory that uses enzymes to break down poisons, manufacture vitamins, and do other jobs. Science cannot begin to duplicate these functions, but an experimental liver has been designed that uses cells from pig livers. Like the artificial kidney, the artificial liver is a large device outside the body through which the patient's blood is circulated.

The blood passes over pig liver cells enclosed in a thin plastic membrane. The membrane allows toxins to pass through, but stops the white blood cells of the patient's immune system, which would otherwise attack the pig liver cells. Such artificial liver devices have been used to keep patients alive for short periods until a donor could be found for a liver transplant.

The artificial pancreas also uses animal cells enclosed in a membrane to produce insulin, but it is small enough to implant in the body. The membrane allows nutrients to pass through to the cells, and allows the insulin they manufacture to get out.

NO BIONIC PEOPLE YET...

In the 1970s, a popular television series called 'The Six Million Dollar Man' made the word bionic a part of everyday language, but promised more than biomedical engineers can yet deliver. On the show, astronaut Steve Austin lost both legs, an arm, and an eye in an accident; he was given atomic-powered, superstrong limbs and a TV camera eye with telescopic and infrared vision.

The television show was based on the science fiction novel *Cyborg* by Martin Caidin. Cyborg, short for cybernetic organism, is a word used – so far only in science fiction – to describe a person who is part human and part machine.

The character in Caidin's book was closer to reality than the one in the TV show: he was strong, but could not lift a car or run 60 miles per hour. His artificial eye contained a spy camera whose pictures could be developed later, but he could not actually see with it. Caidin tried not to go too far beyond current technology, but one part of his story may always be science fiction: all the bionic parts were controlled directly by human nerves. While tiny wires have been used to stimulate muscles and the nerves of the inner ear, receiving nerve signals and sending them on to machinery has proved much harder.

Experimenters have tried placing platinum and iridium wires around a nerve to pick up the tiny electric current that flows when the nerve is activated. In animal experiments, this method has detected and identified nerve signals. But the implants do not last. The body treats them as foreign objects and walls them off by surrounding them with scar tissue. Eventually this insulates the implants from the nerve currents.

If a method could be found to connect wires to nerves, it could restore movement to persons who are paralyzed when nerves in the spinal cord are severed. Such a method would also allow us to fulfill another science fiction prediction and connect the human brain directly to a computer.

The bionic ear

The hearing aid is one of the best-known products of bioengineering. It usually fits in the ear, or just behind it, and transmits sound waves through the bones of the skull to the inner ear.

A hearing aid amplifies sounds, so it is of no use to a person who cannot hear at all. However, some deaf people can use another prosthetic device, a cochlear implant, which electrically stimulates the nerves leading from the ear to the brain. As with the eyes, it is impossible to send signals as complex as those sent by the natural system, which can detect sounds from about 20 to 20,000 cycles per second. Cochlear implants usually use only sounds in the speech range (up to about 3000 cycles per second), and break this range into about ten channels. While this seems very limited, people with cochlear implants can learn to understand speech and can hear sirens and horns. The implant makes lipreading easier and helps deaf people monitor their own speaking voices. Some people can even tell one person's voice from another.

W. STEELE

See also: CYBERNETICS; EARS; EYES; FEET; HANDS; HEART; KIDNEYS; LIFE SUPPORT; LIVER AND GALL BLADDER; PANCREAS.

Further reading:

Blume, S. *Insight and Industry: On the Dynamics of Technological Change in Medicine.* Cambridge, Massachusetts: MIT Press, 1992.

BIORHYTHMS

Biorhythms are natural rhythms of cyclic changes in an organism's behavior or physiology

Humans and many other animals have always responded to light and dark, generally hunting by day and sleeping by night, except for nocturnal creatures, which reverse this pattern. However, we have only recently become aware that these rhythms, and the many other rhythms and cycles throughout the living world that are all known as biorhythms, are not just responses to external conditions but actually preprogrammed internal responses. These cyclic changes, in which organisms adapt to regular changes in their environment by modifying their behavior or physiology in a periodic rhythm, may be daily cycles, such as sleep; monthly cycles, such as human menstruation; and yearly cycles, such as migration and hibernation.

Many animals demonstrate annual rhythms of behavior, of which bird migration is a typical example. In autumn these Snow geese (Anser caerulescens) migrate from arctic breeding grounds to more temperate regions.

CORE FACTS

- Circadian rhythms follow an approximate 24-hour cycle. One example is photoperiodism (the response by an organism to length of day), which is controlled by the phytochrome system in flowering plants and by the brain and its hormones in animals.
- Circannual rhythms follow a yearly cycle; examples include migration and hibernation.
- Most mammals have a reproductive cycle that follows a yearly rhythm, called the estrus cycle. Humans and some other primates have a reproductive cycle that follows a 28-day rhythm, called the menstrual cycle.
- Resynchronization is the process of resetting an internal rhythm. Environmental cues, called zeitgebers, trigger biological pacemakers.

An evolutionary response

To survive, all living organisms must be able to regulate their day-to-day activities in response to changes in the environment. Many scientists believe that biorhythms are a product of natural selection (see EVOLUTION; NATURAL SELECTION); organisms that could "anticipate" external cyclic changes in light, temperature, and available food, and modify themselves or their behavior accordingly, would be better able to survive than organisms lacking this ability. Examples of this capability to cope with a changing world include plants that flower when conditions are favorable; animals that change their coats with the seasons, and those that hoard food in the fall; and birds that migrate south for the winter.

Most biological rhythms are related to environmental cycles, such as the moon phases, seasonal changes, tidal movement, and daylength. However, in 1729, the French astronomer Jean-Jacques de Mairan suggested that biorhythms could occur without environmental cues. He noticed that some flowers, such as tulips, open in the morning and close at dusk. This biorhythm originally evolved to allow the flower to take full advantage of sunlight for photosynthesis and to protect it from the cool of the night, but in experiments the flowers continued this behavior, even when kept in dim light. As a result, it is now known that, although external cues such as the day-night cycle may "set" the biorhythms, the rhythmic behavior is actually controlled by endogenous (internal) rhythms. These rhythms are natural biological timekeepers, and are often referred to as biological clocks.

Most biological clocks in animals, plants, and microorganisms follow a cycle that lasts approximately 24 hours, which is called the circadian rhythm (from the Latin words *circa*, meaning about, and *dies*, meaning day). However, this rhythm is closely related to the rotation of the Earth, which takes slightly longer than 24 hours to make a complete turn on its axis. Experiments have shown that when humans are kept in constant darkness, their sleep and hunger cycles soon settle into a 25-hour rhythm.

Photoperiodism

Photoperiodism is a type of circadian rhythm. It is a biological response to changes in daylength – the most important factor affecting the organism being the length of the dark period, rather than that of the light period. This phenomenon occurs in plants and many animals, including fish, birds, insects, and mammals. It influences such important activities as the metamorphosis from caterpillar to butterfly, molting, and mating. Diurnal animals have their biological clocks set so they are most active during the day and they sleep at night. By contrast, nocturnal animals sleep during the day and are most active at night.

CONNECTIONS

- Many aspects of animal **BEHAVIOR** are dictated by biorhythms, including **REPRODUCTION, SLEEP, MOLTING, MIGRATION,** and **HIBERNATION.**

- In animals biorhythms are controlled by the **BRAIN** and its **HORMONES.**

- Cycles occur throughout the physical world, such as in the swing of a pendulum, the rotations and revolutions of the stars, and the vibrations of microscopic quartz crystals.

Shorter days indicate the onset of low temperatures and a decrease in available food. For many animals this is a cue to hibernate. Diapause is a similar state found in many species of insects, during which the insect can remain dormant for many months or even years. This rhythm is also thought to be triggered initially by decreasing daylength.

One important process affected by photoperiodism is flowering in plants, which depends on alternating periods of light and dark. Flowering plants can be divided into three groups, based on their reaction to daylength. There are long-day plants, such as petunias and spinach, which flower only if the dark period lasts for less than a critical amount of time — usually about 12 hours. By contrast, short-day plants, such as chrysanthemums and orchids, flower only if the dark period lasts longer than the critical length. Some plants, such as geraniums, are called indeterminate or day-neutral plants and flower however long the dark period.

It has been shown that if a period of darkness in a short-day plant's life cycle is interrupted by an "unexpected" exposure to light, the plant will not flower. It is also known that only red light (light of wavelengths between 650 and 680 nm) can produce such a phenomenon, and that this inhibitory effect can be reversed by a subsequent exposure to far-red light (light of wavelengths between 710 and 740 nm). In 1938 Karl Hamner and James Bonner of the U.S. Department of Agriculture suggested that this was due to a light-sensitive pigment in the plant. This pigment was eventually isolated in 1959 and named phytochrome.

The phytochrome system

Phytochrome exists in two interconvertible forms. One form, known as P_r, strongly absorbs red light; in doing so it is converted to the form known as P_{fr}. P_{fr} strongly absorbs far-red light, and as a result is converted back to P_r.

CIRCANNUAL RHYTHMS

Many animals display an internal (endogenous) mechanism for timing cycles that are much longer than the 24-hour photoperiod or the 28-day menstrual cycle. These longer cycles display circannual (yearly) rhythms that continue under relatively constant environmental conditions. Examples of annual rhythms in animals are migration (see MIGRATION), and hibernation and estivation (see HIBERNATION). In humans, circannual rhythms have been identified for hormonal control of ion levels in the urine, body temperature, and cortisol and growth hormone levels.

A Fallow deer (Dama dama) buck shedding velvet. Deer have an annual cycle of antler growth and shedding, controlled by hormones. The velvet (fur-covered skin) carries blood to the growing antlers. In the fall, the velvet dries up and is shed (the animals often aid this process by rubbing against vegetation); in winter, the antlers are shed.

FLOWERING PLANTS

One environmental effect of photoperiodism in plants is the absence of ragweed in the northernmost regions of the United States. Ragweed is a short-day plant, which begins to flower only when there is no more than 14.5 hours of daylight within 24 hours. In northern Maine, the days do not shorten to 14.5 hours until August, when there is not enough time for the ragweed seeds to mature before the first frost.

Another classic example of the photoperiodic control of flowering is seen in the single-flowering Japanese cherry (Yoshino) trees, which were first planted along the banks of the tidal basin in Washington, DC, in 1912. These trees bloom in early spring, with brilliant pale pink and white flowers. One striking feature of these trees is that all members of the species will flower at the same time of year, wherever they are planted, be it in their native Japan, the United States, or elsewhere. These trees were originally given as a gift of friendship from Japan, partly because of the symbolism of the trees blooming at the same time in both countries.

A CLOSER LOOK

In most light-mediated plant responses, P_{fr} has been found to be the active form of phytochrome. Sunlight contains more red than far-red light, and so during the day most phytochrome is converted into the active P_{fr} form. Although it is well established that phytochrome is the receptor pigment involved in photoperiodic responses, exactly how the plant measures daylength is still poorly understood. Experiments suggest that another substance is involved in the control of flowering besides phytochrome. Although this substance has still not been identified so far, scientists think that it may be a hormone-type chemical, which they have named florigen.

Photoperiodism in plants has been exploited fully by horticulturalists, who are able to control the plants' exposure to light and dark, so controlling when they flower. This means that they can produce large quantities of flowers from early- and late-flowering species at the same time.

Melatonin

Sources of biorhythm control in animals have been identified in the brain and its hormones. In birds, rats, and some other vertebrates, the pineal gland (a tiny, cone-shaped piece of tissue found deep within the brain) is thought to influence rhythms by secreting a hormone called melatonin. Melatonin production peaks during the hours of darkness (in humans, it is highest between 11:00 P.M. and 7:00 A.M.) and is lowest during the day. This hormone then influences a variety of other hormones, acting as a natural pacemaker in setting a rhythm for many bodily activities such as cell division. Experiments have shown that when pineal glands are removed from birds, the birds lose their biorhythms completely.

Human biorhythms

Humans can also adapt or respond to rhythmic changes in the outside world. For example, many people have a circadian rhythm that makes them wake up at about the same time every morning without the need for an alarm clock. Another example of the effects of biorhythms is the problem of "jet lag," a condition in which a person may experience various health problems after flying through several time zones in a short period of time. These problems may include sleeplessness, constipation, diarrhea, or other intestinal problems, decreased alertness, and a general feeling of tiredness. The body may be "out-of-sync" for several days (or sometimes weeks) after traveling.

Shift work also interferes with the natural biological clocks in humans. In shift work, a person has a working day other than the traditional "9 to 5" (a midnight to 8:00 A.M. shift, for example). Workers in this situation commonly experience sleep disturbances and physical disorders, such as ulcers and depression. Their bodies are constantly trying to adapt to new rhythms, because their "days off" are usually spent in a normal time frame. The fatigue and tension that results from the disruption of the biorhythm is thought to impair workers' efficiency and judgment.

Recent research has suggested that human biorhythms may also play a role in seasonal affective disorder (S.A.D.), or "winter blues." S.A.D. sufferers feel extremely depressed during the winter months, due to the short days and long nights. One therapy prescribed to alleviate these symptoms is intense bouts of light.

Humans are dependent on circadian rhythms to regulate the levels of hormones circulating in the bloodstream. A classic example of such a hormone is cortisol, which is released from the adrenal glands at regular intervals and controls the body's use of nutrients. A normal day-night schedule sees the peak for blood cortisol levels when a person awakens in the morning, and the lowest levels at night, just before sleep. By contrast, nocturnal animals that hunt in the dark display highest cortisol levels at night and lower levels in the daytime.

FIDDLER CRABS

The Fiddler crab (*Uca vocans*) has two bursts of activity every day, which correspond to times when the tide is low. Then the crabs emerge from their burrows and hurriedly complete all their activities before the tide comes in again. In a laboratory setting (see diagram below), these periods of activity continue, but without the external cue of the tides the crabs' cycles lengthen and no longer remain synchronized with the times of low tide outside.

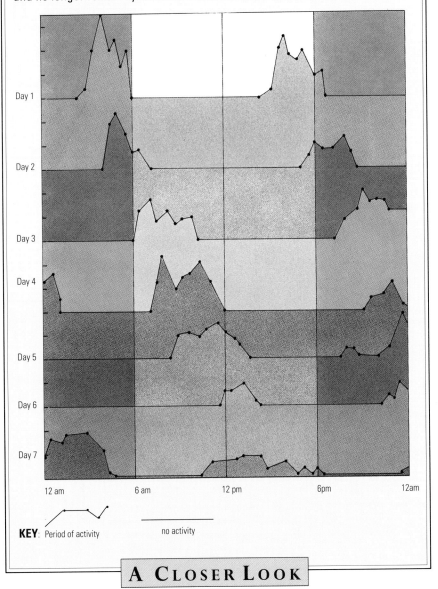

KEY: Period of activity   no activity

A CLOSER LOOK

BIOLOGICAL PACEMAKERS

The development of internal biorhythms requires biological pacemakers to monitor and synchronize these biorhythms and mark the passage of time. To recognize differences in environmental rhythms, the pacemakers receive information from receptors that monitor the external environment. The cues or markers in the environment that trigger the biological pacemakers are called zeitgebers (German for "time-givers"), and the process of resetting the internal rhythm is known as resynchronization. Examples of zeitgebers for circadian rhythms include sunrise and sunset, temperature fluctuations, social interaction, and availability of food.

Although circadian rhythms are internal, they can be modified by outside conditions. Being influenced by external forces allows for adaptability and promotes survival of the species. For example, a plant which receives only dim light in its environment may be able to adapt its daily rhythm if moved to an environment that provides brighter light. The ability to adjust to an external condition in this way is referred to as entrainment. The entrainment will not continue, however, if the new rhythm is too different from the original.

An example of humans adapting to a new daily rhythm occurs when traveling across time zones. Then the travelers' normal circadian rhythms are disrupted and their biological clocks are unable to reset themselves completely in one go. It takes around five days for the rhythm to return to normal. It is usually more difficult for travelers to recover from jet lag if they travel eastward because sunset occurs earlier than usual, and they are trying to sleep when their bodies are still wide awake. When flying westward, they need to try to go to sleep later than usual, which is not so difficult.

Frequent travelers have realized that certain measures can be taken to minimize the effects of jet lag. For example, prior to the trip a person can change his/her eating and sleeping times gradually to those expected in the new time zone; when travelling west, it is best to remain awake and go to sleep at an appropriate hour in the new time zone; when traveling east, it is best to get up earlier and earlier each day before you fly. It also helps to increase exposure to natural sunlight. In addition, recent research has shown that daily doses of the hormone melatonin may reduce the effects of jet lag.

A CLOSER LOOK

Other important hormones controlled by circadian rhythms include a growth hormone, which stimulates normal body growth, and prolactin, which helps a female's body prepare breast milk for her nursing baby. The levels of both these hormones increase at night, and they have been associated with the normal cycle of sleep and activity.

Aldosterone is a hormone that helps regulate blood pressure (see CIRCULATORY SYSTEMS). This hormone also displays an obvious daily rhythm of activity, but in this case it is associated with changes in posture. Peak levels usually occur at around 6:00 A.M., shortly before a person who has been asleep lying down wakes up and needs an increase in blood pressure to assist in the transition from sleep to activity. The lowest levels of aldosterone usually occur in the afternoon.

The hormone thyrotropin stimulates the thyroid gland (an endocrine gland in vertebrates that controls the rate of metabolism and influences development), one of thyrotropin's functions being to prepare the body for sleep. Levels of thyrotropin rise sharply late in the afternoon and evening, and peak just before the onset of sleep, before falling continuously until they reach their lowest point at approximately 4:00 A.M.

Testosterone is a male sex hormone. Testosterone levels are at their lowest in the late afternoon, and rise gradually through the evening and night until they reach their peak in the morning, at about the time of awakening. Many scientists believe this biological rhythm may exist in order that sexual arousal occurs at a time of day (in the morning following a full night's sleep) when the male is most energetic and capable of successful intercourse.

Unlike the hormones mentioned above, levels of the female sex hormone estrogen follow an approximate monthly rhythm, fluctuating throughout the menstrual cycle. Levels are low at the beginning of the cycle, starting from the first day of menstruation when the womb lining begins to shed, and peaks around the 14th day when ovulation (the release of an egg from the ovary) occurs. The estrogen levels then remain fairly high before lowering again for the start of a new cycle.

M. MAHALIK

See also: BEHAVIOR; BRAIN; HIBERNATION; HORMONES; MENSTRUAL CYCLE; MIGRATION; REPRODUCTION; SLEEP.

Further reading:
Solomon, E.P., Berg, L.R., Martin, D.W., and Villee, C. *Biology.* 3rd edition. New York: Saunders College Publishing, 1993.

REPRODUCTIVE CYCLES

Unlike humans, most animals in the wild do not reproduce continuously during the reproductive phase of their life cycle; mating behavior is usually confined to once a year, at a time referred to as the mating or breeding season. This is timed so that the birth of the offspring will occur when food is most plentiful and the climate most favorable for survival.

To synchronize reproductive cycles with the changing seasons, most animals have a rhythm centered around the photoperiod. This rhythm is controlled by the hormone melatonin, which regulates the levels of gonadotrophic hormones, which in turn are essential for successful reproduction.

The yearly reproductive cycle in most female mammals is called the estrus cycle. Estrus itself is the point within this cycle when ovulation (the release of the ovum, or egg, from the ovary) takes place, and when the female will accept the male. In the higher primates (Old World monkeys, apes, and humans), the estrus cycle is replaced by the menstrual cycle, which lasts approximately 28 days. If no fertilization occurs after ovulation, the lining of the uterus breaks down and is discharged from the body, and the whole cycle begins again.

BIOSPHERE

The biosphere is the part of the Earth's land, soil, waters, and atmosphere that supports life

The biosphere is that part of a planet that contains life. Scientists believe that it may be a unique feature of the Earth, as life has not been found elsewhere in the universe so far. The biosphere is a vast layer, extending from the bottom of the ocean to at least 30,000 ft (9000 m) above sea level.

The biosphere is a closed system; it receives no materials from the outside. All materials must be recycled. The only outside contribution is sunlight, which provides the energy to power most life processes. Energy passes through the biosphere from one organism to another (see FOOD WEBS), eventually being lost as heat to the environment or being locked away in organic molecules. These interconnections have led some scientists, however controversially, to suggest that the biosphere behaves much like a living organism (see GAIA HYPOTHESIS).

The term "biosphere" is most often used in debates about the health of the global environment. Factors considered threats to the health of the biosphere include the human population explosion, pollution, deforestation, habitat destruction, and the general overharvesting of the planet's natural resources. Every year the human population increases by over 93 million individuals, or almost three per second. This population puts great pressure on the resources of the biosphere.

The growing population and the needs of people have resulted in two major impacts on the biosphere: the loss of natural habitats and resources, and pollution. Increasing demands for wood and land have resulted in significant losses of temperate and tropical rainforests (see BIOMES AND HABITATS). Many grasslands have been cleared for grain plants such as corn, wheat, and barley. Even the oceans have felt the pressure of human demands for resources; many coastal waters have been overfished and overharvested.

Pollution is another byproduct of human consumption. Although every kind of waste that people create originated in the biosphere, it becomes very difficult to return this waste to the natural resource cycle. For example, we use vast amounts of fossil fuels to run automobiles and manufacture industrial products. Although these resources come from organic matter locked away in ancient times, such as coal, oil, or natural gas, through technology we transform these natural materials into a variety of unnatural byproducts. Pollution from these byproducts of water, air, and soil not only affects our lives, but also the lives of all other organisms on the planet.

Today people are more aware of the threats to the biosphere. Many individuals take steps to conserve energy and recycle waste products, including paper, glass, and aluminium tins. Advances in recycling waste and reintroducing it into the natural cycles of the biosphere offer promise in the future as they help to reduce the demand for new raw materials as well as keeping the planet clean. In addition, new farming techniques, natural forms of pest control, and soil-friendly farming practices (see BIOLOGICAL CONTROL), may ease demands for new croplands. These approaches can help to ensure a long life for the biosphere.

K. HOSOUME/J. KAUFMANN

See also: ECOLOGY; GAIA HYPOTHESIS.

Further reading:
Bradbury, Ian K. *The Biosphere*. New York: Belhaven Press, 1991.

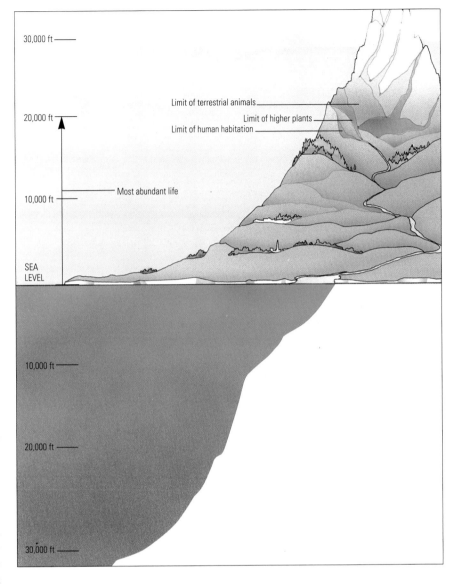

30,000 ft

20,000 ft

Limit of terrestrial animals

Limit of higher plants

Limit of human habitation

10,000 ft — Most abundant life

SEA LEVEL

10,000 ft

20,000 ft

30,000 ft

The biosphere is many thousands of feet thick, but most life is found in a small section between just below sea level and 20,000 ft (around 6000 m) into the atmosphere.

CONNECTIONS

● The Earth is the only planet in our solar system that can support life in a biosphere. This is because just enough **ENERGY** from the sun reaches us to allow water, which is essential to life, to exist as a solid, liquid, and a gas.

● The **GAIA HYPOTHESIS** states that the biosphere is a living organism, with its own mechanisms of **HOMEOSTASIS**.

BIOTECHNOLOGY

Biotechnology is the application of industrial production techniques to exploit biological processes

Biotechnology, the industrial development of biological processes, is steadily increasing its influence on modern life. Already a huge variety of products has emerged, from antibiotics, through genetically engineered vaccines, home pregnancy-testing kits, detergents, and motor fuels, to new sources of food. Using biotechnology, it is possible to dispose, not only of domestic waste and sewage, but of toxic industrial wastes, and even to recover materials from them. The five main areas in which biotechnology plays an important role are: medicine, waste management, fuel production, food production, and agriculture.

During the 1990s, more than 250 companies in the United States were engaged in biotechnological development. Financial problems were considerable, however, since they had not only to obtain the approval of the regulatory agencies for each product, but also convince the public that it was sound. Nevertheless, at any one time, more than 100 new products were in their final phase of clinical tests or had been submitted to the FDA (Food and Drug Administration) for approval.

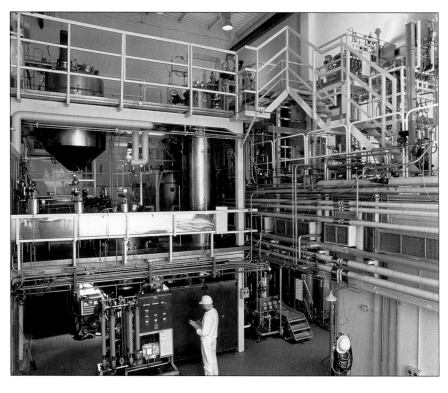

Large-scale technology

Most biotechnological processes use microorganisms, such as bacteria, fungi, and algae. Bacteria are particularly useful because they reproduce rapidly by cell division and so manufacture the required substances in a short space of time. Certain processes depend upon the action of only a single enzyme produced by the organism, and in these cases the isolated enzyme may be used. However, in the manufacture of food and drink, such as wine and beer, cheese, and bread, flavor is of the greatest importance. Since this is due to the presence of a range of metabolic byproducts, the whole microorganism must be used.

To be useful in industry, microorganisms must be grown in vast quantities in order to make them work on a large scale. In the manufacture of industrial chemicals and pharmaceuticals, there are many advantages in employing live agents of this kind,

Industrial biotechnology needs vast quantities of microorganisms. This large-scale (530-gal or 2000-liter) fermenter is used in the commercial production of monoclonal antibodies (see page 174).

compared with undertaking long, and possibly difficult, chemical synthesis. Only moderate temperatures are required, raw materials are relatively cheap, and production time is short. On the other hand, these are living organisms, and they must be nurtured with care. Strictly sterile conditions are necessary to ensure unwanted organisms cannot contaminate the process; close monitoring of temperature, pH, and the supply of gases such as oxygen is necessary; and the quantities of available nutrients must be controlled with precision.

Fermenter technology

Many products are manufactured in fermenters (otherwise known as bioreactors). These are large tanks that can hold as much as 53,000 gal (around 200,000 liters) – or even more. They, and the pipelines that supply them, are sterilized by steam; they are then filled to a fixed level with nutrient solution, and "seeded" with a culture of the appropriate microorganism. The mixture can be stirred, or the movement produced by bubbling air up through the liquid may be sufficient. Heating coils and cooling jackets maintain the optimum temperature for growth. More nutrients can be added during the fermentation process, or it may be halted at a particular point by the addition of substances that inhibit further enzyme activity. Throughout the process, sensors monitor and control the pH, temperature, and other factors.

This technology was first developed during World War II for the manufacture of penicillin, but it has since been applied to a growing range of

---

CORE FACTS

■ Biotechnology uses microorganisms (bacteria, protozoa, viruses, algae, and fungi), cells, and cell products in industrial and commercial settings.

■ Biotechnology has applications in areas of medicine, agriculture, food production, and waste disposal.

■ Biotechnology has a close relationship with other scientific disciplines, including genetics, molecular biology, and chemical engineering. It uses techniques such as fermentation, enzyme technology, genetic engineering, and cell cultures.

CONNECTIONS

● Biotechnology has been used to create biological detergents that contain **ENZYMES.** Ordinary soap is the result of a chemical reaction between a fat and an alkali. This reaction is called saponification.

● Compared with chemical processes, biotechnology usually uses lower pH levels and temperatures; cheaper raw materials; and water rather than organic solvents.

industrial and fine chemicals and pharmaceuticals. These include ethanol and citric acid; antibiotics and vaccines; insulin, interferon, and vitamin B_{12}. Some of the microorganisms used in these processes are genetically engineered (see GENETIC ENGINEERING).

Isolating enzymes

The enzymes used by the organisms in many of these processes can also be concentrated and isolated as pure products. Some break down starches into simple sugars such as glucose. One such important enzyme, glucose isomerase, converts glucose to fructose, which is a much sweeter sugar. The two sugars form a syrup, which is used as a sweetener in many processed foods. Another group of enzymes used extensively in biotechnology include the proteases. These enzymes break down proteins and can be useful in meat preparation, cheese-making, baking, and brewing. Proteases are also used in detergent production.

Enzymes also have many applications in medicine. They can be employed in an easily-used type of indicator called a biosensor. Most enzymes have a high specificity; each particular kind of enzyme recognizes and binds with a specific molecule before initiating a specific chemical reaction (see ENZYMES). This means that enzymes can be used to detect, or sense, those specific molecules. The enzyme is embedded in laser-drilled holes in a protective gel or membrane, which is at the end of a hand-held probe. This is dipped into the solution being tested: the reaction of the enzyme with the specific substance produces a tiny electric signal, which is amplified electronically and read out on an LCD (liquid crystal display).

For example, glucose sensors have been developed, which use the enzyme glucose oxidase to measure levels of glucose in the blood of people suffering from diabetes (see DIABETES). Other enzymes are used in biosensors that can detect a range of compounds from environmental pollutants to hormones and ethanol in blood or urine.

Enzymes can be "immobilized" by trapping them – or the cells containing them – onto the surface of, or inside, fibers, gels, or plastic particles. The advantages are considerable. The enzyme particles can be separated and used many times over, since they are unaffected by the process in which they take part. They are also much more stable: for instance, glucose isomerase will become inactive within a few hours in solution, but can be kept in an immobilized state for over a year at room temperature.

Thousands of natural enzymes have now been identified, but less than 250 have so far been produced commercially in biotechnological quantities.

Currently, much research is being directed to ways of producing synthetic enzymes to perform specific metabolic functions. These may be "designer" enzymes produced by making small changes to the DNA carrying the code for a specific enzyme (see genetic engineering, below), or enzymes that are completely synthetic.

BIOLOGICAL DETERGENTS

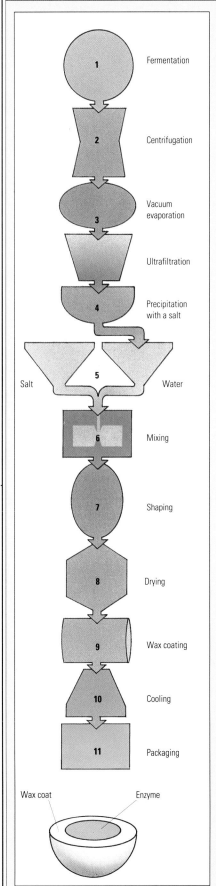

Proteases and other enzymes are present in so-called "biological" detergents, where they break down and remove carbohydrates and proteins present in stains left by food and blood. They are less effective at removing fats, however.

One big advantage of these detergents for the consumer is that they work effectively at very low temperatures, which saves energy and has a gentle action on clothes. However, there are also disadvantages. In the early days of production, many people developed allergic reactions to these detergents; a problem that has mainly been solved by coating the enzymes in wax. Attention has now turned to the question of potential health hazards for workers at the manufacturing plants, and scientists are investigating the possible effects of these protein-destroying enzymes on the skin and mucous membranes.

The first biological detergent was produced in 1913 by Otto Rohm in Germany. The enzyme used was trypsin, taken from the pancreas of animals. Biological detergents became widely available in the 1960s. Today, they are manufactured by bacteria on a huge scale.

The process has a number of stages. First, the enzymes are produced by bacteria in a large tank called a fermenter (1). Then the mixture is spun in a centrifuge so that particles of different densities are separated out and the bacterial cells can be isolated and removed (2). Next the mixture undergoes a process called vacuum evaporation and/or ultrafiltration to remove water (3), and the enzymes are precipitated with a salt to separate them from the liquid culture (4). Now sodium chloride (common salt) is added for preservation, and water is also added to produce a paste (5), which is then thoroughly mixed (6), extruded, or squeezed, and shaped into spheres (7). Once the spheres have been dried (8), they are coated with wax in a wax coating drum (9) and cooled (10), before being added to the other detergent ingredients and packaged (11). When the detergent is eventually used in a washing machine, the wax coat melts in the water and releases the enzyme.

A CLOSER LOOK

GENETIC ENGINEERING

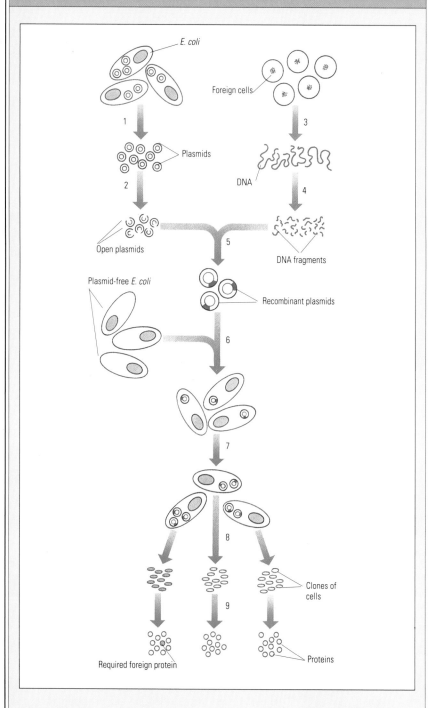

In genetic engineering, using *Escherichia coli* bacteria, plasmids (small rings of DNA) are isolated from a culture of *E. coli* (1), and opened up by the use of an enzyme (2). DNA molecules are extracted from foreign cells in culture (3), and another enzyme is used to cleave them into gene-sized fragments (4). The DNA fragments are inserted into the open plasmids, which are resealed using another enzyme, to form recombinant plasmids (5). Each of these contains a different piece of DNA, which may or may not contain the relevant gene for the required protein. The recombinant plasmids are now mixed with plasmid-free *E. coli* in the presence of calcium ions, which causes each bacterium to take up a separate plasmid (6). The bacteria copy their plasmids (7) and then divide to produce identical copies, or clones, of themselves (8). These clones then manufacture their proteins (9): one or more clones will produce the required foreign protein.

A CLOSER LOOK

Genetic engineering

During the 1980s, scientists developed another industrial use for microorganisms: as producers of vast quantities of substances normally found in other microorganisms, plants, or animals (even humans), using a set of techniques collectively known as genetic engineering, or recombinant DNA technology (see GENETIC ENGINEERING). This form of biotechnology involves the transferral of genes from one organism to another, often between species, to instruct the host organism to produce commercially or medically desirable products, such as human insulin (see the box on page 173).

Special enzymes known as restriction endonucleases will break up chromosomes into gene fragments that represent a specific DNA sequence (see DNA). The gene is then introduced into a "vector," such as a virus, which can enter the cell of a bacterium such as *Escherichia coli* and affect its chromosome structure. Millions of copies of this altered chromosome are then produced by the rapid reproduction of the bacterium. The process is known as gene cloning, and has been very important in developing the large-scale manufacture of drugs such as human insulin. Genes may also be introduced in this way into the reproducing cells of plants and animals: organisms that develop containing such "foreign" genes are described as transgenic.

Biotechnology in medicine

Biotechnology has helped prevent, diagnose, and treat a wide variety of medical conditions.

Vaccines are used as prevention for a vast array of infectious diseases, and have already saved millions of lives worldwide. Vaccination involves introducing a dead or highly weakened microorganism into the body. Its antigens (markers) then stimulate the immune system to produce antibodies to fight the disease-causing microorganism whenever they recognize it in the future (see ANTIBODIES; IMMUNIZATION).

Vaccines are usually produced by growing viruses in cell culture, most commonly in cells taken from monkey kidneys or chicken embryos. However, genetic engineering is increasingly being used in vaccine production. The genes responsible for producing the antigen in the disease-causing microorganism are introduced into a less dangerous organism such as *E. coli*. This is then cultured in large quantities, and the antigen extracted.

Vaccines of this kind have been used to protect young farm animals against diarrhea. Trials are also being carried out on a vaccine for malaria, using a strain of *Salmonella* carrying the surface protein from *Plasmodium falciparum*.

Some microorganisms naturally produce compounds that inhibit the growth of other bacteria. These compounds, called antibiotics, have been used for treating bacterial infections for many years.

Bioconversions, or small changes to a molecule by a microorganism, can greatly alter the effect of that molecule. For example, adding a fluorine atom to a steroid hormone makes it one hundred times more powerful. The hormones in birth control pills and the anabolic steroids used to improve athletic performance are made by bioconversions.

Many important pharmaceuticals are made by microbes through genetic engineering. Interferon to treat leukemia, Factor VIII to treat hemophilia (an inherited deficiency in the blood clotting process; see BLOOD), and growth hormone to treat dwarfism, are examples. Growth factors to heal ulcers, and relaxin, a hormone to ease childbirth, are still in the development stage.

Waste management

Microorganisms in nature break down dead plant and animal matter. This natural activity is put to work in biotechnology as microorganisms are used to break down the organic waste produced by human society.

Large-scale sewage treatment takes place in plants that provide the most suitable conditions for the microorganisms, to allow their natural decay processes to work. These processes may be either aerobic or anaerobic. Solids removed by filtration and settling are broken down aerobically by a mixture of bacteria and protozoa (collectively known as zooglea), to produce methane gas – which may be collected for use as a fuel – and sludge for fertilizer. The liquid remaining after removal of the solids is treated anaerobically in warm tanks called digesters to produce various carbon compounds and hydrogen. Any solid sediment remaining is then used as fertilizer, buried in landfill sites, or dumped at sea. Sewage in rural areas is treated by microorganisms in anaerobic conditions in septic tanks or cess pits.

Phosphates from detergents in domestic waste water, one of the major sources of water pollution, can now be accumulated by bacteria, which are first "starved" of phosphorus and then released into effluent held in special lagoons. After the bacteria have taken up the phosphates they are filtered out and dumped in a landfill.

Composting breaks down garden and food waste into a humus-rich soil. The process is aerobic, takes several months and involves the action of bacteria, fungi, earthworms, and insects.

Bioremediation is the use of microorganisms to break down toxic substances. Many organic compounds produced by industry, such as oil, PCBs, and pesticides, are toxic and harmful if released into the environment. Although this technology is still in its early stages of development, researchers are hopeful that in the future bacteria may be used to convert dangerous petrochemical waste into harmless byproducts, such as carbon dioxide and water, and fungi may be used to degrade other chemicals found in soil, such as selenium.

The Environmental Protection Agency (EPA) is presently charged with decontaminating decommissioned military bases, where one of the most common wastes has been tri-nitrotoluene (TNT). Both

INSULIN PRODUCTION

Insulin is a hormone manufactured by pancreatic cells in vertebrates. It plays an extremely important role in regulating the level of glucose in the bloodstream (see INSULIN). As its name suggests, people suffering from the debilitating disease insulin-dependent diabetes mellitus cannot produce insulin themselves, and rely on injections of this hormone to prevent their blood glucose levels from becoming dangerously high (see DIABETES). Traditionally, insulin was taken from pigs and cattle, but porcine and bovine insulin is slightly different from that of humans. The immune systems of many patients reacted against this "foreign" substance, dramatically reducing its effectiveness. In the early 1980s, however, this problem was solved, when human insulin became one of the first licensed products to be genetically engineered in bacteria. Now this hormone is manufactured in vast quantities.

The first step in producing human insulin on a commercial scale is to locate the gene responsible for human insulin and isolate it using recombinant DNA technology (see GENETIC ENGINEERING). Once isolated, each gene is transferred into an appropriate vector – usually a ring of bacterial DNA called a plasmid. This recombinant plasmid, containing the human gene integrated into the bacterial DNA, is inserted into a bacterium, such as E. coli (see the box opposite), and the bacteria are placed in a large tank called a bioreactor. The bioreactor is full of warm water, essential nutrients needed for the bacteria to grow, and a supply of air. Within a short space of time, the bacteria multiply, with each separate bacterium manufacturing insulin. The bacteria can then be broken open and the insulin extracted.

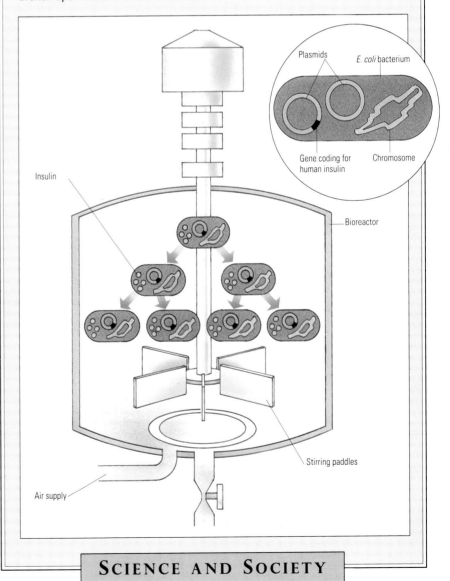

Plasmids
E. coli bacterium
Gene coding for human insulin
Chromosome
Insulin
Bioreactor
Stirring paddles
Air supply

SCIENCE AND SOCIETY

plant and bacterial species that produce large quantities of nitrate reductase – an enzyme capable of breaking down TNT – are being investigated.

Soil contaminated with oil may be treated with microorganisms. The soil is first removed to a pit lined with plastic where it must be fertilized and repeatedly tilled. Some strains of the group of bacteria called *Pseudomonas* are able to break down the hydrocarbons found in oil and petrol. When the ship the Queen Mary was moved to Long Beach in California, 800,000 gal (3,600,000 liters) of oily water in its bilges was decontaminated by bacteria within. Unfortunately, microorganisms are not likely to be effective for oil spills in the ocean, because they require not only the carbon in the oil but suitable concentrations of nutrients, and they would be spread too thinly to develop a high enough temperature for rapid growth.

Some microorganisms will accumulate heavy metals, and this ability has been exploited both in the decontamination of toxic waste and in mining of low grade ores. For example, the sulfur bacterium *Thiobacillus ferro-oxidans* will break down the insoluble copper-bearing chalcopyrites ore and convert it into soluble copper sulfate.

Plastics are difficult to degrade, but one, Biopol (polyhydroxybutyrate), is both made and degraded by bacteria. Biopol can be molded, spun into fibers or made into film. It is used in biodegradable packaging, and for surgical sutures (see SURGERY), where it eventually breaks down in the body. Experiments are now under way to genetically engineer canola plants to produce Biopol in industrial quantities.

Fuel production

The biotechnology industry also aids the production of both liquid and gaseous fuels. For example, new "biological" techniques are used to enhance the recovery of oil. Water pumped into oil wells forces oil to the surface; but oil is sticky, and water is too thin to dislodge and displace it completely. Xanthan gum, a thick liquid produced by the bacterium *Xanthamonas campestris*, can be added to the water to thicken it and make it better able to push the oil

MONOCLONAL ANTIBODIES

Biotechnology has had an important impact on the diagnosis of disease, through the use of monoclonal antibodies. Monoclonal antibodies are artificial antibodies first developed in 1975 by Georges Kohler and Cesar Milstein at Cambridge in Britain. These antibodies are highly and reliably specific: each type of antibody recognizes and reacts with only one type of antigen or foreign protein (see ANTIBODIES). This antigen may be a drug, a hormone, or a protein present on the outside of a disease-causing bacterium. When antibodies are mixed with a sample of the patient's blood, the antibodies interact with the antigen, causing a reaction that can be measured. Monoclonal antibodies can be used to detect a variety of diseases, and some cancers of the colon, lung, breast, ovary, and prostate. Home pregnancy kits use a monoclonal antibody that reacts against a hormone, human chorionic gonadotrophin (HCG). This hormone is secreted by the embryo and is present in the mother's urine.

Monoclonal antibodies can also be used for treatment. Bacterial toxins and snake venoms can be inactivated by injecting specific antibodies that will attack them. Antibodies can be combined with anticancer drugs and targeted at cancer cells. When the antibody binds to the cancer cell, the attached drug may kill the cell.

The process for producing monoclonal antibodies is shown in the diagram to the right. The main difficulty is that the antibody-producing cells die soon after they are removed from the body. To overcome this, the antibody-producing cells are combined with cancer cells, which can be grown quite easily outside the body and which divide indefinitely. The cells most commonly used are mouse spleen cells and mouse melanoma (cancer) cells.

The resulting hybrid cells have the properties of both types of original cell. They secrete the antibody and, like the cancer cells, can be grown in culture. The hybrids are tested to find which clone cell is producing the antibody. This clone (shown in sandy yellow) is grown on a large scale and the monoclonal antibody is extracted from the culture.

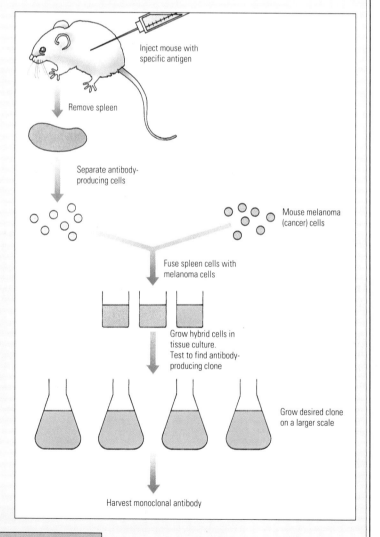

Inject mouse with specific antigen

Remove spleen

Separate antibody-producing cells

Mouse melanoma (cancer) cells

Fuse spleen cells with melanoma cells

Grow hybrid cells in tissue culture.
Test to find antibody-producing clone

Grow desired clone on a larger scale

Harvest monoclonal antibody

A CLOSER LOOK

to the surface. Xanthan gum can also be mixed with the muds in drilling areas, as it helps to lubricate the giant drills used in oil recovery.

Methane and hydrogen are produced from the metabolism of a wide range of microorganisms acting on manure, sewage, paper, and food waste. Biotechnologists are now using them to break down waste material and produce methane for fuel.

Some larger, two-stage, systems in the United States use algae as the material for the bacteria to consume. The algae are harvested from shallow ponds into which the raw material (usually sewage material) has been fed. The algae are then put into a digester where they are consumed by the methane-producing bacteria. This two-stage process produces a larger amount of material for the bacteria to feed on and the algae are grown at no cost, using energy supplied by the sun. One of the main disadvantages is the large amount of water needed. Areas with plentiful sunlight often have limited supplies of water.

There are only a small number of microorganisms that release hydrogen. However, scientists have discovered some bacteria and algae containing the enzyme hydrogenase, which can catalyze the combination of hydrogen ions and electrons to form molecules of hydrogen gas. One bacterium, *Clostridium butyricum*, is able to produce hydrogen from a weak sugar solution. Another method that has been investigated is the use of the alga *Chlorella pyrenoidosa* and the enzyme glycolic oxidase, extracted from plants, to oxidize water molecules into hydrogen and carbon dioxide gas.

Scientists are constantly trying to find new ways to produce energy, using renewable sources that are less polluting than the traditional fossil fuels. Ethanol, alone or mixed with gasoline to form gasohol, is used to run cars in Brazil, the United States, and Zimbabwe. The alcohol is produced by yeast fermentation of sugar cane. In Europe, oil from canola plants is burned in diesel engines. However canola, ethanol, and gasohol are currently more expensive and less efficient than petro-fuels.

Traditional food technology

Biotechnology has been an essential feature of food production for thousands of years. Two of the most traditional fermentation products are yogurt and cheese. To make yogurt, the bacteria *Lactobacillus bulgaricus* and *Streptococcus thermophilus* are added to milk. These microorganisms produce enzymes that convert lactose, a sugar in the milk, to lactic acid, which lowers the pH of the milk and causes proteins to coagulate (thicken) and form yogurt.

Other species of microorganism make cheese (the bacteria *Streptococcus lactis* and *S. cremoris*, and the fungi *Penicillium camemberti* and *P. candidum* in camenbert.) In traditional cheesemaking these organisms are present in the environment, or are added from a previous production, but in factories they are introduced as a culture. The enzymes produced break down the coagulated proteins to form solid fat curds and liquid whey. The whey is drained off, and the curds are dried by heating, mixed with bacteria and/or fungal spores, pressed, and aged or ripened. The type of cheese produced depends on the temperature at which the curds are dried and the particular strains of microorganisms used.

Other microorganisms, such as yeasts, are used in fermentation processes. Typical products include bread and ethanol. Varieties of *Saccharomyces* yeasts convert the sugar in bread dough to carbon dioxide and ethanol. The bubbles of carbon dioxide make the dough rise, and the ethanol evaporates when the dough is baked. Yeasts also ferment the sugar in grapes and grain to make wine and beer, in which the ethanol is the more important product.

Soya beans, rich in protein, are used as the basis of a range of Asian foods, including soy sauce, miso paste, and tempeh. The beans are fermented with the fungi *Aspergillus oryzae* and *Rhizopus oligosporus*, together with lactic acid bacteria and yeasts.

During the 1970s, attention turned to the possibility of using microorganisms as a source of single-cell protein (SCP) for animal food. They could be grown very efficiently on industrial waste in huge fermenters: as little as 0.6 lb (0.25 kg) of initial microorganism was expected to produce up to 5,500 lb (25,000 kg) of SCP per day. Few of these projects succeeded, due largely to high development costs and consumer resistance. One success story so far is the high-protein material for human consumption named Quorn™. It is manufactured in Britain from *Fusarium* fungus grown on waste from flour making. It has a high fibrous content, and when compressed has a texture similar to meat.

Biotechnology in agriculture

Biotechnology can be used to create vaccines and antibiotics for animal as well as human diseases. Veterinary vaccines are also important as tests for techniques that may later be used on humans.

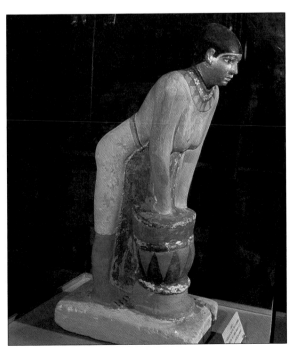

Microorganisms have been exploited in food production for thousands of years. This Ancient Egyptian painted model, dating from around 2400 BC, shows a woman making beer.

Hormones can also be used to treat animal diseases, and genetically engineered bovine somatotropin (BST) is presently being used to increase milk production in cows. However, there is still much controversy over the sale of BST milk, following opposition from animal welfare groups and concerns that traces of the hormone in the milk could pose potential health risks to humans.

Genetic engineering of farm animals is still experimental, although since the late 1980s some work in this area has already been successful. In Scotland, transgenic sheep have been produced that are able to secrete alpha-1-antitrypsin, a protein that is extremely important in the treatment of human lung disease, in their milk. Chitinase, an enzyme found in plants, breaks down the hard shell of some insects; transferring the gene for chitinase into animals can make them resistant to insect pests.

Biotechnology has been used for many years in agriculture. Nitrogen, essential for plant growth, is often applied as fertilizers. But *Rhizobium* bacteria can "fix" nitrogen from the air into soil. The growth of plants can be enhanced by sowing soil with the bacteria, but it may also be possible to transfer the nitrogen fixation gene from *Rhizobium* into plants.

Microorganisms that cause disease in insects can help control insect pests. Most commonly used is *Bacillus thuringiensis*, which creates a toxin that kills insect larvae. Transgenic plants have been developed to contain the gene that produces the toxin.

Genetic engineering can also be used to improve plants that are grown for food. One example of this is the "flavor-savor" tomato now available in many supermarkets. A recent development has been the identification of the gene that regulates plant growth. All plants appear to contain the growth hormone indole-3-ethanoic acid, mostly in an inactive form. The plant's rate of growth is probably controlled by the amount of active hormone available. A gene has now been isolated that controls the inactivation of the hormone, providing hopes that genetic engineering will obtain much bigger plants.

Individual cells from plants might also be used in biotechnology, the cells being removed from the organism and grown in a nutrient broth. About 25 percent of our drugs and medicines are derived from plants, including the steroids used in the contraceptive pill (derived from yams) and codeine, used in painkillers (taken from poppies). Plant extracts are also used in perfumes.

Questions of safety and morality

Despite the benefits of biotechnology there are a number of moral and safety concerns. Many people feel that it is "not right" to interfere with the balance of nature when the effects of such interference are still not known. There is concern that genetically engineered microorganisms released into the environment may cause new diseases, or encourage the development of strains resistant to known drugs. There is also fear that an accident could result in the escape of the cancer cells and

These seedlings of lucerne, a cattle fodder crop, are being grown in spheres of nutrient gel. Plant biotechnology offers the possibility of producing new varieties of plants with desirable characteristics or with a built-in resistance to pests.

viruses used in the first stages of genetic engineering. Many consumers also worry about the health risks of eating food from genetically engineered plants or animals.

A typical case is that of BST used to increase milk production. The FDA has so far found no evidence of the hormone appearing in the milk, but the general public's attitude is less positive. Supermarkets have said that they will resist any requirement to label the milk as being from BST-treated cows, as they are fearful that it would not sell. There is also the question of longer-term effects upon the health of the animals themselves. And the final question remains, "Why do it?". Milk production in the United States and in many other countries is presently in excess of demand. There appears no reason to increase this surplus.

Animal rights activists legitimately question the morality of creating transgenic animals that may suffer. Transgenic pigs grow faster and are leaner than normal ones, but are unable to stand because of arthritis. In order to investigate the effects of new drugs, transgenic mice have been created for medical research that automatically develop cancer, cystic fibrosis, and muscular dystrophy (see ETHICS).

M. ALLEN/B. INNES

See also: AGRICULTURE; ANTIBIOTICS; ANTIBODIES; BACTERIA; ENZYMES; ETHICS; FERMENTATION; FUNGI; GENETIC ENGINEERING; IMMUNIZATION; INSULIN; MICROBIOLOGY; WASTE DISPOSAL; YEASTS.

Further reading:
Bains, W. *Biotechnology From A to Z*. New York: Oxford University Press, 1993.
Davis, S.M. and Davidson, W. *20:20 Vision*. New York: Simon & Schuster, 1991.
Krimsky, S. *Biotechnics and Society: the Rise of Industrial Genetics*. New York: Praeger, 1991.
Spallone, P. *Generation Games: Genetic Engineering and the Future for our Lives*. Philadelphia: Temple University Press, 1992.

BIRDS

The term "birds" covers an enormous range of animals that vary widely in appearance and have very different lifestyles. However, all birds have several characteristic features: they all have a body covered in feathers, a beak, and a pair of front limbs modified into wings. They are the largest group of terrestrial vertebrates, containing more than 8700 species.

Birds represent one of nature's finest examples of adaptation. The ability to fly is found in certain vertebrates (bats, for example) and in insects. However, it is most developed in birds. It has allowed them to penetrate every terrestrial niche on

Earth, and to travel great distances in search of food. Birds are found throughout the world, from the Equator to the poles, living in the air, on land, and in water.

BIRDS AS THE ULTIMATE FLYERS

In order for birds to be able to fly, a wide range of adaptations had to evolve. These include feathers, body weight reduction, and strong muscles for powered flight.

Feathers

Feathers are unique to birds. They provide a light-weight aerodynamic surface for flight. They also insulate birds from high and low temperatures, and help them retain body heat. This allows birds to survive in the coldest regions on Earth. The insulating capacity is exploited by humans, who use the feathers in comforters and jackets.

Feathers, like hair, horn, and fingernails, are made of a protein called keratin. The basic feather

---

CORE FACTS

- Birds belong to the class Aves, which has 27 living orders and more than 8700 species.
- The ability to fly has allowed birds to travel great distances and to penetrate every terrestrial niche.
- Birds have many adaptations that allow them to fly, including hollow bones, powerful breast muscles and a good circulatory system, and feathers.
- All birds hatch from eggs.

CONNECTIONS

- Not all birds have the power of **FLIGHT. FLIGHTLESS BIRDS** include penguins, emus, ostriches, and kiwis.

- Some scientists believe that birds are descendants of the **DINOSAURS.**

- The struts inside birds' bones are very like the struts used to strengthen aircraft wings and bridges.

- Nitrogen extracted from birds' droppings (or guano) is used to make explosives.

The Indian peacock (Pavo cristatus) *fans out his feathers to attract a female. Some scientists believe that the "eyes" on the male's feathers transfix the female, allowing him to mate.*

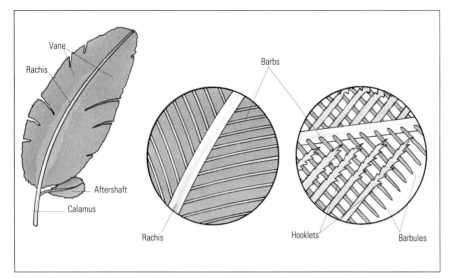

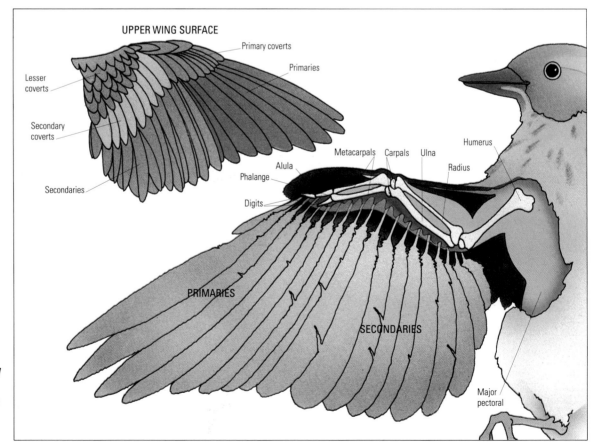

The structure of a basic feather. Feathers differ in size, shape, and texture, according to their function.

has a tubular base (the calamus), a central shaft (the rachis), and a series of branching barbs. The barbs on either side of the central shaft are collectively known as a vane. The shape of the feather is maintained by a series of small hooked barbules along each barb, which interlock like velcro.

There are different types of feathers, each with a particular design and function. Those feathers closest to the skin, called down feathers, are small, soft, and fluffy, with very short shafts. They provide insulation, but are no good for flight. Powder feathers, related to down feathers, produce a fine white powdery material made of granules of keratin. This powder repels water and helps keep the bird waterproof. Contour feathers are longer and stronger than down feathers, and have a smooth

sheet-like texture, providing an airfoil. The flight feathers (known as remiges) and the tail feathers (known as rectices) are larger and more stiffened forms of contour feather.

Most birds molt once a year. The wing feathers are usually lost in stages, allowing the bird to continue to fly. Some ducks and geese lose their wing feathers all at once and are unable to fly for a month or more.

Body weight reduction

One important adaptation to flight is the reduction in body weight. This has been partly accomplished by a reduction in the weight of the skeleton, which is achieved by having thin hollow bones. The skeleton of a pigeon is only 4.4 percent of its total body weight, whereas the skeleton of a rat is 5.6 percent of the rat's body weight. Despite being so light, the skeleton of a bird also has to be strong enough to cope with the stresses associated with flight. Some of the bones under high stress, such as those in the wing, have struts inside them for added strength.

Many of the bones that are separate in other vertebrates are fused in birds, to create a complex that is incredibly lightweight but very strong. For example, the sacral vertebrae and the bones of the pelvis girdle are fused into a thin, tubelike complex, and the bones in the wings and legs are fused together.

To further reduce weight, birds do not have a urinary bladder to store urine. They quickly secrete concentrated nitrogenous waste in the form of paste-like uric acid, known as bird drop-

The wing of a bird has the same bone structure found in the forelimb of other terrestrial vertebrates, but has been specially modified for flight.

pings. The reproductive biology in birds is also geared toward weight reduction. Unlike other vertebrates, most birds have only one functional ovary and oviduct. The reproductive organs enlarge during the breeding season, and shrink for the rest of the year.

Powered flight

The first requirement for powered flight is the ability to generate muscle power to beat the wings. To do this, birds evolved warm-bloodedness, or homeothermy. By maintaining a high internal body temperature, the biochemical reactions necessary to work muscles can take place rapidly.

Birds eat high-energy foods, including seeds, fruits, worms, insects, fish, and other animals, in order to obtain the energy needed to maintain their body temperature and fly. They avoid low-energy foods, such as leaves and grasses. Many species of seed-eating birds also have special structures in their digestive systems for storing and using energy-rich food. The crop, just below the esophagus, is a storage chamber for seeds. This allows a bird to eat rapidly and collect seeds when they are abundant. While they are stored in the crop, the seeds soften and are made easier to digest.

The breast muscles of the bird are the source of propulsion for powered flight. For very strong fliers, such as the pigeon or dove, the breast muscles can account for as much as 40 percent of the adult bird's body weight.

A well-oxygenated blood supply is critical for muscle function. Birds, like mammals, have four-chambered hearts, so oxygen-rich and oxygen-poor blood are kept separate. This ensures that the muscles get maximum oxygen from the blood. Blood pressure is higher in birds than in mammals. This ensures a high rate of red blood cells arriving at the flight muscles.

Birds have a well-developed pair of lungs with a separate array of air sacs. These can store oxygen to supplement the supply in the lungs. They also help to keep the bird cool during long flights.

An enhanced nervous system

Flight requires sharp eyesight and a good sense of balance. The brain has well-developed centers for controlling muscle coordination (see BRAIN). The parts of the brain responsible for sight, the optic lobes, are also large. Birds have a good sense of hearing and can detect almost as wide a range of frequencies as humans can. Nocturnal hunters rely on their excellent hearing to detect prey in the darkness.

Birds that cannot fly

Some bird species have lost the ability to fly in favor of a more terrestrial lifestyle (see FLIGHTLESS BIRDS). These include the ostrich (*Struthio camelus*) from Africa and the emu (*Dromaius novaehollandiae*) from Australia. Penguins have also forfeited the power of flight for the ability to dive and swim.

A kingfisher (Alcedo atthis) *diving to catch a fish. Kingfishers have a straight, strong, pointed beak adapted to stabbing at fish below the surface of the water.*

Beaks and feet

All birds have a beak and two feet, but the size and shape of these can vary widely according to their function. In particular, the size and shape of a beak determines the type of food source a bird can exploit. Finches, with their blunt, wedge-shaped beaks, are seed-eaters, while insect-eaters such as robins and warblers have fine, pointed bills. The long needle-like beaks of hummingbirds are perfectly adapted to feeding on the nectar of flowers. Birds of prey have strong, hooked beaks for gripping and tearing apart their prey. Parrots have large strong beaks for a different function: crushing tough seed cases and nuts. Avocets and curlews are shore and marshland birds with long, slender, curved bills. The bill of the American avocet (*Recurvirostra americana*) has a gentle upward curve, which is ideal

for sweeping from side to side, feeling for minute particles of food below the surface of the water; the Long-billed curlew (*Numenius americanus*) has a downward-curved beak adapted to probing for worms and insect larvae in deep mud.

Feet and claws have their adaptations to lifestyle, too. For example, some waterbirds, such as ducks and geese, have webbed feet adapted to a swimming lifestyle, while others, such as coots and gallinules have long, widely spread toes to prevent them sinking into mud. Birds of prey have strong feet ending in sharp, hooked talons, ideal for seizing and killing their prey. One bird order is called the Apodiformes, or "footless birds." This group contains the swifts and hummingbirds, which are not literally footless but have very short legs and rarely use their feet.

Life history
All birds hatch from eggs. Eggs protect the developing embryo. No species of bird gives birth to live young, probably because of the weight constraint of carrying young birds in the womb. Most birds lay their eggs in nests, which protect both the eggs and the parents who sit on the eggs to incubate them. The materials used usually blend with the background to act as camouflage. Nests are generally built in inaccessible places, such as on the tips of branches or in cliff cavities, so that they are protected from predators.

Eggs contain the embryo, a large yolk to feed the embryo, and sacs for storing metabolic wastes. Eggs range in size from that of the now extinct Giant elephant bird of Madagascar (13 in or 33 cm long) to the tiny Vervain hummingbird (*Mellisuga minima*) egg (less than ⅖ in or 1 cm long). The eggshell is composed mainly of calcium carbonate with a small amount of protein. Most of the calcium carbonate comes from the bones of the mother. Gases and moisture can pass through the eggshell, allowing oxygen to enter and waste carbon dioxide to leave.

A nesting colony of Atlantic gannets (Sula bassana). The Atlantic gannet breeds in the Arctic. The birds usually return to the colony where they were born in order to breed.

THE DIFFERENT KINDS OF BIRDS

The Class Aves, to which all birds belong, is divided into 27 living orders and several extinct orders.

ORDERS	DESCRIPTION
Archaeopterygiformes	A single extinct species, *Archaeopteryx lithographica*.
Hesperornithiformes	Several genera of extinct flightless marine birds.
Icthyomithiformes	9 known species of extinct tern-like birds.
Struthioniformes	A single living species, the flightless ostrich.
Rheiformes	2 living species of large-legged flightless birds from South America, the rheas.
Casuariiformes	4 species of flightless walking birds: the emu of Australia, and the cassowaries of Australia and New Guinea.
Aepyornithiformes	At least 11 species of extinct flightless birds, known as the elephant birds of Madagascar.
Dinornithiformes	9 species of extinct flightless birds.
Apterygiformes	3 species of chicken-sized flightless birds from New Zealand, known as the kiwis.
Tinamiformes	More than 40 species, known as the tinamous.
Sphenisciformes	17 species, better known as the penguins.
Gaviiformes	5 species, known as the loons.
Podicipediformes	About 18 species, known as the grebes.
Procellariiformes	Over 100 species containing marine birds, including albatrosses, storm petrels, and shearwaters.
Pelecaniformes	About 60 species, including marine birds such as pelicans, gannets, and cormorants.
Ciconiiformes	116 species of long-legged wading birds, such as hernons, ibises, and flamingos.
Anseriformes	Around 150 species, containing the ducks, geese, swans, and the screamers.
Falconiformes	About 300 species of day-active birds of prey.
Galliformes	Over 260 species, including game and domestic fowl, such as turkeys, pheasants, and the domestic chicken.
Gruiformes	About 200 species, containing the long legged, strongly flying cranes, and the short legged, weakly flying rails and coots.
Charadriiformes	About 320 species of shorebirds, gulls, terns, and auks.
Columbiformes	About 300 species of pigeons and doves. Also includes the extinct dodo *(Raphus cucullatus)*.
Psittaciformes	About 350 species, containing the parrots, and macaws.
Cuculiformes	About 146 species of cuckoos and their relatives.
Strigiformes	Over 150 species of owls.
Caprimulgiformes	About 100 species of birds with unusual names, such as the frogmouths, goatsuckers, nightjars, and poorwills.
Apodiformes	398 species of very small birds, including the insect-feeding swifts and the nectar-feeding hummingbirds.
Coliiformes	6 species found in South Africa.
Trogoniformes	Around 35 species of trogons and quetzals.
Coraciiformes	194 species of kingfishers, mot-mots, todies, bee-eaters, cuckoo-rollers, hoopoes, and hornbills.
Piciformes	Around 380 species, including the well known toucans and woodpeckers, as well as honeyguides.
Passeriformes	Over 5000 species (60 percent of all known species), including swallows, robins, bluebirds, and thrushes.

Most eggs are drab in color, although some are blue or green as the result of the release of bile by the female during shell development. Many eggs are colored to blend in with their environment. This is particularly important for birds that do not build nests but lay their eggs on the ground: the eggs of the killdeer (*Charadrius vociferus*) look like pebbles.

Eggs are produced one at a time. Some species lay one egg a day, though the Masked booby (*Sula cyanops*) leaves a gap of up to seven days between successive eggs.

The eggs are incubated by one or both parents sitting on them. In some birds, a brood patch forms on the belly. This patch lacks insulating feathers so heat can pass from the adult bird to the eggs.

The hatching time depends on the species. It can be as short as ten days for the Great spotted woodpecker (*Dendrocopus major*), or as long as 81 days for the Royal albatross (*Diomedea epomophora*). At hatching, the young bird must escape from its shell on its own. A special structure called the egg tooth on the upper bill helps the bird chip through the shell and is lost just after hatching. Even with the egg tooth, it can take up to six days for a young albatross chick to hatch out of its egg.

The maturity of the chick on hatching also varies. In some species, such as the domestic chicken, the chick is moving around in less than a day. Young birds with this degree of maturity on hatching are called precocial. The most advanced chicks are those of the megapodes. After escaping from their shell, the young birds have to dig their way out of the large nest mound. They are already feathered and ready to take care of themselves without any help from the parents. By contrast, many chicks have a low degree of maturity and are completely helpless at birth. Naked and blind, these altricial young are dependent on their parents.

Depending on the degree of maturity, the parents tend to the hatchlings by feeding them and keeping them warm until the adult plumage grows and the young birds can take care of themselves.

Adult birds enter a period of courtship and reproduction. Courtship can involve a complex set of behavioral displays and bright plumage. Some species, such as the cranes, conduct elaborate and flamboyant dances (see COURTSHIP).

Bird sounds

The most conspicuous aspects of bird courtship are bird songs. These can be used to entice a mate, or to warn other males about territorial limits. With few exceptions (the pelican, stork, and some vultures), all birds have some kind of voice.

Bird sounds are not produced by the larynx or vocal cords, as in mammals, but by the syrinx, a structure unique to birds. It is located at the base of the trachea (windpipe) where the bronchi branch off to the lungs (see RESPIRATORY SYSTEMS). Air from the lungs vibrates as it passes one or two pairs of elastic membranes in the syrinx. Changes in the tension of the membrane alter the pitch of the sound.

EVOLUTION OF BIRDS

The earliest accepted fossil bird is *Archaeopteryx lithographica*, which lived between 160 and 150 million years ago during the time of the dinosaurs. It had some of the characteristics of modern birds, as well as more reptilian features. The bird features include well-developed feathers and the beginning of wings. Like the reptiles, it had a long tail, toothed jaws, and a poorly developed breastbone. *Archaeopteryx* was probably a poor flyer but a good glider (see ARCHAEOPTERYX).

During the Cretaceous Period, between 135 and 65 million years ago, birds evolved and diversified. Fossil birds from this period were more bird-like than *Archaeopteryx*. They had lost their reptilian tail and had a well-developed sternum.

With the beginning of the Tertiary Period, 65 million years ago, more recognizable types of birds had evolved. By the end of the Eocene Epoch (50 to 40 million years ago), most orders of modern birds were represented.

Some people believe that not all dinosaurs died out in the mass extinction at the end of the Cretaceous Period, but live on today as birds. They claim this view is supported by similarities between the skeletons of birds and certain dinosaurs known as therapods.

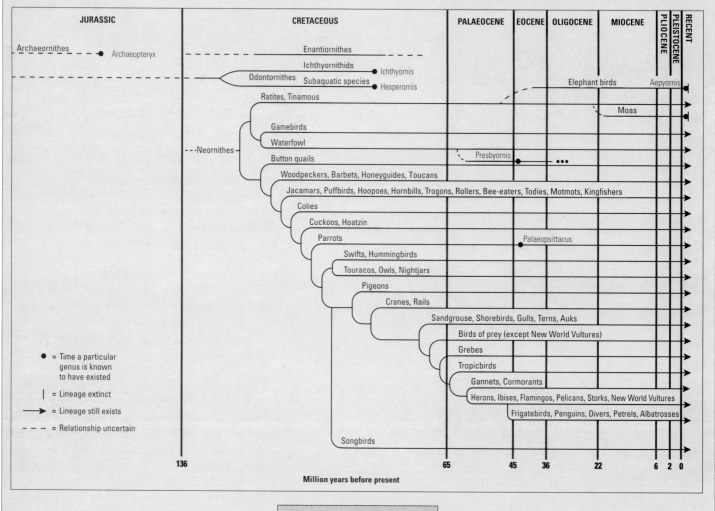

EVOLUTION

The size and shape of the syrinx varies greatly between different species.

What is the difference between bird calls and bird songs? Bird calls are usually short and have a relatively simple pattern. They rarely include more than four or five notes. Calls are used to influence the activities of other members of a flock: to warn them about predators or to coordinate the time to migrate or feed. Bird songs are more complex and more melodic. They are usually produced by the male to attract a mate. Songs are sometimes used as a form of musical combat between mature males to vie for the attention of a female.

K. HOSOUME/J. KAUFMANN

See also: ADAPTATION; ARCHAEOPTERYX; BIRDS OF PREY; COURTSHIP; EGGS; FLIGHT; FLIGHTLESS BIRDS; FOREST BIRDS; GRASSLAND BIRDS; NESTING; PERCHING BIRDS; SEABIRDS; WATERBIRDS AND WADERS.

Further reading:
Clements, J.F. *Birds of the World: a Checklist*. 4th edition. California: Ibis Publishing Co., 1991.
Handbook of Avian Anatomy: Nomina Anatomice Avium. 2nd edition. Cambridge, Massachusetts: Nuttall Ornithological Club, 1993.
Shaw, Frank. *Birds of Western North America* and *Birds of Eastern North America*. New York: Smithmark, 1990.

BIRDS OF PREY

Birds of prey are birds that have developed adaptations to a predatory lifestyle

With vision twice as sharp as that of humans and feet strong enough to kill a mammal in one swift pounce, birds of prey reign as the master hunters of the skies. Birds of prey capture and kill animals for food. Many are found soaring among the clouds in search of their prey, everywhere from Toronto to Tierra del Fuego, Tijuana to Tokyo.

Birds of prey are often called raptors. This term generally covers birds belonging to the order Falconiformes, although some biologists also include owls, which are placed in the order Strigiformes.

There are approximately 292 diurnal, or day-time, species of falconiformes, including hawks, falcons, eagles, and vultures. They range in size from mouse-size falconets to vultures and eagles, which are as big as the fattest Thanksgiving turkeys. The 162 species of owl share the falconiforms' hooked bills, powerful legs, sharp talons, and taste for animals, but differ in several important ways. For one, most species hunt at night, sleeping from dawn until dusk. These species also have unusually broad heads and forward-facing eyes. Some owls have a face ruff and decorative tufts that resemble cat ears.

The life span of the raptors varies with size. Smaller species are shorter lived. In captivity large vultures and eagles live for 45 to 55 years, while small falcons and hawks reach 15 years. Wild birds face many more hazards and their average life span is shorter.

Adaptations for hunting

From their oversized eyes, to their hooked bills, strong legs and razor-sharp talons, raptors are designed to hunt. As a group they prey on everything from insects and tiny mammals to ducks, fish, and monkeys. Individual species have more specialized diets. The Everglades kite (*Rostrhamus sociabilis*) eats only one species of snail, the Apple snail (*Pomacea sociabilis*). Ospreys eat only fish. Falcons prey mostly on birds.

Most raptors search for prey from the air, using their long wings to coast along on air currents. The heaviest raptors — eagles and condors — have difficulty in flapping flight, but their broad wings make

Bald eagle (Haliaeetus leucocephalus) *in flight, clearly displaying the hooked beak typical of birds of prey.*

soaring virtually effortless. Smaller species that favor open spaces, such as falcons and kestrels, have long, narrow wings and muscular bodies for quick aerial acrobatics. Hawk-eagles, goshawks, and other forest-dwelling species have long tails and broad wings to help them maneuver quickly among the trees.

Few animal feats are more impressive than a raptor diving at speeds of up to 200 mph (320 km/h) toward its prey. Streamlined, bullet-shaped bodies speed their dives and allow raptors to overtake birds they could never catch in flapping flight. Owls prefer to hunt from a perch and make only short flights to seize their prey. Their soft, dense plumage gives most owl species silent flight.

A raptor's most valuable hunting tool is its vision. Raptors have unusually large eyes and an abundance of color-sensitive cells called cones in their retinas (see EYES). These features enable raptors to focus clearly on distant objects. Owls, on the other hand, are color blind, but see well in the dark. They have few cones in their eyes and many rods — cells in the retina that function at very low light intensities. Their eyes are large and cannot be moved in their sockets. To make up for this, their necks are long and flexible and can be rotated up to 270 degrees.

CORE FACTS

- Most birds of prey capture and kill animals for food, although vultures eat carrion (dead meat).
- The term birds of prey generally covers birds in the order Falconiformes, which contains hawks, eagles, falcons, and vultures. Owls belong to the order Strigiformes.
- The two orders are not closely related, but they share many adaptations for hunting, including hooked bills, strong legs, and sharp talons. These adaptations have evolved in response to the orders' similar lifestyles.

CONNECTIONS

● Many birds of prey have been poisoned by chemical **PESTICIDES**, such as **DDT**. Although **CONSERVATION** projects and captive breeding programs have helped some birds, the only long term solution is to reduce the use of chemical pesticides.

● Falcons are accomplished flyers, and often kill their prey in full flight. The designers of modern fighter planes try to incorporate the features that make these birds so maneuverable.

However, owls' most important hunting tool is their keen hearing. This is sharpened by the fact that one eardrum is higher than the other. Scientists believe this allows owls to pinpoint sounds coming from different locations at the same time.

Few birds have a good sense of smell, but some New World vultures, such as the Turkey vulture (*Cathartes aura*), are rare exceptions. The Turkey vulture can smell covered or hidden carcasses.

Another important adaptation in raptors is their strong legs, ending in razor-sharp talons. Some raptors kill their prey with their claws, while others grasp the prey and kill it with a blow from the beak. Then their sharp, hooked bills are used to tear the prey's flesh.

Scientists once believed raptors hunted alone, but recently discovered that many species work together. Some hawks, for example, fly with vultures to disguise themselves from their prey. Harris's hawks (*Parabuteo unicinctus*) in the southwestern United States hunt in groups of up to six, and then share their catch.

SURVEY OF THE FALCONIFORMES

The order Falconiformes consists of five families: Cathartidae, Falconidae, Accipitridae, Pandionidae, and Sagittariidae.

Family Falconidae

If raptors were pilots, the 60 species of falconids would be the Top Guns, diving at speeds of 200 mph (320 km/h). One of the most widely recognized falconids is the Peregrine falcon (*Falco peregrinus*), whose hunting prowess makes it a favorite of falconers. The Peregrine falcon is about the size of a crow. It can be identified by the black, hood-like feathering on its head and black "moustache" marks on both sides of its beak.

The characteristic facial disc of an owl is part of a highly specialized hearing apparatus.

Like many birds of prey, Peregrine falcons were nearly wiped out by the pesticide DDT (see DDT). By the early 1970s, there were no known nesting pairs left east of the Mississippi River and only 19 pairs to the west. But the 1972 ban on DDT, combined with efforts of some dedicated ornithologists, brought about a remarkable recovery. By the mid-1990s, the number of breeding pairs had climbed to more than 900, enough for Peregrines to be removed from the endangered species list.

Family Accipitridae

With 217 species, the Accipitridae family is the largest group of raptors. Accipiters include eagles, hawks, buzzards, Old World vultures, and goshawks. Members of the family vary greatly in shape, size, hunting habits, and flying skills. Their similarities are in their eggshells, molting patterns, oil glands, and other features unnoticeable to the casual observer.

One of the most familiar accipiters in North America is the Red-tailed hawk (*Buteo jamaicensis*). It is found in every terrestrial habitat except the Arctic and very dense forests. Coloration varies from lightly speckled white to almost black among several subspecies, although all are distinguished by their reddish tails.

Bald eagles (*Haliaeetus leucocephalus*) are found most often in wilderness areas near water. They are characterized by their dark plumage, sharply contrasting white heads, and wingspans of up to 8 ft (2.4 m). Bald eagles were was once common throughout the United States. But hunting and DDT diminished the population of this majestic bird

EVOLUTION OF BIRDS OF PREY

The falconiforms seem to have branched off the bird evolutionary tree 20 million years ago, making it difficult for scientists to determine their evolutionary links. Fossils suggest that raptors most likely evolved from storks. The first raptor to evolve was probably a New World vulture, which scientists trace back to the Paleocene Epoch during the Tertiary Period.

The many features falconiforms and owls share – hooked bills, sharp talons, strong legs, keen eyesight – illustrate the concept of convergent evolution. Though unrelated, both orders depend on similar food sources and have developed the same basic characteristics in response to their feeding habits.

Another unusual characteristic of birds of prey is that the female is larger than the male in most species, including owls. This trait, called sexual dimorphism, is the opposite of most birds, in which the male is larger. Size differences increase in relation to the agility of raptors' prey. Among falcons, which prey on birds, females are twice the size of their mates. Scavenging vultures, on the other hand, show little or no weight difference between the sexes. Scientists can not explain raptors' dimorphism, but suspect their large size is an evolutionary adaptation to help females attract mates and also protect them from males who could view them as potential prey.

EVOLUTION

PEREGRINE FALCONS IN THE CITY

Window washers working the upper stories of skyscrapers have the constant worry of not falling off. Now they have an additional concern: they never know when a Peregrine falcon might attack. Dozens of window washers have become victims of these high-rise squatters, as cities have become the newest frontier for falcons on the rebound from near extinction.

These urban newcomers seem as comfortable among the glass and concrete skyscrapers as their ancestors were among snow-topped mountain peaks. In the cities, the gull-size raptors have an adundant supply of prey, including pigeons and starlings. At the same time they are protected from their main enemy, the Great horned owl. By the end of 1993, some 75 pairs of Peregrine falcons had made their homes in more than 50 cities coast to coast.

A CLOSER LOOK

almost to extinction. By 1963, the number of nesting pairs in the lower 48 states had fallen to 417. But like the Peregrine, the eagle population has recovered. The U.S. government in 1993 counted 4016 nesting pairs and proposed that the species be removed from the endangered species list.

Family Cathartidae

The Carthatidae family contains the seven species of New World vultures. These birds can be distinguished by their open nostrils, which create a hole straight through their beak.

To the casual observer, New World vultures and Old World vultures look alike. Both have bare heads and necks, nest in large colonies, and eat carrion. Yet the 15 species of Old World vultures, which make their home in Africa, Europe, and Asia, are related to eagles and hawks, while the New World vultures are more closely related to storks.

The largest raptor in North America is a cathartid, the California condor (*Vultur californianus*). Weighing 30 lb (13.6 kg), it is twice the size of most eagles and its wingspan reaches nearly 10 ft (3 m). The California condor is mostly black with an orange head and large, triangular white patches under each wing. By the mid-1990s, California condors hovered on the brink of extinction. Only three birds lived in the wild and fewer than 90 were in zoos and captive breeding programs.

Family Sagittariidae

The Secretary bird (*Sagittarius serpentarius*) is the sole member of the Sagittariidae family. With its long legs, short toes, and habit of hunting on foot, the Secretary bird looks more like a stork than a raptor. Like storks, these African natives feed their young by regurgitation, and share the task of infant care between both parents. Yet the Secretary bird's calls, feathered thighs, and other physical features are more like an eagle's, leading scientists to believe it was an early offshoot from the Accipitridae family. The Secretary bird is named for the head feathers that make it look like an old lawyer's clerk carrying a bunch of quill pens behind his ears.

An osprey (Pandion haliaetus) with prey. This bird is highly specialized for catching fish. It has very strong feet, and one of its three front toes can be moved to face backward (as in owls). This, in addition to the horny spines on the undersides of its toes, helps to give a firm grip on a slippery fish.

Family Pandionidae

The Pandionidae family's only member, the osprey (*Pandion haliaetus*), is the falconiform order's best angler. It makes its home along waterways in the Northern Hemisphere and Australia.

Ospreys weigh between 2 and 4 lb (0.9 and 1.8 kg). They have dark wings and back, white chest and head, and a dark band running through their eyes. Females have a dark streak running across their breast, which looks like a necklace.

Ospreys soar with their wings bent slightly downward, much like gulls. They feed mostly on fish, but occasionally eat birds, turtles, and small mammals. They typically build their nests on top of dead trees, but also often choose artifical structures such as channel markers and telephone poles.

SURVEY OF THE STRIGIFORMES

Scientists divide the order Strigiformes into two families: Strigidae and Tytonidae. Some recognize a third family, Pholididae, for the Bay owls, whereas some place the Bay owls in the Tytonidae.

Family Strigidae

This is the largest owl family with 125 species. They range in size from the 5 in (12.7 cm) tall Elf owl (*Micrathene whitneyi*) to the 33 in (83.8 cm) Great gray owl (*Strix nebulosa*). They are found throughout the world, except in Antarctica and a few isolated islands. The family Strigidae are commonly called "typical" owls.

Like their cousins from the Tytonidae family, typical owls have broad heads, large, forward-facing eyes, hooked beaks, long, rounded wings, short tails, and sharp talons. The most obvious difference between the two families is in the shape of their face. Typical owls' faces are shaped like two discs joined at the nose. Members of the Tytonidae have a face shaped like a heart.

The most common owl in North America is the Great horned owl (*Bubo virginianus*), which makes

HISTORY OF FALCONRY

Falconry ranks among the world's oldest sports, dating back as far as the 8th century BC. But the ancient sport and its modern version are about as alike as a chariot and a Corvette.

The earliest evidence of falconry comes from Assyria. Travelers to the Orient brought the sport back to Europe during the Middle Ages, where it flourished among the elite of Western Europe and Great Britain. The 17th century brought an abrupt halt to the sports' growth, as open lands were enclosed and hunters took to the shotgun. Only the members of a handful of hawking clubs throughout Europe kept the sport alive.

Early settlers in the United States were too busy establishing the colonies to practice falconry. The sport didn't catch on here until the late 1930s, after twins Frank and John Craighead began writing articles for National Geographic about their unusual hobby.

Thirty years later, the discovery that DDT was killing raptors forever changed the ancient sport. Until the U.S. government banned DDT in 1972, there were no successful captive breeding programs. Falconers simply took young birds from the wild. The falcons' demise prompted the establishment of captive breeding programs. Taking falcons from the wild is now illegal, and breeders supply all the birds used for the sport. The raptors' decline also inspired strict governmental control of falconry, including an exam, two-year apprenticeship, and government inspection of raptors' mews.

In spite of the tight controls, interest in falconry is growing. According to the North American Falconers Association, some 3700 people practice falconry in the United States. Between the mid-1980s and the mid-1990s, membership grew 10 percent.

Modern technology has also reshaped the sport. Earlier falconers tracked their birds with bells. Today, many falconers use radio-telemetry to follow their raptors during the hunt. This enables falcons to pursue faster, more challenging prey with less risk of being lost.

Only about a dozen raptor species have the flying skills and temperament for falconry. Traditionalists favor swift Peregrine falcons. Others use accipiters, including the goshawk and European sparrow hawk. Apprentice falconers in the United States may own only an American kestrel falcon or a Red-tailed hawk.

---

its home from the Arctic to the Straits of Magellan. The bird takes its name from its large size (about 25 in (63.5 cm) in height) and the two large, hornlike tufts topping its head. The Elf owl, found in Texas and East Mexico, often nests in woodpecker holes in the giant Saguaro cactus.

Family Tytonidae

Only ten species make up the owl family Tytonidae. Like most raptors, they are distributed throughout the world, except in polar regions and on a few oceanic islands.

The most familiar family member in the United States is the Barn owl (*Tyto alba*), named for its fondness for nesting in barns. The Barn owl is the size of a crow and has a white, heart-shaped face, dark eyes, and pale brown and gray speckled back and wings. By night, ornithologists identify Barn owls by their strange hisses, screams, and grunts.

Raptors in danger

Since the 1972 ban on the pesticide DDT, several endangered raptor species have made remarkable comebacks. But threats to their survival are far from over. PCBs, the pesticide dieldrin, and other toxic chemicals still endanger raptors. One of the few California condors bred in captivity and released into the wild died after drinking antifreeze.

The greatest threat to birds of prey today is loss of habitat. Development continues to diminish the open spaces large raptors need. With less wilderness left, some raptors take to the cities and suburbs, where they are felled by power lines, factory exhausts, and chemicals carelessly left outside.

Yet another threat to some species is the demise of the animals they prey on. A prime example is the Everglades kite, which depends on the Apple snail. Efforts begun in the early 1990s to save the Everglades from agricultural drainage brings some hope to the kites' survival.

The California condor population has failed to rebound in spite of captive breeding. Land development has overtaken their limited habitat, while the large animals they feed on have diminished. Unlike eagles and falcons, California condors can not readily adjust to being released in new habitats. A glimmer of hope comes from a sanctuary established in the Los Padres National Forest, north of Los Angeles. This gives condors the wide spaces and the large animal prey they need to survive.

C. WASHAM

See also: ADAPTATION; BIRDS; CARNIVORES; DDT.

Further reading:

Hendrickson, John. *Raptors, Birds of Prey.* San Francisco: Chronicle Books, 1992.
Scholz, Floyd. *Birds of Prey.* Mechanicsburg, Pennsylvania: Stackpole Books, 1993.

A group of Rupell's griffon vultures (Gyps ruppellii) feeding on a zebra carcass. The lack of feathers on their heads is believed to aid unobstructed feeding.

BLOOD

Blood is a fluid body tissue that carries nutrients to every cell in the body and helps fight disease

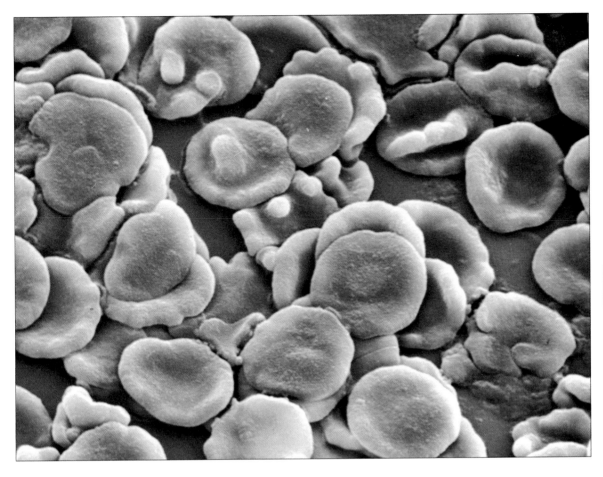

People often talk about "injecting new blood" when they mean to give something a new lease of life. In fact, blood is literally a life-sustaining substance. It circulates around the body of many animals, supplying the cells with the nutrients and oxygen needed for energy and growth. It collects waste material and takes it away for disposal. Blood also helps the body fight disease by attacking and destroying foreign invaders, such as bacteria.

Plasma, the liquid portion of blood, contains a large amount of sodium chloride (common salt) and is often compared to dilute seawater. Like blood in animals today, seawater provided the essential elements for growth in our primitive ancestors.

The blood is pumped by the heart through blood vessels (arteries, capillaries, and veins). An adult man has approximately 11 pints (5.5 liters) of blood in his body. As the actual amount of blood depends on body size, women generally have slightly less.

BLOOD COMPONENTS

Each of the functions of the blood is carried out by a different type of blood cell. The red blood cells, or erythrocytes, carry oxygen from the lungs to all the cells in the body. The white blood cells, or leukocytes, are the body's defense force. Platelets, or thrombocytes, form the plugs that stop wounds from bleeding. All of these specialized cells are suspended in the plasma.

Erythrocytes

The erythrocytes (from the Greek *erythros*. red, and *cytos*, cell) tranport oxygen around the body. In humans and other mammals red blood cells do not contain a nucleus. They measure 8 μm in diameter and are flattened disks, with a thick lip around their rim. This makes them look like doughnuts or rubber balls with the air removed. In other vertebrates, red blood cells are larger and oval-shaped, with a nucleus. Erythrocytes can change shape, stretching or rolling up to squeeze through the

CORE FACTS

- Blood consists of a liquid (plasma), containing red blood cells (erythrocytes), white blood cells (leukocytes), and platelets.
- Blood is a fluid body tissue. It acts as a transport system within an animal's body and helps fight disease.
- Red blood cells transport oxygen around the body.
- White blood cells defend the body from invasion by microorganisms and parasites.
- Platelets are cell fragments that help begin the blood clotting process when blood vessels are damaged.

CONNECTIONS

- The bloodstream is essential in helping to maintain the body's **HOMEOSTASIS**. It constantly circulates nutrients and **HORMONES** around the body, via the **CIRCULATORY SYSTEM**, transporting them to where they are most needed.

- The **IRON** (Fe) in red blood cells binds readily to **OXYGEN** (O_2) and, to a lesser extent, **CARBON DIOXIDE** (CO_2). However, most carbon dioxide is carried as bicarbonate ions (HCO_3^-) dissolved in the plasma.

- **AIDS** can be transmitted through blood transfusions. It is a disease caused by a **VIRUS** that attacks the T-helper cells and depresses the **IMMUNE SYSTEM**. Without an effective defense system, the sufferer may eventually succumb to a microbial infection or **CANCER**.

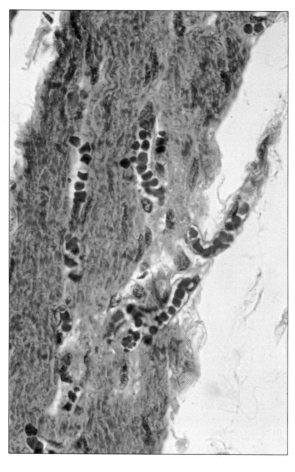

smallest blood vessels, the capillaries, which are only 4 to 9 μm wide. A single milliliter of blood (around 20 drops) contains approximately 4 to 6 billion erythrocytes in men and 3 to 5 billion erythrocytes in women.

Erythrocytes get their red color from a pigment called hemoglobin. Hemoglobin is made up of an iron-containing pigment (heme) attached to a protein chain (globin). It is the iron that binds to the oxygen. Each hemoglobin molecule contains four atoms of iron, so it can carry four oxygen molecules. Nearly all the oxygen carried in the blood is bound to hemoglobin, with a very tiny percentage dissolved in the plasma. The oxygen-carrying capacity of the blood depends on the amount of hemoglobin it contains. Normally each 10 ml of blood can carry 2 ml of oxygen.

Low oxygen levels in the blood, or a reduction in the amount of hemoglobin (for example, after heavy bleeding), stimulates the release of a hormone called erythropoietin, which increases the production of erythrocytes. People who live at high altitudes, where the air contains less oxygen, make more erythrocytes than people living at sea level.

Leukocytes

The white cells, or leukocytes (*leukos* is Greek for white), maintain the body's immune system by fighting off invasion by microorganisms and parasites. Much of their work is done outside the bloodstream, which acts as a transport vehicle, carrying them to sites of infection. Leukocytes are 12 to 15 μm in diameter – almost twice as large as

Red blood cells squeezing through a capillary. The cells have an internal elastic framework that allows them to bend and twist, and squeeze through blood vessels that are narrower than they are (light micrograph x 400).

The hemoglobin molecule is made up of four chains. Each of the chains has one heme group, the iron-containing molecule that transports oxygen and gives blood its red color.

erythrocytes. Normal blood has between 4000 and 10,000 leukocytes per milliliter.

There are two different types of leukocytes, granulocytes and mononuclear cells. The granulocytes have multilobed nuclei and are full of granules. In 1878, Paul Ehrlich, a German scientist, discovered that granulocytes could be stained on a microscope slide and divided into types based on the color of their granules. Neutrophil granules stain poorly, giving them a gray appearance; eosinophil granules stain bright red; and basophil granules stain dark blue. The mononuclear cells can be divided into monocytes and lymphocytes. They have round or oval nuclei, and few granules in their cytoplasm.

Neutrophils

Most leukocytes are neutrophils. They account for about 70 percent of the leukocytes circulating in the blood, although a large number spend part of their life span stuck to the inside of blood vessels (usually capillaries), while others migrate out of the blood vessels and into infected areas of tissues.

Neutrophils are the first line of defense against invading microorganisms. They move rapidly to areas of tissue injury, attracted by the toxins that the invading bacteria release. When the body is infected, the bone marrow produces and releases extra neutrophils. An increased number of neutrophils is a classic sign of an infection, and a blood count is often used by doctors to diagnose illnesses. Many of these extra neutrophils will also look "immature," that is, they have fewer than the usual number of lobes in their nuclei.

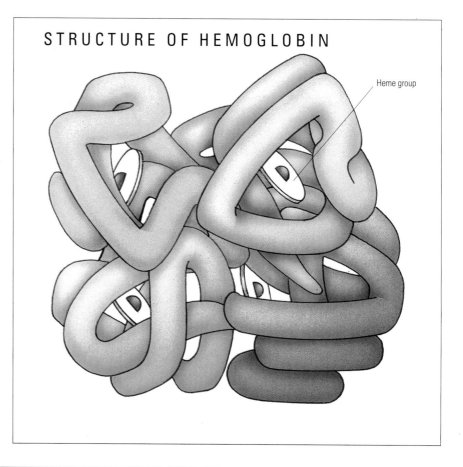

STRUCTURE OF HEMOGLOBIN

Heme group

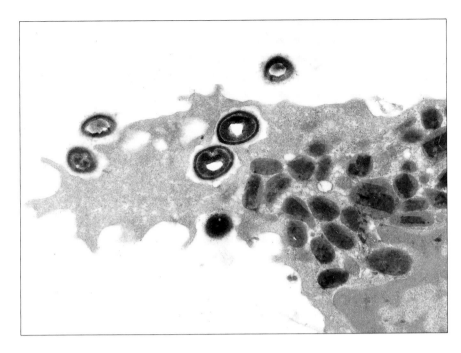

An eosinophil leukocyte consuming bacteria. The bacteria will be destroyed by enzymes in the leukocyte's granules (electron micrograph x 10,000).

Neutrophils respond to infection or tissue damage by producing proteins called adhesion molecules, which bind to corresponding adhesion molecules on the endothelial cells lining the inside of the blood vessels. This attachment halts the movement of the neutrophils, which had been traveling in the direction of the blood flow. Once stationary, the neutrophils, which are very pliable, squeeze between the endothelial cells and migrate out of the circulatory system into the tissues.

Having left the blood, the neutrophils travel rapidly to the site of a bacterial invasion, moving through the tissues by producing pseudopods, or false feet. These are thin extensions of the cell, which move forward into a space. The cell cytoplasm pours into this forward section closely followed by the rest of the cell.

At the site of the invasion, neutrophils ingest the bacteria by enclosing them with pseudopods in a process known as phagocytosis (from *phagein*, the Greek for consume; see CELLS). The bacteria are then killed and digested by enzymes in the neutrophil's cytoplasmic granules. Pus, the yellow-white liquid that seeps from abscesses and sores, is a mixture of dead neutrophils and the microorganisms they have engulfed.

The neutrophil uses several enzymes to digest bacterial cells. Neutrophils also kill bacteria by producing toxic substances, superoxide, hydroxyl, and hydrogen peroxide. These chemicals are usually present in the neutrophil's granules, but when a neutrophil comes into contact with an invading microorganism it becomes activated and produces increased amounts. The main bactericidal (bacteria-killing) agent is hydrogen peroxide.

If the number of neutrophils circulating in the blood drops, or if their function becomes impaired, the consequences are drastic. In either case, the body will soon fall prey to infection by viruses, bacteria, or fungi. A low neutrophil count over a long period allows the body to become over-

Two neutrophils with ingested bacteria (electron micrograph x 8500).

whelmed by infections, and this is likely to be fatal. Likewise, when neutrophils are not functioning properly, they may be unable to ingest or kill invaders. In the condition known as chronic granulomatous disease of childhood (this disease, still known by the same name, can also occur in adults), neutrophils are unable to produce the chemicals for killing bacteria. This results in repeated, and often severe, infections.

Certain medications can reduce the number of neutrophils or affect their function. Cytotoxic drugs, used in the treatment of cancer, often decrease the number of neutrophils, while corticosteroids, such as hydrocortisone and prednisone, impair their function. Prolonged use of these drugs often leads to infection.

Eosinophils and basophils

Eosinophils also contribute to the body's defense, particularly against invasion by multicellular parasites such as tapeworms. There are far fewer eosinophils than neutrophils. Mature eosinophils are released into the bloodstream, but move quickly into the tissues, hence there are usually few eosinophils circulating in the bloodstream.

Like neutrophils, eosinophils are mobile and contain several highly toxic proteins in their cytoplasmic granules. Eosinophils' major basic proteins, the enzyme peroxidase and cationic protein, are poisonous to invading parasites. In certain cases, such as in allergy, they can even poison the body's own tissues. Allergy is an overreaction of the immune system to an antigen (a foreign substance such as a viral or bacterial protein). A common example is pollen, which causes hay fever (see IMMUNE SYSTEM).

Basophils are the least plentiful of the leukocytes. They are mobile cells with phagocytic properties and can migrate into the tissues. Basophil granules contain histamine, which they release in injured tissues or in the presence of an antigen,

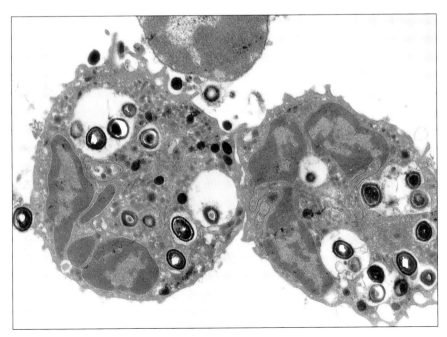

causing an allergic response. Histamine makes the capillaries at the site dilate (expand), allowing more white cells to flood into the area.

Monocytes

The mononuclear cells, monocytes and lymphocytes, have a major role in coordinating the response of the immune system to infection.

Monocytes are larger than the other leukocytes, measuring between 15 and 20 μm across. They have large, distinctive, kidney-shaped nuclei, which look like fried eggs under the microscope. Monocytes are released into the blood from the bone marrow where, after a day or two, they mature and migrate into the tissues, particularly the liver, spleen, lymph nodes, and lungs. Once in the tissues, monocytes are called macrophages. These are mobile cells, which serve as scavengers, ingesting bacteria and injured or dead cells by a process called phagocytosis.

Lymphocytes

Lymphocytes can vary from 5 to 20 μm in diameter. They are divided into two different classes: B-cells and T-cells.

B-cells, or B-lymphocytes, synthesize antibodies, which are specialized proteins that can bind to foreign substances and neutralize them. This happens after the B-cells have been "challenged" by an antigen, a process known as the humoral immune response (see ANTIBODIES). Few B-cells circulate in the blood; most are found in the lymph nodes and in lymphoid tissues such as the spleen.

B-cells only produce antibodies when mononuclear leukocytes are present. The increase in B-cells and antibody production depends on the function of a type of T-lymphocyte called a T-helper cell. These cells release substances known as cytokines, which stimulate the multiplication and differentiation of B-lymphocytes.

As well as stimulating B-cells, T-cells can recognize foreign cells and kill them. This is what happens when the body rejects a skin graft or a transplanted organ: the T-cells identify the new organ as foreign. The drug cyclosporin can be used to suppress killer T-cells. This drug has revolutionized transplant surgery by interfering with the T-cells' powerful immune response.

Plasma

The liquid plasma consists of water and various dissolved substances, including the gases oxygen, carbon dioxide, and nitrogen, and the ions (charged particles) sodium, potassium, calcium, chloride, and phosphate.

About 10 percent of the total volume of plasma consists of the plasma proteins. Most plasma proteins fall into two groups, albumin and globulins. Albumin is synthesized by the liver. It acts as a carrier molecule, binding to fatty acids (organic acids that usually have a long chain) and some drugs and transporting them through the bloodstream. The

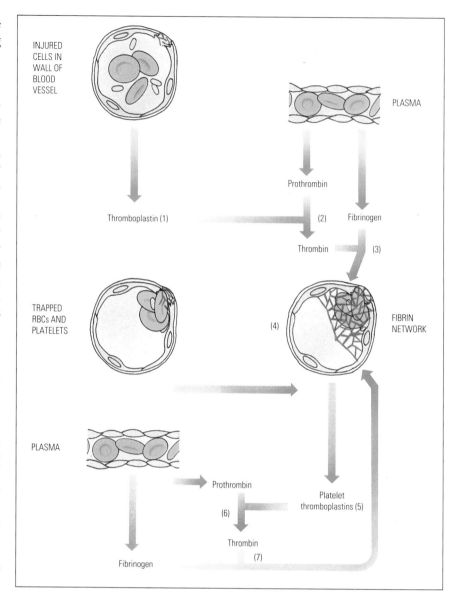

globulins are a diverse family of proteins. They include the antibodies synthesized by lymphocytes in the lymph nodes. The other globulins are clotting factors such as fibrinogen, enzymes and enzyme inhibitors, and proteins that transport lipids (organic compounds including fats and waxes), such as the triglycerides and cholesterol, through the blood.

The plasma proteins play an important role in maintaining the blood's osmotic pressure. This is the driving force behind the movement of water molecules across semipermeable membranes from areas of high water concentration to areas of low water concentration, a process known as osmosis.

Platelets and blood clotting

Cuts and scrapes that damage the blood vessels do not normally endanger life, because a complex process called blood clotting (or coagulation) occurs to prevent excess bleeding. Clotting is a built-in mechanism, which is triggered automatically by the injury.

Clotting requires many components. Among the most important are the platelets. These are small disk-shaped cell fragments with an average

Blood clotting is a complex process, which takes place in a series of stages.

diameter of 2 to 4 μm. Platelets have a sticky coating, which is very important in the clotting process. There are between 150,000 and 350,000 platelets in every milliliter of blood.

When a blood vessel is torn or injured, a protein called collagen, which is normally found inside the endothelial cells that line the blood vessel, becomes exposed. As platelets gather at the site of injury, receptors on the platelet cell membranes bind to the collagen to patch the edges of the wound together. The platelets also stick to each other to form a plug. At the same time they release a substance called serotonin, which makes the blood vessel contract. This slows down blood flow and reduces loss of blood. The platelet plug is only temporary. To stop the bleeding permanently, a clot made out of fibrin must form. The stages of blood clotting are shown in the diagram opposite.

First, the damaged tissue cells release a chemical called thromboplastin into the blood (1). This converts prothrombin (an inactive plasma enzyme produced by the liver) into its active form, thrombin (2). Thrombin acts on the plasma protein fibrinogen, which is also produced by the liver. As a result, the fibrinogen is converted into fibrin (3).

Fibrin is a protein made up of long branching fibers. The fibrin fibers create a web-like network in the wall of the damaged blood vessel. This traps red blood cells and platelets to form a plug (4). The trapped platelets release more thromboplastin (5), which stimulates the conversion of even more prothrombin into thrombin (6). The thrombin stimulates conversion of fibrinogen to fibrin (7). The enmeshed platelets release contractile proteins, which pull the edges of the wound together. This makes a firm clot.

Blood clotting takes place all the time. Blood vessels are often damaged and repaired without our being aware of it – in bruising, for example. Once they have fulfilled their function, blood clots cannot stay in place forever. However, if they were simply released into the blood, the entire circulatory system would eventually become clogged. To prevent this, a substance called plasminogen, which is found in the plasma, is incorporated into the blood clots. An activating factor released by the endothelial cells in the blood vessels converts plasminogen into a clot-dissolving enzyme called plasmin. Once the wound has healed, the plasmin dissolves the clot so well that any remaining particles from the clot are so small they can be excreted from the body via the kidneys.

Clotting disorders

Any of the steps in the clotting process can be affected by disease, or by inherited defects. One of the most common hereditary defects is hemophilia. This is caused by the absence of factor VIII, one of the proteins involved in the complex series of reactions leading to the formation of fibrin. This condition is mainly found in men, although it can be carried in the genes of women. In hemophiliacs,

even slight injuries can cause uncontrollable bleeding. Bleeding is most likely to occur in the joints. This is painful and can lead to crippling progressive deformity. Today, hemophiliacs can be treated with transfusions and injections of factor VIII.

There are two other significant hereditary diseases caused by a deficiency of clotting factors. These are deficiencies of factor IX and of von Willebrand's factor (a protein that circulates as a complex with factor VIII and affects both coagulation and platelet function). Prothrombin and some of the clotting factors (factors VII, IX, and X) are synthesized in the liver via a process that requires vitamin K. Deficiency of this vitamin, as well as liver disease (such as hepatitis, cancer, or excessive alcohol consumption), can also affect coagulation.

The clots themselves can cause problems. Abnormalities of the lining of the veins, particularly in the legs, often cause clots to form in the blood vessels. These clots, known as thromboses, can form as the result of certain kidney diseases and some cancers, and during pregnancy. Long periods of immobilization, for example in convalescing patients, also increase the risk of thrombosis formation, probably because blood does not return as rapidly as normal from the leg veins. The clot may eventually grow large enough to block the blood vessel. If they break off, the clots can travel through the blood vessels to the heart or to the brain, and may cause a heart attack or stroke.

BLOOD OF NONMAMMALS

Primitive single-celled animals, such as amebas, do not need a blood system – they can absorb oxygen and nutrients directly from their surroundings and discharge their waste products into the environment. Sponges and cnidarians (sea anemones, jellyfish, hydras, and corals) also lack a blood system. In these animals, food and oxygen is transported by the sea- or fresh water that is pumped through their internal spaces.

As animals increase in size and complexity they need their own internal transport system. In most animals, blood picks up oxygen and expels carbon dioxide (metabolic waste) by passing over the respiratory exchange membrane of the gills, lungs, or skin.

Nonmammalian blood cells are slightly different from those of mammals, although they function in a similar way. Amphibians and reptiles have fewer red cells than mammals, but these cells are larger, contain nuclei, and are derived from lymphocytes in the spleen. The evolutionary trend is that the oxygen-carrying capacity becomes greater in the higher vertebrates. Athough the red cells in the higher vertebrates are smaller, there are far more of them. The nucleus becomes smaller, until in mammalian erythrocytes it has been lost altogether. Mammalian red blood cells are generally circular, with the exception of those of the camel, which are elliptically shaped. In birds, the red blood cells are also elliptical in shape, and they contain nuclei.

Hemoglobin is used to carry oxygen in almost all orders of animals above the flatworm. Mollusks, crustaceans, and some other animals, however, do use other pigments, such as hemocyanin, which contains copper rather than iron for carrying oxygen. Hemocyanin is blue-green in color.

While mammals use platelets in the process of blood clotting, nonmammals use thrombocytes. These cells are nucleated and spindle shaped, and are very fragile, breaking down easily to release thrombin. In some salamanders the thrombocytes fragment into smaller nonnucleated cells, similar to platelets.

How blood cells are made

All blood cells develop from stem cells, which are found in the bone marrow. Stem cells begin life in the developing embryo, and move to the liver, spleen, and bone marrow as the embryo develops. By birth, the stem cells are being produced almost exclusively by the bone marrow.

The stem cells divide and reproduce throughout life. Some of them simply reproduce to produce more stem cells, but most develop into one of four cell types. One type will eventually become the erythrocytes, another, the granulocytes and monocytes, the third, lymphocytes, and the fourth, cells known as megakaryocytes. Once the stem cells have undergone this change, they are known as committed cells. They divide and differentiate until they mature into specific blood cells.

The committed cells that develop into erythrocytes are called proerythroblasts, which then become basophilic erythroblasts. The basophilic erythroblasts have very little hemoglobin, and large nuclei. The nuclei shrink as the cells evolve and they acquire more hemoglobin. Eventually they become reticulocytes, or immature erythrocytes, which still contain a tiny amount of nuclear material. This nuclear core is pushed out of the cell before the mature erythrocytes leave the marrow to enter the circulation.

Erythrocytes normally circulate for around 120 days before being destroyed. In an adult, around two million new cells are produced and destroyed every second. Erythrocytes can metabolize glucose to provide energy. However, in humans and other mammals they lack a nucleus and so cannot manufacture new enzymes or make cellular repairs. With time, they become more fragile and eventually rupture before being removed by the spleen. The spleen is an efficient recycler. It breaks the erythrocytes down into their components, some of which can be used again in new cells.

The monocytes and granular leukocytes develop from committed cells called myeloblasts. The granulocytes are all derived from promyelocytes, which divide into myelocytes. The myelocytes still have single-lobed nuclei, but, as they mature, the shape of the nuclei changes until it takes on the characteristic multilobed appearance of the mature cells. Granulocytes develop from stem cells over a period of eight to nine days.

Mature granulocytes are stored in the bone marrow. They are released into the circulation as they are needed. Once they have been released, granulocytes have a relatively short life: they are often in circulation for only five to ten hours before migrating into the tissues, where they live for between five and 14 days. In contrast, the monocytes, which spend only a short time in the blood (ten to 20 hours), can live for months or years as macrophages in the tissues.

The lymphocytes begin life as lymphoblasts in the bone marrow. Once they enter the circulation they move to the lymph nodes, where they multi-

KARL LANDSTEINER

In 1930, Karl Landsteiner won the Nobel Prize for his discovery of the ABO blood typing system that has allowed blood transfusion to become the safe and routine medical practice that it is today.

Karl Landsteiner was born on June 14, 1868 in Vienna, Austria. He was educated at the University of Vienna, where he received his MD (doctorate) in 1891. Between 1898 and 1908 he worked at the Vienna Pathological Institute, where he began his search for the differences in human blood that explained why it could not be transfused safely. In 1900 he discovered that human blood falls into three major types, according to different antigens on the membranes of red blood cells. He labelled these types, A, B, and O. In the following year, he discovered a fourth type, AB, which possesses both the A and B antigens. He later discovered that there were further antigen systems involved in distinguishing blood types. In 1927 he discovered one of the minor blood typing systems, the M and N system, and in 1940 the rhesus factor. Landsteiner was appointed Professor of Pathology at the University of Vienna (1909-19) and at the Rockefeller Institute for Medical Research in New York City (1922-43). He died on June 26, 1943.

Karl Landsteiner's work has had a major impact on health and medicine (and even law) in the 20th century. People who once would have died during wars, surgery, and childbirth can now be saved by blood transfusion. Blood typing also has implications in law, where it has been used as evidence in paternity suits and murder trials. Karl Landsteiner's classic text *The Specificity of Serological Reactions* helped to establish the science of immunochemistry (the study of the chemistry of immunological reactions).

DISCOVERERS

ply. The lymphocytes then reenter the circulation from these sites, and return to the lymph nodes via the lymphatic system.

T-cells are thought to mature in the thymus. This is a small spherical organ essential to the immune system, which sits behind the breastbone in adult mammals.

The origin of the B-cells is less clear. In mammals, B-cells first develop in the bone marrow or liver of the embryo. In birds, they mature in the bursa of Fabricus, an appendix-like organ in the hind part of the gut. The names T- and B-cells refer to "thymus-derived" and "bursa-derived" (even though few vertebrates have a bursa and their B-cells come from the bone marrow).

The other type of blood cell, the platelets, are actually fragments of larger cells called megakaryocytes, which are found in the bone marrow. Platelets do not have nuclei. They bud off from the megakaryocytes and are formed from the cell membrane and cytoplasm of these larger cells.

BLOOD TYPING AND TRANSFUSIONS

Since the Middle Ages, doctors and scientists had been fascinated by the idea of treating blood loss by injecting blood from one person into another. One of the earliest known attempts was by an Italian physician, Giovanni Colle, in 1628. Nearly all of these early attempts killed the patients, and so blood transfusion was banned in France, England, and Italy after the late 17th century. No one understood why the blood of one person could not just be transferred into another.

Then in 1895 a Frenchman called Jules Bordet discovered that when the red blood cells of one animal are mixed with the serum (blood plasma, which has had fibrinogen and the other clotting proteins removed) of another species, the red cells of the first animal agglutinate (clump together). Karl Landsteiner, an Austrian, found that the same thing happened when the red blood cells and serum of individuals of the same species are mixed.

It soon became clear that blood contains antigens (see IMMUNE SYSTEMS), which can trigger reactions when one sort of blood is mixed with another. There are two major groups of antigens that determine a person's blood type. These are called the ABO and the rhesus (Rh) systems. They were both discovered by Landsteiner, the ABO system in 1900, and the Rh system in 1940. Blood groups are particularly important to identify when people need a blood transfusion after an operation or an accident. A transfusion of the wrong sort of blood will be rejected by the patient's own blood, causing more harm than good. It is important to match the blood of the donor with the patient's own blood as closely as possible.

The ABO system

In the ABO system, the blood type depends on the presence or absence of two related antigens, A and B, on the surface of the red blood cells. A person with blood type A has the A antigen on the surface of the red blood cells, someone with blood type B has the B antigen, AB blood type has both A and B antigens, while a person with blood type O has neither antigen on their red blood cells.

The different blood types also have a characteristic combination of antibodies anti-A and anti-B in the plasma. These are proteins that will attack the type of antigen that the person lacks on their own red blood cells. This reaction causes the cells to clump together and this can plug the smaller blood vessels. Thus blood type A has anti-B antibody in the plasma, type B has anti-A, type AB contains neither antibody, and type O has both anti-A and anti-B antibodies. The type of blood that people can be given in a transfusion depends on

In blood transfusions the blood types of the donor and the recipient have to be matched carefully. This shows what happens when different blood types are mixed together in a dish in a laboratory. For example, type B blood causes type A and type AB blood cells to clump together. This is because type B blood contains anti-A antibodies, which attack the A antigens found in both A and AB blood.

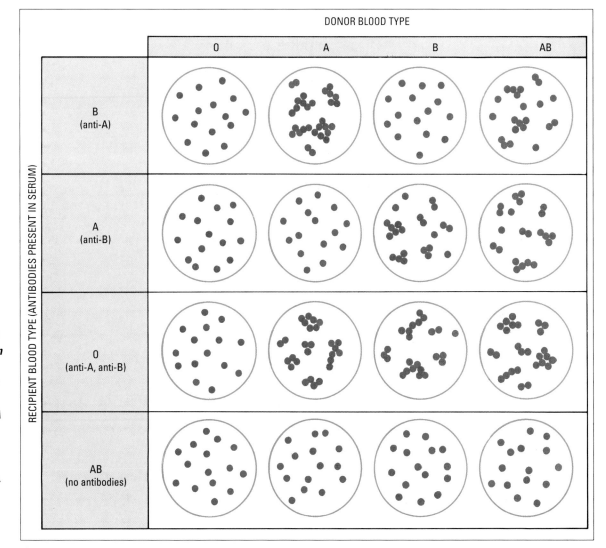

their own blood type. Care must be taken to ensure that the antibodies in the recipient's plasma will not react with the blood cells in the donor blood. The antibodies in the donor plasma do not usually represent a problem, because the plasma is quickly diluted in the recipient's bloodstream. Blood of type O contains neither antigen and can be transfused into patients with any of the other blood groups. Type O individuals are known as universal donors. However, people with blood type O can only accept donor blood type O.

A person with blood type A produces antibodies that attack both B and AB type blood. He or she can only receive transfusions from another person with blood type A or O. Likewise, a person with blood type B can only receive blood from another person with type B or from someone with type O. People with AB group blood are able to accept A, B, or O type groups. They are known as universal recipients. In fact, the terms universal donor and universal recipient are not entirely accurate, since there are other antibody systems that influence transfusion.

ABO blood types are inherited. A person with group A blood type will have parents both of group A, or one parent with group A and one with group O. Likewise a person with B group blood will have parents of B and B, or O and B groups. A person with group O blood will have parents who are both group O, and a person with AB blood will have one parent with group A and one parent with group B. This system used to be a common way of establishing paternity (fatherhood) in legal cases, but it is not conclusive.

The Rh system

The second major antigen system in blood is the Rh system, first found in the blood of rhesus monkeys. The Rh system consists of at least eight Rh antigens. The most important of these is called antigen D. A person who is Rh-positive has the antigen D on the surfaces of his or her red blood cells, while the cells of someone who is Rh-negative have no antigen D. Around 85 percent of the population are Rh-positive. The remaining 15 percent are Rh-negative.

Rh typing is particularly important during pregnancy. If a Rh-negative woman has a baby with a Rh-positive father, the baby may be Rh-positive. Even though the mother's bloodstream and the fetal bloodstream are separate, some Rh-positive red cells cross the placenta at birth. When the mother's immune system comes into contact with the Rh-positive blood from the fetus, it makes antibodies against the antigen D.

This does not cause a problem in a first pregnancy, because the antibodies are produced very slowly. However, the immune system retains a "memory," and the same event a second time can cause a much higher antibody production. These antibodies cross the placenta into the fetus's bloodstream, causing the fetal red cells to clump together. The Rh-positive baby may die unless it receives a transfusion of Rh-negative blood.

During pregnancy and after the birth of each baby, Rh-negative mothers are treated with antibodies to antigen D. They quickly clear the mother's blood of any Rh-positive fetal red blood cells, reducing the chance of her immune system producing antibodies against antigen D.

Other transfusion reactions

There are at least 12 other minor antigen systems in humans, which can sometimes cause transfusion reactions. Before any blood is transfused, the donated blood must be mixed with the recipient's blood and checked carefully for any signs of clumping (agglutination) or bursting (hemolysis), which indicate incompatibility.

Blood for transfusion is stored in blood banks, but whole blood cannot be kept longer than six weeks. However, various components can be separated and frozen and stored for up to a year. Components that can be kept in this way include platelets to control bleeding; concentrated red blood cells to correct anemia; plasma fractions such as fibrinogen to aid clotting; and gamma globulin to help fight certain infectious diseases.

Infections such as hepatitis and AIDS can be acquired as a result of transfusion, although the blood supply (collected and distributed in the United States by the Red Cross) is carefully

---

CHARLES DREW

During World War II, U.S. physician Charles Drew set up the National Blood Bank program with the American Red Cross. His pioneering work in blood research meant that, for the first time, blood could be preserved and stored for future use in emergency life-saving transfusions.

Charles Drew was born on June 3, 1904. He graduated from McGill University in 1933 and went on to teach pathology at Howard Medical School in Washington, D.C., and train in surgery at Freedman's Hospital. In 1938 his important research began with a two-year fellowship at Columbia-Presbyterian Medical Center in New York. Here Dr Drew concentrated on how blood could be stored without becoming spoiled: at that time, even when refrigerated, it could not be preserved for longer than a week. His breakthrough came when he removed the blood cells and attempted to preserve the plasma. He found that this could be kept fresh for longer, without refrigeration, and worked better than whole blood in transfusions. During World War II Dr Drew directed plasma supplies to Great Britain, where they were used to save the lives of many injured soldiers. And, despite his death in 1950, Charles Drew's work is still helping to save many lives today.

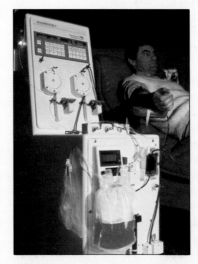

Following Dr Drew's blood research, people are able to donate blood plasma for use in later emergencies.

DISCOVERERS

ARTIFICIAL BLOOD

Scientists have been occupied for years by the question of how to develop a safe and effective replacement for blood, a compound that will fulfil the function of carrying oxygen around the body. The advent of AIDS has increased the urgency to find a blood substitute that is free of viral contamination and, since highly selective screening methods have contributed to a diminishing supply of donated blood, is available in large quantities. Now it seems likely that the end of this search is in sight. Using techniques such as genetic and protein engineering, scientists have developed artificial hemoglobin, the oxygen-carrying protein present in all red blood cells.

In looking for a safe subsitite for blood, researchers have considered a range of criteria. As well as having the correct oxygen-carrying capacity and being virus-free, the blood substitute must be compatible with all blood groups, must remain stable in the circulation for an appropriate length of time, and must not upset the osmotic balance in the blood.

Because the molecules responsible for blood type occur on the surface of the red blood cells, researchers have believed that a safe blood substitute should be cell-free. This suggested free hemoglobin as the key to artificial blood. However, early experiments in the 1940s demonstrated that transfusion with free natural hemoglobin is not practicable. One reason is that free hemoglobin, unbound by cellular membranes, easily splits into two halves, each consisting of one α- and one ß-globin. Unlike larger blood cells and plasma proteins, these are able to pass through the kidneys, where they are excreted via the urine or where they clog the kidney's capillaries.

Another problem is that hemoglobin is usually helped in its task of delivering oxygen by a small molecule known as DPG, which occurs in red cells, one for each 280 million hemoglobin molecules. Free

hemoglobin does not have DPG and so yields little oxygen. By 1984, scientists had discovered how to produce large amounts of human hemoglobin inside bacterial cells. The gene responsible for producing hemoglobin was introduced into the bacterium *Escherichia coli*, which was "tricked" into producing large amounts of the protein. This provided a method of producing unlimited amounts of identical human hemoglobin.

However, this technique could only contribute to the development of artificial blood if the hemoglobin molecules, introduced into bacteria for mass production, could be "redesigned" to remain intact and to release their oxygen easily.

The considerable work by Max Perutz (for which he received a Nobel Prize for chemistry) on the atomic structure of hemoglobin shows that the end of one α-globin chain is close to the beginning of the other α-globin. Using genetic engineering, scientists have managed to join the genes for the two α-globins and introduce them into bacterial cells together with the gene for ß-globin. The bacteria have used these "redesigned" genes to produce hemoglobin with the two α-globins securely linked together and attached to two separate ß-globins.

Researchers have also found a solution to the problem of improving oxygen delivery. There are around 300 abnormal hemoglobins that occur as natural mutations in humans, some of which will release oxygen readily, even in the absence of DPG. Scientists have introduced the gene for one of these mutations into the gene for the ß-globin chains, which are used to manufacture hemoglobin in the bacteria. These bacteria can now produce vast quantities of genetically identical hemoglobin, which does not disintegrate and provides readily available oxygen.

SCIENCE AND SOCIETY

screened. Medical staff should always consider the risks of infection and of unforeseen reactions when deciding whether a transfusion is necessary.

BLOOD DISEASES
The different blood components can become diseased as a result of deficiency, reactions to drugs, or inherited disorders.

Red blood cell disorders
One of the most common red blood cell disorders is anemia. In anemia there are too few red blood cells in the blood, and consequently a low level of hemoglobin. This means that the blood carries less oxygen, and sufferers tire easily. There are several types of anemia. Some are caused by deficiencies in the nutrients needed to produce red blood cells, such as iron, folic acid, and vitamin B_{12}. Other anemias are inherited.

Iron-deficiency anemia
A deficiency in iron is the most common cause of anemia, since iron is needed for the production of hemoglobin. In this type of anemia, reduced hemoglobin production leads to a reduction in red blood cell production. Iron deficiency is generally diagnosed by measuring the concentration of iron in

the blood, which will be low, as well as testing the iron-binding capacity of the blood, which will be increased, as though the body were trying to overcome the deficiency in iron. This type of anemia has several causes. The deficiency may be the result of not taking enough iron in the diet, but this is an unusual cause except in strict vegans (who eat no animal products).

A more common cause of deficiency is loss of iron from the body. This loss is generally the result of heavy bleeding. Blood loss through menstruation can lead to iron deficiency, and can be overcome by taking iron supplements. However, in men and in nonmenstruating women, iron deficiency may be caused by bleeding occurring anywhere in the body, often from the gut. This could be the result of serious illness, such as stomach and colon cancer. It can be detected by the presence of blood in the feces. Pregnant women sometimes become anemic because they are supplying most of their iron to the developing baby.

Macrocytic anemias
Deficiencies of both folic acid and vitamin B_{12} cause macrocytic anemias. In these disorders, there are fewer red blood cells, but the cells themselves are much larger than usual.

Folic acid deficiency may be the result of inadequate intake, often in pregnancy or malnutrition, or because the gut is not absorbing it properly. This happens in some chronic diarrheal diseases. Anemia caused by a deficiency of vitamin B_{12} can eventually lead to serious disease of the nervous system, so it is particularly important to find out the cause of macrocytic anemia. Vitamin B_{12} deficiency is virtually always the result of insufficient absorption, often as part of a syndrome known as pernicious anemia. In this disease, the stomach fails to produce a substance known as intrinsic factor of Castle, without which B_{12} cannot be properly absorbed (see DIGESTIVE SYSTEMS).

Thalassemias and sickle cell anemia

Red blood cell production can also drop in certain hereditary diseases. Thalassemias are caused by an inherited defect in which the blood cells are very small. They are most common in countries around the Mediterranean Sea, in southern Europe, and in the Middle East. The word thalassemia actually means "anemia of the sea." These disorders vary in severity from mild to life-threatening (see HEREDITARY DISEASES).

Sickle cell anemia is most common in people of African descent. In people who have this disease, the red blood cells are shaped like half-moons. This distortion happens in the veins after the hemoglobin has released its oxygen. These so-called "sickle" cells slow the blood flow and clog the capillaries, causing tissue damage and severe pain. This clogging gradually destroys the spleen, leading to severe and sometimes fatal infections. Sickle cell anemia occurs in people who have inherited the relevant gene from both parents. If the gene is inherited from only one parent, the person has what is known as sickle cell trait, in which he or she is a carrier of sickle cell anemia and usually has no symptoms.

Both thalassemia and sickle cell trait probably evolved as a defense against malaria. When the red blood cells of someone with sickle cell trait are attacked by the parasite that causes malaria, the abnormal red blood cells collapse. This slows the parasite's growth.

Leukemia

Leukemia is a type of cancer in which the white blood cells divide uncontrollably (see CANCER). The most serious type is acute leukemia, which mainly affects children. An excessive number of immature white blood cells are produced, which "take over" the marrow and prevent it from producing red blood cells and platelets. The immature white blood cells are incapable of fighting disease. The reduction in the number of red blood cells leads to anemia, while the lowered number of platelets makes blood clotting less effective. As a result people with acute leukemia suffer from internal bleeding and are like to develop serious, and often fatal, infections.

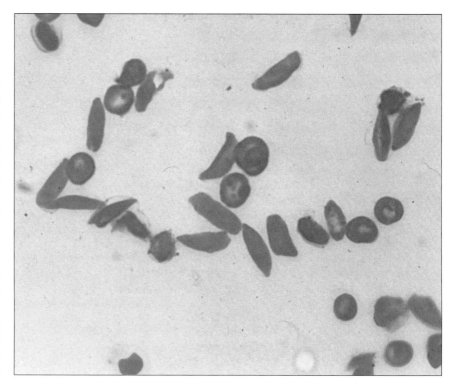

This blood sample has been taken from someone with sickle cell anemia. It shows normal red blood cells and crescent-shaped sickle cells (light microscopy x 200).

Chronic leukemias take longer to develop and are most common in people over the age of 40. They are less dangerous than the acute form. Leukemias are usually diagnosed by looking at a blood smear, and then carrying out a bone marrow biopsy (examination of small tissue samples to check for disease).

Platelet disorders

Because of the role platelets play in forming blood clots, abnormalities can lead to significant bleeding problems. The most common cause is thrombocytopenia, or a reduced number of platelets. This may occur because the bone marrow produces fewer platelets, or because the platelets are destroyed too quickly. Thrombocytopenia can be caused by an adverse reaction to drugs, or by more serious conditions, such as leukemia.

The only significant result of a low platelet count is increased bleeding. This may be trivial, such as bleeding gums during tooth brushing, and easy bruising, or it may lead to a life-threatening hemorrhage, especially in the gut, lungs, and brain. Thrombocytopenia is diagnosed by a low number of platelets in a blood count. It can be treated with corticosteroid drugs (see CORTICOSTEROID DRUGS) or, in rare cases, by removing the spleen.

A. FRYER

See also: AIDS; ANEMIA; ANTIBODIES; CIRCULATORY SYSTEMS; IMMUNE SYSTEMS; LEUKEMIA; LYMPHATIC SYSTEMS; SPLEEN; TRANSPLANTS.

Further reading:
Belcher, Anne E. *Blood Disorders*. St. Louis, Missouri: Mosby, 1993.
Greene, W.C. "AIDS and the Immune System." *Scientific American*, **269**, pp.98-105, Sept. 1993.

BONE

Bone is a calcified connective tissue that forms a supportive skeleton in higher vertebrates

Like the steel girders in a skyscraper, bone acts as a framework for the vertebrate body, providing internal structural support, giving shape to the body, and helping to maintain posture.

Bone is not lifeless material. Indeed it is a living connective tissue capable of growth and repair. It provides the points of attachment for the skeletal muscles, without which movement would be impaired, and is the framework on which the internal organs of the body are suspended and protected. Bone also has other important functions in the body. It is involved in the production of red blood cells, and it acts as a store for the minerals calcium and phosphate.

CORE FACTS

- Bone forms the skeleton, the framework of the vertebrate body.
- A typical vertebrate skeleton has 200-300 bones.
- Bone develops from cartilage.
- Mature bone is composed of osteons, which collectively make up haversian systems.

The typical vertebrate skeleton is a flexible framework of 200 to 300 bones, linked by connective tissue such as muscle, ligaments, and cartilage. Bones meet at the joints. Some joints, such as those of the pelvis (which has three distinct bones) do not allow bones to move much, whereas other joints, such as the shoulder joint, allow for a wide range of movement. The articulating, or moving, surfaces of more mobile bones are covered with thin layers of cartilage. This frictionless surface reduces wear on the bones as they move relative to each other.

Formation and structure

There are two distinct types of vertebrate bone: dermal bone and endochondral bone. Dermal bone forms directly from mesenchyme, or embryonic connective tissue. Groups of mesenchyme cells deposit bone in plates. In bony fishes, dermal bones are formed over almost the entire body as plates over the head and as scales over the rest of the body. These bony parts act like armor to protect the soft inner tissues from damage by impact or predators. In birds and mammals, dermal bones are normally found only in the skull, jaws, and pectoral (shoulder) girdle.

All the main bones of the vertebrate skeleton are endochondral bones. These bones are developed from cartilage by the action of osteoblasts, or bone-depositing cells. For example, in the fetal development of a long bone such as the femur (upper leg), in the earliest stages of development,

Cross section of compact bone shown under the light microscope. The network of osteons that make up haversian systems are clearly visible. Each haversian system consists of a haversian canal, surrounded by lamellae – ring-like layers of calcified bone.

CONNECTIONS

● Bone injured beyond repair can be replaced by a porous glass called bioglas. The body fills the bioglas pores with collagen fibers, making a strong resilient material. The design and manufacture of new body parts is called **BIONICS.**

● Bone is immensely strong, with a compressive strength, or resistance to pressure, comparable to that of reinforced concrete.

---

the mesenchyme cells are altered to create hyaline cartilage, a precursor of bone. This cartilage provides a form or shape for the developing bone (see diagram overleaf). A membrane called the perichondrium forms around the hyaline cartilage and becomes the periosteum, which contains a network of blood vessels and nerves and is capable of laying down fresh layers of bone to increase the bone's diameter.

Cartilage cells deep inside the structure break down leaving cavities (epiphyses), which will become the center of bone deposition. Blood vessels from the perichondrium invade the hyaline cartilage and enter the newly formed central cavities. Calcium salts for the new bone matrix and the special bone secreting cells, the osteoblasts, are carried in the blood. The osteoblasts use the calcium salts to create a thin-walled network of central bone called spongy bone.

While the spongy bone is forming at the center of the hyaline cartilage, a different kind of bone is forming at its edges. Cells from the periosteum begin to deposit a layer of bone, known as a bone collar, around the cartilage. Unlike the spongy bone, this peripheral bone is dense and compact. As it continues to be deposited, the long bone grows in width and strength. The bone grows in length at regions called epiphyseal cartilage plates at each end of the long bone. These regions contain actively dividing cells that allow the bone to elongate as more bone-producing cells are deposited. How tall a person becomes mainly depends on when this epiphyseal plate growth ends, usually between the ages of 16 to 21 years.

The interior structure of mature bone is intricate and it functions very actively. A cross section through the compact mature bone shows a complex web-like network of structures called osteons, which collectively make up what is known as the haversian system. At the center of each osteon is a blood vessel, surrounded by ring-like layers of calcified bone called lamellae. The lamellar rings contain osteocytes (bone cells), and each osteocyte has a small cavity (called a lacuna), which is connected to other osteocytes via small canals called canaliculi. The bone cells exchange materials through these canaliculi.

The bone marrow, the spongy center of long bones, vertebrae, ribs, and the sternum, is an important blood-producing region of the adult vertebrate body (although it is not the only region where red blood cells are formed). The marrow tissue that produces blood cells is called myeloid tissue. In mammals, both erythrocytes (red blood cells) and lymphoid cells (immune system cells) are produced in the marrow. Bone marrow transplants are an attempt to introduce healthy bone marrow into a patient suffering from a blood disease such as leukemia, a rare form of blood cancer.

Bone repair

Like other connective tissues, bone is able to repair itself when damaged. After a fracture, for example, the broken bone begins to heal itself immediately. For this reason, the bones need to be aligned as soon as possible so that the bone will maintain its original shape. The bones may then be held in place by a plaster cast or metal pins. First, blood from broken blood vessels within and around the bone pours into the gap between the two broken ends of bone and forms a clot, sealing the damaged vessels. After a few days, connective tissue cells from the periosteum, called fibroblasts, enter the blood clot and lay down collagen fibers, forming a mesh called the callus, which spans the gap between the two ends of broken bone. Then osteoblasts from the periosteum convert the callus to bone, knitting the two ends together.

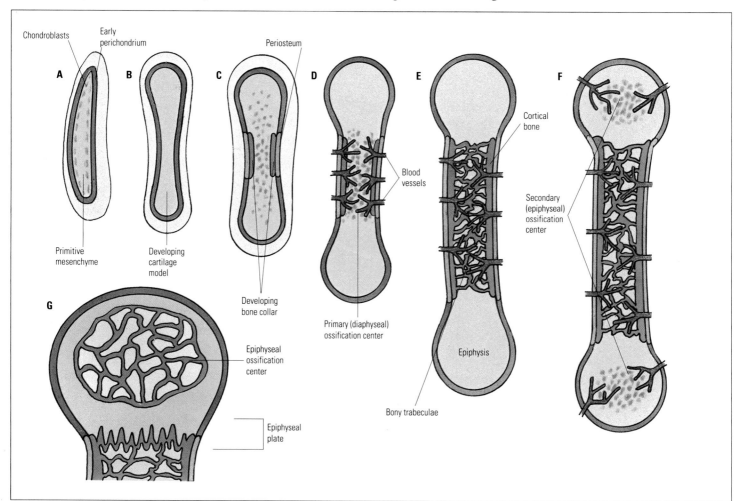

Development of fetal long bone. (A) Developing chondroblasts in primitive mesenchyme. Formation of perichondrium and cartilage blueprint. (B) Developing cartilage model takes on the shape of new bone. (C) Perichondrium transforms to periosteum, which produces a collar of compact bone. Calcium salts are deposited in enlarging cartilage model. (D) Blood vessels grow through the periosteum and bone collar bringing ossification cells with them. These establish a primary ossification center in the center of the developing bone. (E) Bony processes spread into the primary ossification center to occupy the entire central space. At this stage, the terminal club-shaped epiphyses are still composed of cartilage. (F) Establishment, around birth, of secondary, (epiphyseal) ossification centers in center of each epiphysis by ingrowth of mesenchymal cells (which become osteoblasts) and blood vessels. (G) After birth, the secondary (epiphyseal) ossification center enlarges to leave an epiphyseal plate of cartilage and a surround of cartilage, which will eventually become the articular cartilage that protects the joints.

BONE DISEASES AND DEFORMITIES

A number of bone diseases have plagued humans over the centuries. In a condition known as osteoporosis, which affects around 20 million Americans, changes in the production and destruction of bone can cause the mass of bone to decrease after the age of 20 to 30 years, making the bones more fragile and likely to fracture. This happens because more bone is lost than is replaced. Some degree of osteoporosis is part of the normal aging process in elderly people, particularly women, but in severe cases the bone becomes extremely brittle.

No one fully understands what causes osteoporosis, although certain risk factors have been identified, such as smoking, calcium deficiency, lack of exercise, and alcohol consumption. Severe osteoporosis occurs most often in post-menopausal women and, although the full cause is not known, scientists believe that the female sex hormone estrogen may play a significant role in maintaining bone mass. There is evidence that administering estrogen in hormone replacement therapy (HRT) can help in reducing the rate of bone loss in these women. Other preventative measures include taking regular exercise and ensuring an adequate supply of calcium in the diet. Food rich in calcium includes milk and milk products, green leafy vegetables, citrus fruits, and shellfish.

In a disorder called rickets, bones lose their rigidity and become softened, causing bow-knees in toddlers, and knock-knees in older children. Untreated, rickets leads to short stature and bone deformity. Rickets is usually related to a lack of vitamin D, which affects the deposition of minerals. This can be caused by a dietary deficiency of vitamin D, which is added to dairy products, or by an intestinal disease, which interferes with its absorption. Vitamin D is also manufactured by ultraviolet light, hence lack of exposure to the sun can sometimes be a factor. Rickets can also be caused by inherited abnormalities of bone metabolism, and chronic kidney failure. Rickets was once common, but with increased standards of nutrition, rarely occurs now in developed countries. The best prevention is vitamin D supplements.

Bone deformation may also be the result of achondroplasia, a defect in bone development, which affects individuals known as dwarfs. Achondroplasia is inherited and mainly affects the long bones.

The joints can also become a site for injury and disease. The bursa are fluid-filled sacs that minimize friction between muscles, tendons, and bone. They can become inflamed, resulting in a condition called bursitis. Arthritis is a more serious disorder, which affects the mobility of joints; it can be brought on by trauma, a previous disease such as gonorrhea or Lyme disease, malfunctions of the immune system, or genetic defects (see ARTHRITIS).

AT RISK

STRUCTURE OF THE LONG BONE

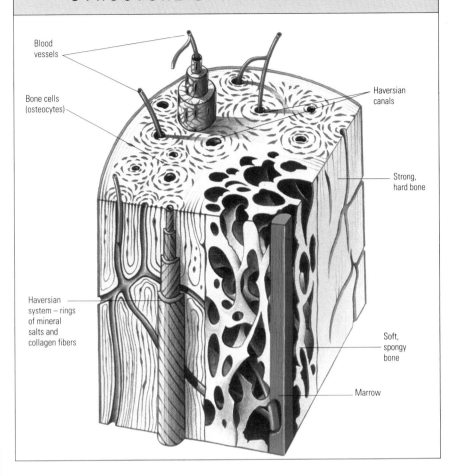

Blood vessels

Bone cells (osteocytes)

Haversian canals

Strong, hard bone

Haversian system – rings of mineral salts and collagen fibers

Soft, spongy bone

Marrow

Adaptations

The interior structure of bone varies between animals, as it has adapted to meet different challenges. Birds, which need a lightweight skeleton in order to fly, have many hollow bones. For example, the skeleton of the frigate bird, which has a wing span exceeding 7 ft (2.1 m), weighs only 4 oz (114 g). This is less than the weight of its feathers! This hollowing of bone was also a weight-reducing strategy seen in some of the bones of larger dinosaurs. Surprisingly, hollowing the bone does not significantly reduce its structural strength. This is because most bone is largely circular in cross section, and most of the bone's structural strength is found in the dense outer layer.

The outward shape of the bone reflects its function in the living vertebrate. For example, in digging animals, such as the badger, the long bones of the forelimb are thick and dense, suggesting powerful muscle action, while in running animals, such as the cheetah, the limb bones are thin, so that minimum energy is needed to move the limbs.

K. HOSOUME/J. KAUFMANN

See also: BLOOD; CALCIUM; CARTILAGE; SKELETAL SYSTEMS; VERTEBRATES.

Further reading:

Chiras, D.D. *Human Biology: Health, Homeostasis, and the Environment.* St. Paul: West Publishing Co., 1991.

BOTANY

Botany is the scientific study of plants

Botany, the scientific study of plants, probably has very early origins. Our early ancestors, living as hunter-gatherers, would have needed to identify which plants were safe to eat and which were harmful. When humans began to lead more settled lives, and practice agriculture, they developed a knowledge of the types of plants that made good crops and provided fodder for domestic animals. Plants are essential to humans and all living things. We depend on plants for food, wood, energy, and oxygen. A thorough scientific knowledge of plants is essential for human survival.

HISTORY OF BOTANY

The scientific study of plants can be traced to Theophrastus in Greece in the 4th century BC. His work is known from *Enquiry into Plants*, which may have been put together from the notes of his students. Dioscorides, of Cilicia (in present day Turkey), compiled the first illustrated catalogue of plant species, known as a herbal, in the 1st century AD. Herbals gave information about plants' botanical, medicinal, and mythological properties.

A more modern style of botanical catalogue appeared in the 17th century. Caspar Bauhin's *Pinax* (Greek for a list or table) was produced in 1623. It was a basic checklist of plant names, and it became the standard reference work on European plants known at that time.

Bringing order to botany

The earliest botanists were mainly concerned with identifying and naming plants. By the early 18th century, many new plants had been discovered and named, but in such a disorganized way that communication between botanists was almost impossible. The next important stage in botany was to bring order to the naming of plants.

In the 18th century, Carl Linnaeus (1707-1778), the famous Swedish botanist, introduced the modern binomial system of naming plants, based on a two-part name and using Greek and Latin words. In the binomial system the basic unit is a species. This is a group of plants that can cross-pollinate each other and produce viable seeds. A group of related plants forms a genus (see CLASSIFICATION). Plants are known by their generic name and

Herbarium sheet from 1896 showing dried specimens of the poppy (Papaver rhoeas).

by a specific name. For example, *Pinus aristatis* is a Bristlecone pine and *Pinus divaricata* is a Jack pine.

Plant explorers

With European colonization of Asia, Africa, Australia, and the Americas, European naturalists became very interested in finding out about other parts of the world. Botanists and plant collectors traveled across the continents. New plant species were "discovered" and brought back to Europe. The plants were transported either as living material or as dried and pressed specimens. Botanic gardens were established for the living plants, and herbaria were set up to house the dried specimens.

THE STUDY OF BOTANY TODAY

The modern science of botany has a number of distinct branches, many of which are interlinked.

Plant anatomy

Plant anatomy is the study of the internal arrangement of plant parts, for example the cellular structure of tissues and the vascular bundles that transport water and nutrients. Plant anatomists work closely with plant physiologists.

Plant physiology

Plant physiologists are interested in the life processes that take place in the plant such as tran-

---

CORE FACTS

■ Botany is the scientific study of plants.

■ The modern science of botany is divided into a number of branches: anatomy, physiology, morphology, taxonomy, cytology, genetics, ecology, paleobotany, and ethnobotany.

■ A scientific knowledge of plants is important in agriculture, horticulture, forestry, and medicine.

CONNECTIONS

● More than 25 percent of our drugs and medicines are derived from plants. Many of these are rainforest species, which are endangered by the destruction of **TROPICAL RAINFORESTS**.

● Botany helps us understand the scientific basis of the processes taking place inside plants. For example, **PHOTOSYNTHESIS** is the process that converts radiant **ENERGY** from the sun into chemical energy, and **TRANSPIRATION** is loss of water from a plant's surface.

spiration (the movement of water into, through, and out of a plant) and photosynthesis (the solar-powered manufacture of carbohydrates from water and carbon dioxide).

Plant morphology

Plant morphology is the external arrangement of plant form and parts. This can mean large obvious features, such as the shape of a tree's trunk and crown, leaf shape and structure, flower structure, number of petals, etc. But it also includes much smaller and even microscopic details. Morphology has long been the main basis for classifying plants.

Plant taxonomy

The identification and classification of plants is still an important area of study. As new plants are discovered, taxonomists name them and arrange them in a recognized scheme. Plants have common names but these change from country to country and even from one part of a country to another. For example, Yellow adder's-tongue and Trout lily are both common names for the lily *Erythronium americanum Ker*. Taxonomists help devise an effective and systematic way of classifying and naming plants that is recognized by all scientists.

Plant cytology

Plant cytology, or cell biology, is the study of plant cells, including the chromosomes inside them. Chromosomes contain the DNA (deoxyribonucleic acid) molecule chains that determine the nature of the life form and how genetic information is passed from one generation to the next. Chromosomal characteristics, their numbers and shapes, are being used increasingly in classification.

Plant genetics

Plant genetics is the study of inheritance in plants. Modern plant geneticists not only study characteristics passed from one generation to the next, they also extract, study, and manipulate the plants' DNA chains. This genetic engineering is producing new cultivars (plants found only in cultivation) specially suited to particular growing conditions. Like detectives, taxonomists can also use genetic profiles to work out relations between plant populations or individual plants.

Plant ecology

Plant ecology considers a plant's relationship to its surroundings. Plant ecologists look at how plants adapt to their environment and to the other living organisms within it. This can give clues about the effects of human interference by showing how plants adapt to pollution, for example. Plant ecology is important for the effective conservation of natural areas.

Paleobotany

Paleobotany is concerned with fossil plants. The principles of classification are different here since a genus and species might only be known from a single fossil. The study of prehistoric plants helps us understand how plants have evolved.

Dendrochronology

Dendrochronology, or tree-ring dating, involves counting the annual rings present in tree trunks, and is used to date archaeological sites or to correct dates already obtained by radiocarbon testing (see CARBON CYCLE).

Ethnobotany

Ethnobotany looks at the relations between humans and plants. Observing how other cultures use plants can have an effect on the agricultural practices of industrialized societies. This might include the introduction of plants with resistance to pests and diseases, or the introduction of new economically important plants. Ethnobotanists can also identify potential new medicine-producing plants, and new crops for societies with food shortages.

N. TURLAND

See also: AGRICULTURE; CLASSIFICATION; CONSERVATION; SELECTIVE BREEDING.

Further reading:
Reveal, James L. *Gentle Conquest: the Botanical Discovery of North America with Illustrations from the Library of Congress.* Washington, DC: Starwood Publishing Inc., 1992.

PLANT COLLECTORS

One of the earliest plant collectors was the English gardener-botanist, John Tradescant (1570-1638). He collected plants from France, Holland, the Mediterranean, and Russia. Tradescant's son, John the younger (1608-62), was also a collector, but he specialized in the plants of the New World, visiting Virginia in 1637, 1642, and 1654. The Tradescants are commemorated by the Virginian spiderwort *Tradescantia virginiana*.

Other famous plant collectors included the wealthy amateur English scientist Sir Joseph Banks (1743-1820) who traveled widely and found many new species with Daniel Solander (1733-1782), his Swedish employee. Banks went with Captain Cook on his voyage around the world from 1768 to 1771 and was a founder of Kew Gardens in London, Britain. The Australian genus *Banksia* is named after him.

Ernest Henry "Chinese" Wilson (1876-1930) was a professional collector employed by the nurserymen Veitch and Son. As his nickname suggests, Wilson specialized in Chinese plants, but he also traveled to Australia, Tasmania, New Zealand, India, Singapore, Japan, Kenya, and Zimbabwe. In 1919, Wilson was appointed assistant director at the Arnold Arboretum in Boston, part of Harvard University, and became the keeper eight years later.

John Tradescant (top) with his son John the younger (below).

DISCOVERERS

BRAIN

The brain is the control center of the body, organizing and coordinating the electrical and chemical signals of the nervous system. It receives information through the senses, analyzes and combines that information, and uses the result to supervise the functioning of the body. The brain governs the body's other organ systems, such as the circulatory, respiratory, and endocrine systems, and controls the body's movement through the muscles. In humans, the brain is the organ of thought, language, and consciousness.

Not all organisms have brains. Sponges completely lack a nervous system while cnidarians, such as Hydra, and echinoderms, such as sea urchins, function with simple nerve nets (see NERVOUS SYSTEMS). Structures that might be compared to a brain appear in bilaterally symmetrical animals (arranged in two symmetrical halves). Planarian flatworms have a collection of nerve cells referred to as "cerebral ganglia," which function as a primitive brain, as do annelids, such as earthworms, and arthropods, such as grasshoppers. Cephalopods, such as cuttlefish, squids, and octopuses, have a more developed nervous system than other invertebrates, probably because of their dextrous tenta-

---

CORE FACTS

- The brain is composed of specialized cells called neurons.
- The brains of birds, mammals, and humans have three parts: the hindbrain, the midbrain, and the forebrain.
- Most brain activity is based on learning and memory, a process of constant remodeling in which the brain alters the connections between its cells.
- Reflexive memory forms habits, such as learning to ride a bike; declarative memory involves conscious association or learning; working memory calls on reflexive and declarative memory combined with data from the senses, and would be used in holding an everyday conversation.

---

cles and carnivorous lifestyle. In these organisms, the ganglia are more or less fused to form a brain that encircles the esophagus. The ganglia themselves are differentiated so that areas within them control certain regions or functions of the body.

The brain is a product of evolution. When multicellular animals first arose, between one and two billion years ago, they needed an internal communications system that would help their cells exchange information. The brain developed as an organized collection of nerve cells, or neurons, from the noncentralized nervous systems of simple animals. Newer vertebrate species tend to have more complex brains than species that evolved earlier, but the features of complicated brains are still based on the features of simpler ones.

The neuron

Like other cells, neurons have a nucleus, set in cytoplasm and surrounded by a membrane that permits the passage of some substances and keeps others out of the cell. But a typical neuron also possesses structures not found in other types of cells. Extending from the neuron's cell body is a very long, thin fiber called an axon and shorter branching projections called dendrites. The longest human axon, which controls toe muscles, extends for more than 3 ft (about 1 m) from the middle of the back. Some whale axons are more than 33 ft (10 m) long. The cell body of a neuron is tiny: most are very much smaller than the period at the end of this sentence.

Neurons communicate via their axons and dendrites; the dendrites of one neuron collects nerve impulses from the axons of distant neurons. The point of communication is called a synapse.

BRAIN WAVES

The brain is a site of constant electrical activity, which is generated by its billions of cells. This activity can be recorded using a machine called an electroencephalograph (EEG). There are different types of brain wave, each with a different frequency and amplitude. When the brain is alert and actively processing information (as when you read this, for example) it generates irregular rapid waves. In a relaxed state, the waves are regular and rhythmic. The brain produces electrical waves even during sleep, and EEGs have been used to study this activity. Opening the eyes changes the normal resting pattern.

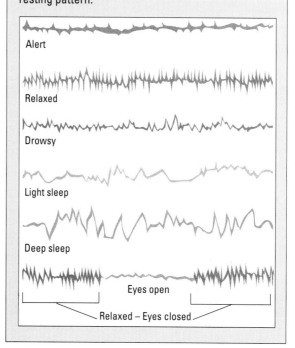

Alert

Relaxed

Drowsy

Light sleep

Deep sleep

Eyes open

Relaxed – Eyes closed

CONNECTIONS

- **NUTRITION** and **METABOLISM** are important to brain function since the brain relies on sufficient levels of glucose to operate efficiently.

- A branch of technology called artificial intelligence (AI) aims to imitate the problem-solving and decision-making functions of the human brain using computer systems. Essential information from a particular area, such as law, medicine, or finance, can be programmed into computers, which then imitate the knowledge and decision-making abilities of a real person.

- The brain is the seat of **COGNITION**, the process of knowing, and perception.

- Neurotransmitters, chemicals transmitted from the end of an axon, and the receptors on the receiving dendrites, are highly specific for each other, fitting together like a lock and key. **ENZYMES** are **PROTEINS** that catalyze biochemical reactions by converting one molecule (the substrate) to another molecule. Enzymes are also highly specific for the substrates they convert, again, employing a "lock and key" mechanism.

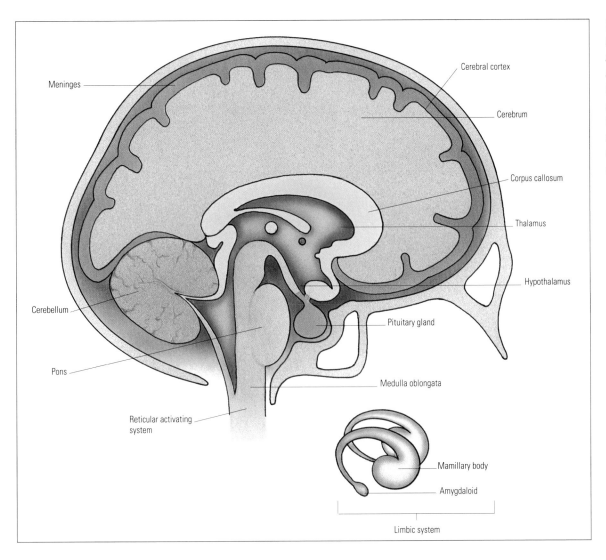

This cross section through the human brain shows the major parts. The limbic system, shown at the bottom of the diagram, actually lies deep beneath the cortex within the thalamus. It is thought to control our moods and emotions.

Labels in figure: Meninges, Cerebral cortex, Cerebrum, Corpus callosum, Thalamus, Hypothalamus, Pituitary gland, Cerebellum, Medulla oblongata, Pons, Reticular activating system, Mamillary body, Amygdaloid, Limbic system

ANATOMY OF THE BRAIN

In all vertebrates, including humans, the brain has three divisions: the hindbrain, the midbrain, and the forebrain.

Hindbrain

The hindbrain, which consists of the brain stem and the cerebellum, is the control center for many of the body's automatic functions. The cerebellum (a wrinkled ball of tissue at the lower rear of the brain) coordinates body movements, especially skilled movements, and maintains the sense of balance. Heartbeat and breathing are governed from centers deep within the medulla oblongata in the brain stem. This is part of the reticular formation, originally thought to be an activating system that oversees alertness in the brain. Now it is known that the reticular formation also maintains muscle tone and reflexes, and so helps to control movement, and also modifies the sensation of pain. The reticular formation is notable for the abundant connections its neurons make with other parts of the nervous system, such as the spinal cord, the thalamus, and the hypothalamus.

Midbrain

The midbrain governs some automatic functions, such as some reflexes, but also controls some voluntary movements. It handles much of the information collected by the eyes and ears, which is also relayed to the higher brain centers.

Forebrain

The forebrain contains the higher brain centers. The thalamus is located in the center of the forebrain, above the midbrain, and it functions as a kind of central processing unit. Almost all infor-

STROKES

The brain needs a constant supply of oxygen and glucose (a simple sugar) for energy. It obtains this fuel from its blood supply. When the flow of blood is disrupted for even a few minutes, brain cells die. Such brain damage usually results from a blood clot blocking a blood vessel, and is known as a stroke.

In the United States strokes are the third leading cause of death and the most common cause of disability in adults. Every year half a million Americans fall victim to strokes, which kill a third of them, and permanently disable another third. Strokes cause coma, paralysis, blindness, and mental deterioration.

Physical therapy (a kind of "habit" learning that helps nerve cells forge new connections that can bypass a damaged area in the brain) can help some stroke patients regain lost abilities, such as speech and movement. However, although the brain contains 100 billion (100,000,000,000) neurons at birth, no new neurons develop subsequently, and consequently, there is currently no way to avert or fix the tissue damage caused by a stroke. The injury becomes permanent just a few hours after the stroke.

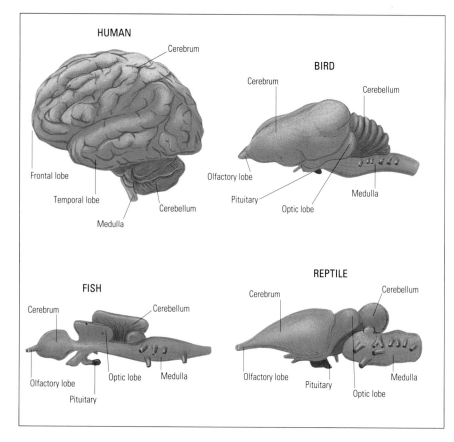

HUMAN

Cerebrum

Frontal lobe

Temporal lobe

Cerebellum

Medulla

BIRD

Cerebrum

Cerebellum

Olfactory lobe

Pituitary

Optic lobe

Medulla

FISH

Cerebrum

Cerebellum

Olfactory lobe

Optic lobe

Medulla

Pituitary

REPTILE

Cerebrum

Cerebellum

Olfactory lobe

Pituitary

Optic lobe

Medulla

This diagram shows the typical brain structures for a human, a bird, a fish, and a reptile. All vertebrate brains have certain features in common, including a large cerebellum to coordinate movement, optic lobes for sight, and olfactory lobes to interpret smells (although whales, dolphins, and porpoises have no olfactory lobes and probably lack a sense of smell).

mation from the senses passes through the thalamus, which relays it to the higher processing areas. Surrounding the thalamus are groups of nerve cells known as the basal ganglia. The basal ganglia are important for the control of movement.

Just underneath the thalamus is the hypothalamus, the main coordinating center for automatic and semiautomatic functions, especially those under the control of the hormone system. The hypothalamus regulates water balance and body temperature, controls sleep cycles and other body rhythms, and plays a role in thirst, hunger, reproduction, and aggressive behavior.

The hypothalamus maintains many connections with the limbic system, a set of structures that circle the brain stem and appeared early in vertebrate brain evolution. One component of the limbic system is the hippocampus, located beneath the lateral ventricles in the cerebrum. The hippocampus functions as a kind of index of the memories, which are stored in various spots elsewhere in the brain.

The limbic system is believed to be the seat of emotions, a reminder of how important emotion is to memory. Near the hippocampus in the limbic system is the amygdala. The amygdala helps coordinate emotional responses to experience. It coordinates information from the senses with some of the automatic functions of the nervous system, such as control of breathing and heartbeat.

Although neuroscientists have made many important discoveries about how brains work in animals, the human brain is the best source of information about itself. Much of this information has been collected through studies of people with brain injuries. That is how scientists identified the

significance of the amygdala. They found that while damage to the hippocampus alone can cause amnesia, damage to the amygdala is usually involved as well. The amygdala apparently attaches emotional significance to our experiences, and these associations are an integral aspect of memory. Partly because of emotional associations, the amygdala can link memories formed in different senses. It connects with the sensory systems in the cortex, as well as with the thalamus and hypothalamus.

The cerebrum

In the more recently evolved vertebrates, the forebrain grows increasingly complex. It is most complicated in the primates, especially humans (*Homo sapiens*). The topmost part of the forebrain is the cerebrum. In the earliest vertebrates, such as fishes and amphibians, it is devoted primarily to the sense of smell. In vertebrates that evolved later, such as reptiles, birds, and mammals, the cerebrum controls most activities, especially conscious activities, by gathering information from the senses, analyzing and interpreting it, and initiating voluntary action based on this analysis. In humans the cerebrum is also the site of thinking, reasoning, and the use of complex language.

The cerebrum is covered by thin sheets of neurons called the cerebral cortex. The cerebral cortex of most vertebrates is fairly smooth, but the human cerebral cortex is heavily folded and pleated, which greatly increases the brain area available for information processing. The cerebralcortex is known as the brain's "gray matter." It consists of the neurons' cell bodies and dendrites. The main central region of the brain, the cerebral medulla, is often known as the "white matter." It contains the neurons' axons that are sheathed in insulation, called myelin, which is white. Myelin helps action potentials travel faster.

In higher vertebrates, such as reptiles, birds, and mammals, the cerebrum is divided into left and right halves; in mammals the two halves are called cerebral hemispheres. The two halves appear very similar, but often have somewhat different functions, especially in humans. The two halves of the cerebrum are not completely separate. They communicate via bundles of axons. The chief connecting axon bundle is known as the corpus callosum. Each side of the brain controls the opposite side of the body.

The cerebrum is further divided into several areas, each with its own functions (see diagram above). The front half, the two parts of the cerebrum that, in humans, lie just behind the forehead, are called the frontal lobes. The frontal lobes are the site of thought, imagination, and planning. The prefrontal cortex, at the front of the frontal lobes, is the storage site for certain kinds of memories. The motor cortex, at the back of the frontal lobes, helps control intentional movements.

The parietal lobes lie just behind the frontal lobes. In the front of the parietal lobes is the sen-

EVOLUTION OF THE BRAIN

The simplest kind of nervous system is the nerve net. This is a network of basic neurons without axons and dendrites. Simple animals, such as jellyfish and corals, have nerve nets. Nerve nets do not have a central place for coordinating information.

As multicellular animals evolved, they began to develop more and more specialized kinds of cells. The nerve net became a nerve cord, a nerve bundle that runs along the front of an animal's body. Nerve cords contain swellings filled with many neurons. These swellings are called nerve ganglions. They are centers where neurons exchange information and commands. An earthworm has a nerve cord with a ganglion in each body segment. The ganglion in its head is connected to its mouth.

As new species evolved, the head end of an animal (with its ganglion) became increasingly important. The head end generally led the way as the animal moved about. This end contained not only the animal's mouth (where the sense of smell began), but also the light-sensing organs that eventually became the eyes. Cerebral ganglions specialized in the sense of smell. The insect head ganglion or "brain" evolved about 550 million years ago. Half of it is reserved for handling information signals from the sense of smell.

The vertebrate brain is large and complex. The portion of the hindbrain that controls automatic functions, such as breathing, heartbeat, and digestion, is well developed in all vertebrates. Most of them also have a cerebellum for muscle control and balance. Vertebrates also possess a midbrain, which processes information from the eyes and ears.

Vertebrates all have forebrains, but in fishes and amphibians it is small and devoted to the sense of smell. In reptiles, the forebrain includes larger cerebral hemispheres. The cerebral cortex, a major advance for information processing in the brain, appeared with the crocodile, a reptile. Mammals arose about 180 million years ago from a group of mammal-like reptiles. Over about 150 million years,

mammals developed very large cerebral hemispheres, which are covered with cerebral cortex. The first folding and grooving of this cortex, and of the cerebellum, which greatly increased the data-processing capacity, took place in this group of animals.

The brain is most highly developed among the primates, the group of mammals that includes monkeys, apes, and humans. The major features of human evolution are the increase in brain size and changes in the shape of the brain.

The human line began around four million years ago with a group of African primates known as *Australopithecus*. *Australopithecus* was much smaller than modern humans, and possessed an ape-sized brain. But the Australopithecines also had a unique human characteristic: unlike the apes, they walked upright on two legs. Some experts believe this development helped encourage brain growth by freeing the hands for more complex activities, including tool-use and other tasks.

Australopithecus was still in existence about two million years ago, when the first true human, *Homo habilis*, evolved in Africa. *Homo habilis* was the first primate to make stone tools, and had a brain almost 50 percent bigger than that of *Australopithecus*. The shape of *Homo habilis*'s brain was also distinct, suggesting a greater capacity for learning and memory. It is quite proable that *Homo habilis* may have used language.

Modern humans, *Homo sapiens sapiens*, probably appeared between 200,000 and 100,000 years ago. The brains of today's humans are very large, three times as large as that of an ape of comparable size and build.

But brain size is not the only explanation for skills that are uniquely human. The human brain is also organized somewhat differently from the brains of other primates, and these special characteristics may account for a number of uniquely human traits, especially language.

The complex vertebrate brain evolved from the noncentralized nervous systems of invertebrates. Vertebrate brains all have three main divisions - forebrain, midbrain, and hindbrain - which grow larger and more complex in the evolutionary sequence from fish to reptiles to birds to mammals.

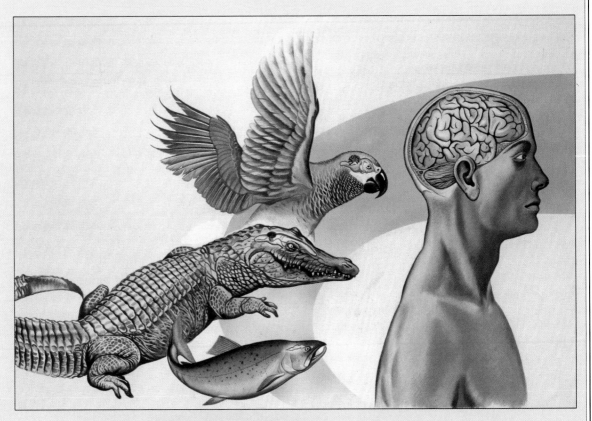

EVOLUTION

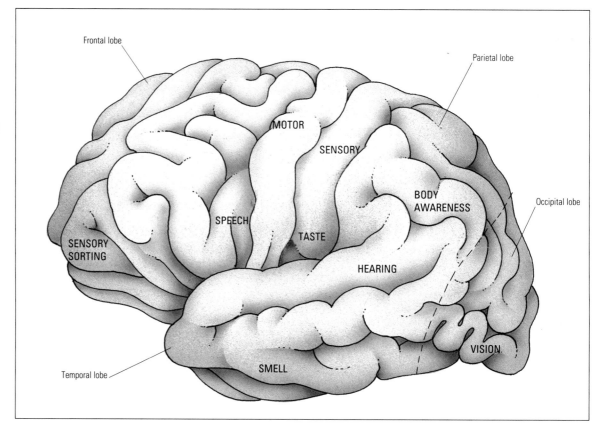

The cerebral cortex of the human brain is divided into four lobes: frontal, temporal, parietal, and occipital. Each lobe has distinct functions, some of which are shown in this diagram. These areas make up the brain's so-called higher centers.

Labels on diagram: Frontal lobe; Parietal lobe; Occipital lobe; MOTOR; SENSORY; BODY AWARENESS; SPEECH; TASTE; HEARING; SENSORY SORTING; VISION; SMELL; Temporal lobe

sory cortex, where information from the sense of touch is processed. The bulge at the back of the head comprises the occipital lobes, which handle information from the eyes. The temporal lobes are located just above and behind the ears, and is where information from the ears is acquired.

The brain is protected by the bones of the skull and by three layers of protective tissues called meninges. A clear colorless fluid, the cerebrospinal fluid, flows through channels within the brain. It acts as a shock absorber, cushioning the brain against the bones of the skull. It also transports nutrients, gases, and wastes, acting as a medium of exchange between the brain and the blood.

THE HUMAN BRAIN
The human brain is the most complex object in the living world. An average human brain weighs approximately 3 lb (1.4 kg) and is about the size of a cantaloupe.

How the human brain develops and grows
The human brain grows remarkably quickly before birth. The brain of a newborn baby contains about 100 billion neurons. This means that, from its beginnings in the early embryo, the brain grows an average of 250,000 nerve cells every minute during pregnancy. Events before birth affect every aspect of brain function for the remainder of life.

Early development of the brain follows a similar pattern in all mammals, but in humans the process takes longer. By three weeks after conception, the human embryo is about $^1/_{10}$ in (2.5 mm) long, and a hollow tube, the neural tube, runs along its length. This will become the spinal cord, and a bulge at one end of the tube will become the brain. A week later, the three major brain regions – hindbrain, midbrain, and forebrain – have begun to form from the neural tube.

NONHUMAN BRAINS

Within the vertebrates, different parts of the brain are specialized in different groups of animals. In lower vertebrates, each of the three major sense organs (nose, eye, and ear, plus lateral line in fish) are associated with one of three subdivisions of the brain: the cerebrum (forebrain), tectum (midbrain roof), and cerebellum (hindbrain), respectively.

The centers of nervous activity are situated in the anterior (front) regions of the brain stem, with the tectum the center of coordination. Going up the vertebrate "scale,", this area becomes rivalled, and then overtaken, by association centers in the cerebral hemispheres that develop from the forebrain. In birds, the tectum is still prominent, but in mammals it is reduced to a reflex center.

The cerebellum plays a major role in locomotion, posture, and equilibrium. In any group, the extent of its development correlates with the intricacy of the movements that it controls. This means that it has an elaborate construction in some fish, birds, and mammals, while in more sluggish vertebrates such as some reptiles and amphibians, it is less developed. Although the cerebellum coordinates movement, actual decisions of where and when to move are arrived at in the cerebrum.

In mammals, the size of the cerebral hemispheres is often thought to give a clue to the mental abilities of an organism, but this is not quite strictly the case. The degree of convolution of the cerebral cortex is often more important. For example, hedgehogs have little convolution, while the hemispheres of whales are elaborately folded.

Different parts of the cerebrum are more prominent in some animals than others. For example, the olfactory bulbs that control the sense of smell are poorly developed in birds. On the other hand, birds have a highly developed corpus striatum that controls instinctive behavior like nest building.

Halfway through a human pregnancy, about 15 to 20 weeks after conception, cells of the cerebral cortex, produced by cells that line a hollow in the forebrain, are increasing by the millions every hour. They must then undertake a complex migration to their eventual locations. The location determines a neuron's behavior and function; neurons with similar characteristics often lie close to one another. Once they reach their final destinations, neurons get bigger. Axons lengthen and dendrites branch out from the cell body.

With brain growth so fast and complex, things can sometimes go wrong. But brain growth is also adaptable, so that many errors get corrected. Still, experts suspect that many human disorders and abnormalities (for example, some kinds of learning disabilities and mental illness) may result when brain cells fail to connect as they should during pregnancy. A mother's use of the illegal drug cocaine during pregnancy, for example, can disturb the normal links between nerve cells.

A neuron will not survive unless its axon reaches a target cell to synapse with. The target cell provides small proteins, called trophic factors, that are essential if the neuron is to survive. Between half and three-quarters of neurons fail to forge these connections, and so they die.

By six months of pregnancy, the fetal brain is functioning as it will after birth. The fetus itself is an active participant in this process, employing its brain to make its muscles work. It kicks, turns, and even sucks its thumb. Each action causes axons and dendrites to branch, creating new synapses in the developing brain, and these new structures help the fetus to acquire additional skills.

By month seven, a fetus's electrical brain waves can be measured through its mother's abdomen. Toward month nine, neurons increase more slowly, and then stop increasing. From then on, humans lose the ability to grow new neurons. But the existing neurons go on getting bigger, and their axons and dendrites get more complicated, so the young human brain's rapid growth continues.

By nine months the infant brain is so enormous that the human birth canal cannot accommodate any more growth. As a result, humans are born at a much earlier stage of development, and with many fewer skills, than other primates. This makes them much more dependent on adult care (see CHILD DEVELOPMENT). The brains of newborn chimpanzees weigh more than half the weight of adult chimp brains. A human newborn's brain weighs less than a quarter of its adult weight. By contrast with other animals, the human brain does most of its growing after birth, which is why human infancy and childhood are so long.

This growth takes place along with massive elimination of synapses, a process known as pruning. The adult rhesus monkey brain possesses only half the number of axons it had as a fetus. Humans are believed to lose at least ten times as many axons and synapses as monkeys do, in a pruning process that goes on at least to the age of 12. Pruning is essential for normal development. Because it is guided and shaped by the unique experiences each individual animal undergoes, the pruning process permits mammals to adapt flexibly to a variety of environments, and makes possible the emergence of new behavioral traits and new skills. Pruning also eliminates incorrect neuron connections, helping to ensure that the brain functions well.

The human brain increases in size until about the age of 18. But even after growth ceases, the human brain continues to increase in complexity.

STUDYING THE LIVING HUMAN BRAIN

For ethical reasons, studying the living human brain directly is difficult, although scientists have been able to learn a great deal indirectly from research on the effects of damage that occurs as a result of disease or accident. For well over a century, for example, scientists have been gathering information about how the brain handles language. Split-brain studies remain the source of what experts know about the differing functions of the two brain hemispheres.

More recently, however, scientists have turned to technologies that permit them to peer into the working brain without harming it. One of the earliest of these techniques was the electroencephalogram (EEG). The EEG can trace the activity of large groups of neurons via electrodes on the scalp. Scientists also use the EEG to study arousal, sleep, and dreaming, and also to help manage coma and epilepsy. An EEG does not measure action potentials, but rather the tiny amounts of voltage generated by the chemical traffic around the outsides of neurons. Specific patterns of this chemical traffic are characteristic of particular brain states, such as sleep, relaxation, or arousal.

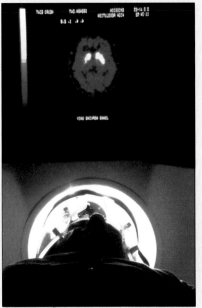

This picture shows Dr Henry Wagner, director of nuclear medicine at John Hopkins Hospital, Baltimore, demonstrating positron emission topography (PET) to produce an axial image of his brain. This technique involves injecting a positron-emitting radioisotope into the body.

The most exciting recent technological innovation for investigations of the brain has been the development of machines that use noninvasive scanning techniques to visualize the human brain. Several kinds of scanners have become available; each has special features that make it useful in specific situations.

The oldest such method, called computed tomography (CT), uses x-rays to picture the living brain (see CT SCAN). CT scanning has been eclipsed somewhat by two more recent scanning methods. Positron emission tomography (PET) creates computerized images of activity levels in different parts of the brain by measuring cerebral blood flow, revealing information about brain activity. It takes snapshots of the brain several minutes apart.

Magnetic resonance imaging (MRI) detects changes in neurons exposed to a strong magnetic field. These images give information about brain structure. Some research centers are now employing both types of scanners at the same time, and then combining the resulting images, so that a research subject's PET activity can be mapped onto MRI scans of the same subject's brain structure.

PARKINSON'S DISEASE

Parkinson's disease, which affects one in every 200 people over the age of 40, is the best-known of the diseases that involve the basal ganglia. These disorders produce distinct sorts of involuntary tremors and jerking movements.

In this disorder, named for the British doctor, James Parkinson, who described it in 1817, the basal ganglia neurons that produce a neurotransmitter called dopamine die. The basal ganglia constitute only a very small part of the brain, but they produce 80 percent of its supply of dopamine. A normal supply of dopamine is necessary for coordinated muscle control. Drugs that increase the level of dopamine have been useful to treat Parkinson's disease, but the drugs have side effects and they do not cure the disorder.

There is an experimental treatment that might offer a cure for Parkinson's disease, but it is very controversial. It consists of transplanting dopamine-producing tissue from the brains of dead fetuses into the brains of Parkinson's patients. The treatment has been opposed by those who fear that it would encourage abortion, so for many years the United States. government prohibited experimentation with fetal tissue. The ban was removed in 1993.

Responding to experience, the neurons of adults alter their shape, their neurotransmitters, their synapses, and their second messengers, and all these changes in turn alter the way the brain functions. Even though the brain cannot grow new neurons, its ability to remodel its connections allows the human brain to recover some function after injury. In general, however, brain injury often results in permanent deficits.

Learning and memory

The brain uses sensors to gather information about the world. Sensors in the eyes collect data about the shape, color, and motion of objects, and sensors in ears register vibrations as sound. The tongue and nose experience tastes and smells, and sensors all over the body report on touch, pressure, temperature, and pain.

The brain uses this data to guide the body's actions, and it does this by learning. Learning is the process by which the brain analyzes incoming information, compares it with past experience, and uses the results of this assessment to change the connections between cells. Learning can strengthen or weaken the relationship between neighboring neurons. It can cause axons and dendrites to branch, forging new links with adjacent cells. It can create or abandon synapses, which changes the routes along which nerve impulses travel. Learning is the birth of new pathways in the brain.

The brain is constantly remodeling itself. The brain begins to develop shortly after conception, but experiences after birth are essential for creating and preserving the brain's connections. At every age, the brain establishes these new connections in the nervous system in response to experience. Learning ceases only at death. The complexity of this brain remodeling is hard to comprehend. To store even a brief, insignificant memory, the brain makes changes at millions of places in the nervous system. Because of this constant brain remodeling,

no two brains are alike, and every human being is unique. Even identical twins, who have exactly the same genes, have very different brains.

Neuroscientists use the terms learning and memory interchangeably. For them, learning and memory are not two different processes, but rather two aspects of the same process. Those who study learning and memory have classified the process in many different ways. Most neuroscientists believe that while there are several different ways in which the brain stores and uses memories, it probably has only two major systems for acquiring those memories. One of these systems is known as reflexive memory, or implicit learning, or habit. The other system is called declarative memory, or explicit learning.

Reflexive memory

Reflexive memory, or habit, was the first form of learning. It evolved soon after animal life began, perhaps as long as 600 million years ago. Even very simple animals engage in habit learning; scientists have discovered a lot about reflexive memory by studying the sea snail *Aplysia*, which has only 20,000 neurons.

All animals, including humans, learn by habit. Humans use the reflexive memory pathways in the brain to acquire skills, such as learning to walk, or ride a bike, and also for other kinds of rote-memory abilities, such as learning the multiplication tables or memorizing irregular verbs. Conscious processes, thinking, and general knowledge are not involved in reflexive memory. In this form of habit learning, the brain and body use rules and procedures automatically, after acquiring them slowly by repeating them constantly. When people say "Practice makes perfect" they are talking about reflexive memory.

How does reflexive memory work? By studying animals, neuroscientists have learned that reflexive memory alters neuron connections. As an organism learns a skill, the stream of neurotransmitters increases at some synapses and decreases at others; this makes some nerve impulses stronger and others weaker. Learning creates new routes in the nervous system, encouraging nerve impulses to travel along certain pathways rather than others. Sometimes the learning is temporary because the new routes are temporary. When the learning alters neurons by producing new synapses, it can be long-lasting, or may even be permanent.

Declarative memory

Declarative memory, sometimes called explicit learning or simply memory, evolved millions of years later than reflexive memory. It is used only by comparatively complex animals. Neuroscientists believe that the brain probably employs reflexive and declarative memory in different ways, using distinct parts of the brain. However, the two systems can interact.

Declarative memory results from an animal's specific experiences and factual knowledge. It frequently rests on conscious links between stimuli occurring at the same time. Declarative memory is not automatic or the product of habit but involves thinking. To engage in this form of learning, the brain analyzes experiences, compares them with other experiences, and draws inferences about them. The thought processes of declarative memory can often be expressed verbally, by contrast with the processes of reflexive memory, which are unconscious and cannot be put into words. Declarative memory can also be fast: learning that takes place as the result of a single experience, rather than through constant practice.

Committing something to memory proceeds in stages, often divided into short-term memory and long-term memory. Short-term memory (sometimes called telephone-number memory) is brief, temporary, and easy to interrupt. It is also small; few people can hold more than about seven items in short-term memory.

Neuroscientists believe that many kinds of permanent memories are stored in the parts of the brain that processed the original sensory information. Thus, in humans, long-term visual memories reside mainly in the occipital lobes, which handle visual data. But before those memories can be made permanent, they must be processed by the hippocampus, a structure in the temporal lobe. A person with damaged hippocampi cannot form new memories, although he or she may recall perfectly old memories that were laid down before the damage occurred.

Exactly how the hippocampus makes long-lasting memories possible is not yet understood. But scientists suspect that the physical basis of these memories comes about through a process called long-term potentiation. In long-term potentiation, neurons in the hippocampus react to an increase in action potentials by strengthening their synapses.

Long-term memory storage involves more than the brief strengthening of the links between neurons involved in temporary memories. In order to create long-term memories, the brain must alter the anatomy of neurons. Axons and dendrites grow new branches, neurotransmitter-release patterns are changed, synapses are created or abandoned, and the arrangement of second messenger activities within neurons is modified. There are no special neurons where memories are stored; memories are built from ordinary neurons that the brain adapts in special ways.

Working memory

Another of the brain's systems for remembering is often called working memory. Sometimes, confusingly, it is also called short-term memory, although it is much more complicated than the telephone-number type of short-term memory. Working memory, which appears to be situated in the prefrontal cortex (above and behind the eyes), differs from what goes on in the hippocampus. The hippocampus helps shape memories by joining together various types of data gathered by the senses. The prefrontal cortex retrieves those memories from their long-term storage sites elsewhere in the brain. Working memory combines stored

The surface of the cerebrum, the cortex, has one area that receives incoming sensory information and another area that is concerned with outgoing motor information. The different parts of the body have different amounts of the cortex devoted to them. A map of the sensory or motor cortex is called a homunculus, from the Latin for "little person." The diagrams below are proportioned to show how much of the cortex is devoted to each body part.

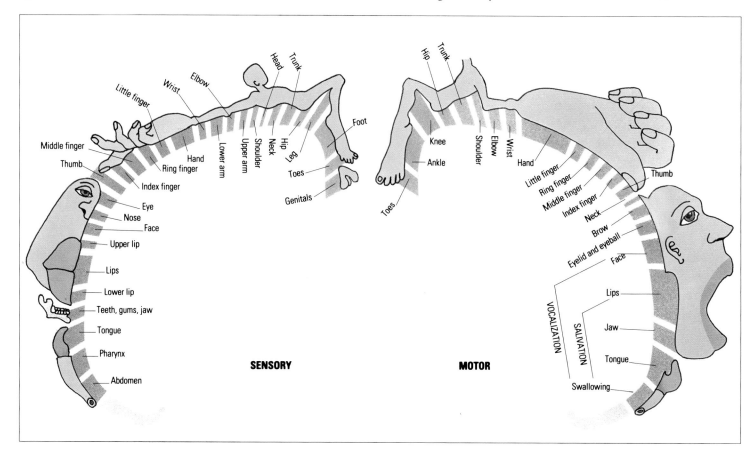

SENSORY **MOTOR**

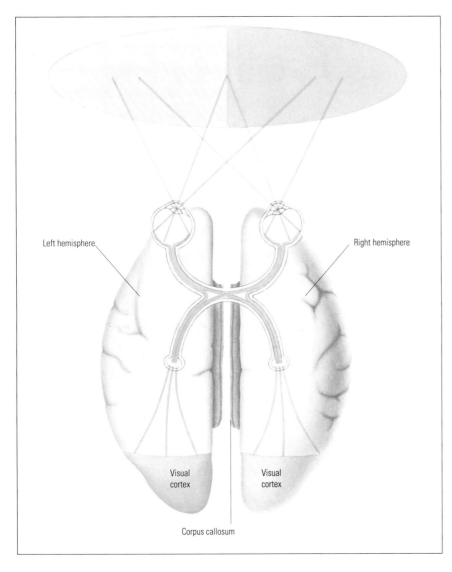

Left hemisphere

Right hemisphere

Visual
cortex

Visual
cortex

Corpus callosum

The cerebral hemispheres process information acquired from opposite parts of the body. When you fix your eyes on a point straight ahead, information from the left field of vision is sent to the right cerebral hemisphere, and information from the right field goes to the left cerebral hemisphere.

knowledge (short-term and long-term) with the data coming in from the senses, and also calls on both reflexive and declarative memory learning systems. It uses the results of this blended analysis as a guide to action.

The process of having an ordinary conversation provides a good example of how all these systems work together. Reflexive memory guides the muscles used in speech. Using language usually calls on both reflexive and declarative memory. Information about the subject of the conversation comes from declarative memory, with the aid of the hippocampus. Many of these are long-term memories, and some are probably permanent. Records of what the other person says, and possible replies, are held briefly in short-term memory. Working memory can help recover the necessary recollections, both short-term and long-term, and help coordinate the way they function together to make the conversation possible.

Two brains in one
The ancient Greeks believed that we had two brains in one. In fact, the cerebrum is divided into two distinct halves, the cerebral hemispheres, joined by the 200 million axons of the corpus callosum. The left cerebral hemisphere processes information from

the right side of the body, the right cerebral hemisphere processes information from the left side of the body. The left cerebral hemisphere is dominant over the right in 90 percent of people. The two hemispheres are attached by a giant bundle of 200 million axons called the corpus callosum, and can therefore communicate with each other. Each cerebral hemisphere has its own distinct functions. The left cerebral hemisphere is in charge of language comprehension and speech production. For this reason, it is sometimes called the verbal brain.

The right cerebral hemisphere, or nonverbal brain, is associated with spatial relationships and recognizing objects by shape. If the corpus callosum is cut, a person looking at an object can recognize the object but is unable to name it (see diagram). This is because the nonverbal memory of the object is stored in the right hand side of the brain, but language is a function of the left hemisphere.

Epilepsy and the split brain
Epilepsy is a disorder that results from damage to a small group of neurons somewhere in the cortex. The damage can occur before or during birth, perhaps due to a shortage of oxygen, which is essential for neurons. But the damage is often the result of a later event, such as infection, high fever, a tumor, or, frequently, a motor vehicle accident. In epilepsy, the damaged neurons give off bursts of uncontrolled rapid electrical signals that can spread all over the brain, causing a seizure. When severe, seizures make the body jerk and twitch, and the person loses consciousness. Seizures are particularly dangerous for small children, because they can lead to mental retardation or even death.

About four million Americans suffer from epilepsy. Drug therapy can help most of them control seizures. Anticonvulsant drugs lessen the frequency of the seizures, but may have side effects such as drowsiness. About one in ten patients may need surgery; sometimes surgeons remove the entire cortex of the injured hemisphere. Infants seem to recover best from this drastic measure, because their brains are still developing quickly enough to allow the remaining hemisphere to assume many of the functions of the injured hemisphere. Adult brains, however, cannot adjust like those of children. To keep severe seizures from spreading from the injured area to the other side of the brain, surgeons sometimes disconnect the two halves of the brain by cutting the corpus callosum, the communications cable that links the cerebral hemispheres.

Research on animals and human patients who have undergone this surgery is our most important source of information about the different functions of the two brain hemispheres. Roger Sperry, who pioneered these split-brain studies, was one of the recipients of the Nobel Prize for Physiology or Medicine in 1981 for this work.

When the left and right hemispheres can no longer exchange information across the corpus callosum, it becomes possible to study each hemisphere separately. These studies have revealed that, for most people, the left brain handles the majority of tasks associated with language. Speaking and writing are located here, although the right brain can understand some simple language. The right brain apparently deals with the rhythms of language. The ability to understand spatial relationships is centered mostly in the right hemisphere too.

BRAIN FUNCTION DURING SLEEP

Complex animals spend a large part of their lives sleeping. Among humans, most adults function best if they sleep for eight hours, a third of every day. Teenagers need even more sleep, as much as nine and a half hours. It is the brain, more than any other part of the body, that requires this amount of sleep. Physical performance is not much reduced by loss of sleep, but intellectual performance and mood are greatly affected. Tired people do less well on tests, have more accidents, and lose their tempers more easily.

Sleep is a dynamic condition with five stages. Stage 1 is light drowsiness. Stage 2 is the first stage of real sleep. Stages 3 and 4 are both times of deep sleep. Stage 5 is the best-known and most-studied stage of sleep, rapid eye movement (REM) sleep. Most dreams occur during REM sleep.

During REM sleep, the eyes move behind the eyelids, but the body is paralyzed from the neck down as the result of a signal from the brain stem to the spinal cord. This REM paralysis occurs in humans and in many animals. Scientists are not sure why it happens, but the paralysis may protect the sleeper from being injured by acting out dreams. Muscles function normally during the other sleep stages, and sleepers move and turn over as often as every 20 minutes.

A typical sleeper moves through a complete set of five stages, lasting about 90 minutes, approximately five times on an average night. The first third of the night is devoted mostly to deep sleep, and most REM sleep lasts only five or ten minutes, but the last stage of REM sleep can go on as long as half an hour. Sleepers often wake just after this last REM stage, so the dream occurring then is the one they are likely to remember. Measurements of electrical activity in the brain during each stage of sleep have shown that it slows down substantially during deep sleep. Gamma camera scans (see diagram above) have shown that a resting brain also appears to need less oxygen (and therefore has a lower blood flow) than an active brain. But brain activity during REM sleep is more like that generated by a brain that is awake.

Deep sleep probably helps to repair daily wear and tear on the body. People who miss a night's sleep spend extra time in deep sleep the following night. The reason for REM sleep, and the dreams that accompany it, is less clear, even though most mammals spend hours every day, about 25 per-

cent of total sleep, in REM sleep. REM sleep has evolved only in mammals. Many experts believe this means that dreaming began with the mammals, although, of course, it is impossible to be sure that other creatures dream just as humans do.

There are many theories about the purpose of dreams. Dreams may offer a safe way of acting out fantasies and fears. Or they may simply be the higher brain centers' way of attempting to make sense out of random electrical discharges from the brain stem. There is also evidence that these brain stem impulses trigger signals in the hippocampus that are a prelude to the neuron changes that are important for learning. Some neuroscientists think that this finding, plus other experimental evidence, suggests that REM sleep may aid learning.

T. POWLEDGE

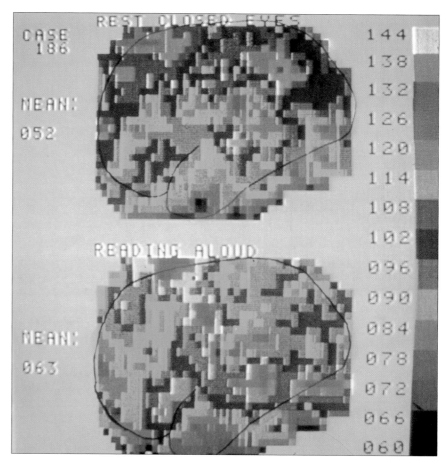

These false color scintigrams show the density of blood flow in a resting brain (top) and the brain of someone reading aloud (bottom). The image below shows an increase in oxygen requirement. The main regions of blood flow are the brainstem (at bottom left of the image), the frontal lobes (right), and the central area.

See also: AGING; ALZHEIMER'S DISEASE; COGNITION; EMOTIONS; INTELLIGENCE; MEMORY; MENTAL DISORDERS; NERVOUS SYSTEM; PSYCHOLOGY; SLEEP.

Further reading:
Changeux, Jean-Pierre. "Chemical Signaling in the Brain." *Scientific American*, **269**, pp.58-62, Nov. 1993.
Iaccino, James F. *Left Brain–Right Brain Differences: Inquiries, Evidence, and New Approaches.* Hillsdale, New Jersey: Lawrence Erlbaum Associates, 1993.
Powledge, Tabitha M. *Your Brain: How You Got It and How It Works.* New York: Charles Scribner's Sons, 1994.
Scientific American, **267**, Sept. 1992 (Entire issue).

BULBS AND CORMS

Bulbs and corms are underground food reserves in plants

Bulbs and corms are underground plant stems, which are modified to store food and water. They are invaluable to many plants, because they enable them to survive extreme climatic conditions, such as cold, drought, or fire. At such times, the plant goes into a period of dormancy, which means it is alive but resting. When conditions are favorable, the plant comes out of the resting state, drawing on the food stored in the bulb or corm, and grows quickly.

Food is usually stored as starch, although some species, such as the onion (*Allium cepa*), store the food as sugar. To deter animals that would dig up their bulbs or corms for food, many plants contain foul-tasting or noxious chemicals.

CORE FACTS

- Bulbs and corms are highly modified underground stems.
- They act as food storage organs and in vegetative reproduction.
- Bulbs and corms are most common in monocotyledons, although they are also present in some dicotyledons, such as *Cyclamen* and *Oxalis* spp.
- Bulbs and corms are common in habitats that have long cold winters or hot dry summers. They are also found on the floor of temperate deciduous forests, which are in dark shade except for brief periods in early spring.
- Many bulbs and corms are popular garden plants, such as tulips, irises, and crocuses. Several are vegetables, including onions and garlic. Some, such as the Autumn crocus *(Colchicum autumnale)*, have medicinal uses.

Bulbs

A bulb is an underground stem that includes roots at its base and layers of compact, fleshy leaves, which extend upward and form the bulk of the bulb. The leaves contain stored food. In the middle of the bulb is a bud, which will grow to produce a leafy shoot and flower above ground when the plant resumes active growth.

The food reserves in the underground leaves are used to support the plant's growth until the foliage leaves begin to photosynthesize. In between the underground leaves, new buds develop. These will eventually enlarge to form daughter bulbs. Well-known bulbs include onions, daffodils, tulips, hyacinths, and lilies.

Corms

The food supply in corms is stored in a swollen stem base. The outside of the corm is usually covered in old leaf bases from the previous year's growth. During the growing season a leafy shoot is produced from the top of the corm. The food reserves from the corm are used for the production of leaves and flowers above the ground, and the old corm starts to wither. However, by the time flowering has finished, a new corm is forming on top of the old one.

The new corm stores extra food made by the plant during the growing season. By the end of the growing season the corm is fully formed; only the remains of the old corm are visible at its base. To make sure the new corm is at the right depth in the soil, contractile roots pull the new corm down to the level of the old corm. Crocuses, gladioli, and cyclamens are among the most familiar corms.

Common habitats

On high mountain meadows, plants cannot photosynthesize in winter because they are buried under snow and cut off from energy-giving sunlight. However, the bulbs and corms are able to survive this period because of their food reserves. When the snow melts in the spring, leaves and flowers are quickly produced. Having flowered, set seed, and replenished its food supply, the plant soon dies down again, ready to face another long winter under the snow.

In regions of the world with a Mediterranean climate (the Mediterranean basin in Europe, coastal California, Chile, South Africa, and southern Australia) many of the plants that are able to survive the intense heat are those with bulbs or corms. These plants live through the summer droughts safely underground; for added protection the outer layers of the bulbs or corms are often hard and leathery.

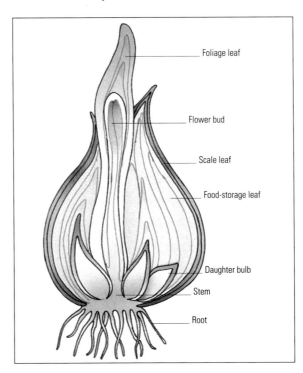

A cross section of a tulip bulb. A bulb is an underground storage stem distinguished by overlapping fleshy leaves.

- Foliage leaf
- Flower bud
- Scale leaf
- Food-storage leaf
- Daughter bulb
- Stem
- Root

CONNECTIONS

- The therapeutic properties of garlic have long been recognized by many cultures. We now know that garlic juice is a powerful agent against many **BACTERIA** and **FUNGI**. It also inhibits **BLOOD** clotting and therefore prevents the formation of thromboses, making it useful in the prevention of coronary **HEART** disease and strokes.

- The thick storage leaves of bulbs are used to conserve **ENERGY** in the form of starch. However, the usual function of the leaves is as the site of **PHOTOSYNTHESIS**.

- Plants store energy in the form of starch. The energy storage molecule of animals is glycogen. Both starch and glycogen are complex **CARBOHYDRATES**.

In temperate deciduous forests there is a short spell in spring when sunlight can reach the forest floor and warm the soil before the trees produce their leaves and cast the forest floor into shadow. Several species of bulbs or corms take advantage of this time. Trout lilies, sometimes called Dogtooth violets (*Erythronium americanum*), carpet woodland floors in eastern North America with yellow flowers. In western Europe, spring-flowering bluebells (*Hyacinthoides non-scripta*) cover the forest floor in a solid blue carpet, before dying down again by midsummer.

Vegetative reproduction

Bulbs and corms are important as a form of vegetative reproduction (see REPRODUCTION). New bulbs form alongside the parent bulb and new corms (cormels or cormlets) form around the edges of the corm's base. Each new bulb or corm can grow into a new plant. One of the advantages of vegetative reproduction is that the plant does not have to rely solely on pollination to reproduce. This is particularly important for plants with a short flowering period.

Unfortunately, the ability to reproduce vegetatively means that some of these plants have become serious weeds that are difficult to eradicate. Ordinary herbicides are often ineffective because the plant has hidden underground resources. Digging or ploughing the soil can make the problem worse as clumps of young bulbs or corms are simply broken up and spread around. One example is Crow garlic (*Allium vineale*), which was native to the Mediterranean but has spread throughout the world, including North America, and is often a serious agricultural weed.

Bulbs and corms in cultivation

The bulbs of onions (*Allium cepa*), garlic (*A. sativum*), and shallots (*A. ascalonicum*) are widely grown as vegetables. Unlike perishable vegetables, they will keep for a long time if stored in a cool, dry, dark place.

Many species of bulbs and corms are popular garden plants, including crocuses, tulips, hyacinths, daffodils, and freesias. They are easy to care for and have bright colorful flowers. Unfortunately, their popularity has had a high price. A considerable trade in bulbs and corms collected from the wild has built up over the years. Many wild populations have suffered, with once common species becoming extremely scarce. A cyclamen (*Cyclamen mirabile*) and a Winter daffodil (*Sternbergia candida*) from Turkey are threatened in the wild as a result of over-collection. The Chilean blue crocus (*Tecophilaea cyanocrocus*) is seriously endangered and may be extinct in the wild for the same reason.

This problem has now been addressed. The trade in endangered bulbs and corms is strictly controlled in many countries by an international treaty called the Convention on International Trade in Endangered Species (CITES). This imposes penalties on countries that have signed the treaty but continue to trade in endangered species.

K. McCALLUM

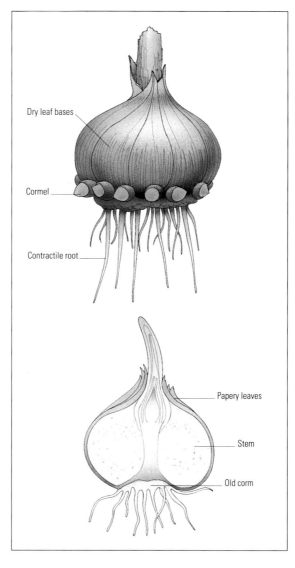

External view of a Gladiolus corm. Although corms look similar to bulbs, their structure is very different. The cross section below shows the internal structure of a corm. In contrast to the bulb, which is mostly leaf tissue, the entire corm is made up of stem tissue. Food is usually stored in the form of starch.

Dry leaf bases

Cormel

Contractile root

Papery leaves

Stem

Old corm

See also: PLANT KINGDOM; STEMS AND STEM SYSTEMS.

Further reading:

Hobbs, J., and Hatch, T. *Best Bulbs for Temperate Climates*. Portland, Oregon: Timber Press, 1994.

COLCHICINE

Colchicine is an alkaloid (a type of organic compound; see ALKALOIDS) obtained from the dried seeds and corms of the Autumn crocus *(Colchicum autumnale)*. The Autumn crocus grows in moist meadows throughout most of Europe. Since medieval times the dried corms have been used to relieve the pain of the disease called gout. Small doses of colchicine are still used as a painkiller in the treatment of gout, arthritis, and rheumatism. In large doses, colchicine is very toxic. It works by interrupting the mitotic cycle leading to cell division (see CELLS) resulting in the production of cells with multiple chromosomes (known as polyploids). This condition is lethal in animals but polyploid plants are often larger and more vigorous than normal plants. Because of this, colchicine is widely used in plant genetics (see GENETICS, SELECTIVE BREEDING).

SCIENCE AND SOCIETY

BUTTERFLIES AND MOTHS

Butterflies and moths are winged insects belonging to the order Lepidoptera

Butterflies and moths, belonging to the order Lepidoptera, are one of the largest orders of insects after the beetles, with over 120,000 described species. They are an extremely diverse group in appearance, with a wide range of subtle and brilliant colors and patterns on their large wings. Because of this, they have received more attention from naturalists and entomologists than any other group of insects; the more showy the species, the more intense the interest. Countless professional researchers and amateur collectors have butterfly and moth collections.

This collecting fervor has been so intense in the past, particularly during the 19th century, that laws have been implemented in some parts of the world to protect butterfly species that are already in decline due to other reasons, such as loss of habitat.

CORE FACTS

- There are over 120,000 described species of butterfly and moth, which form the order Lepidoptera.
- Both butterflies and moths have a life cycle comprising an egg stage, a larval stage, a pupal stage, and an adult stage.
- Adult moths and butterflies may communicate with each other chemically, through the use of pheromones, or visually, through the use of color.

Some species of butterfly have beautiful colors and patterns on their wings. This is a Common swallowtail butterfly (Papilio machaon), which is found throughout Europe and North Africa, and in some parts of Asia.

Features

Although butterflies and moths are so diverse in color, they are perhaps the most uniform insects as regards diet and ecological role. Adults almost always feed on nectar, honeydew, pollen, fermenting sap, or similar sugar-rich plant products such as fruit. (A few species of moths, such as the Vampire moth (*Calpe eustrigata*) in Asia, suck blood.) The larvae feed on fungi and other plant material. Butterflies and moths are the dominant insect herbivore in most habitats, and have successfully invaded all insect ecological niches, except the plant sapsucking niche occupied by the true bugs (order Hemiptera).

All butterflies and moths share a unique body covering made up of large, flattened, scale-like hairs called macrotrichia (from the Latin for "large hairs"). These scales easily detach, perhaps as a means of allowing the insect to escape predators. In butterflies, the scales can be brightly pigmented; some have an iridescent quality. The bright colors have a role in species recognition, and may also warn potential predators of the insect's disagreeable taste. Moths, most of which are nocturnal,

CONNECTIONS

- Butterflies and moths secrete chemical compounds called **PHEROMONES**, which act as signals to other members of the species. These compounds may be used to locate food, or as an aid to **DEFENSE** or **COURTSHIP**.

- **BIOCHEMISTS** can identify the active compound in pheromone secretions by separating the components using a gas chromatograph and analyzing them using a mass spectrometer. This tells them the compound's molecular formula and relative molecular mass.

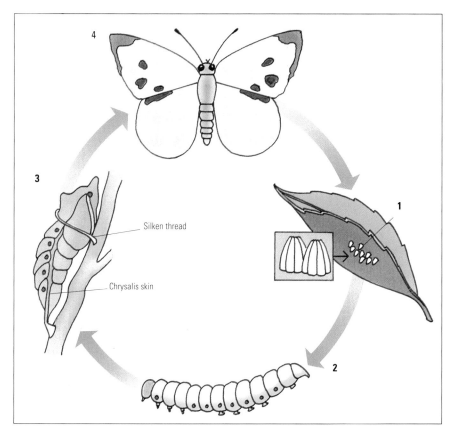

The life cycle of a butterfly or moth moves through a series of stages: first the eggs are laid on a host plant (1), from which the larvae, or caterpillars (2), hatch. Once fully mature, each larva develops into a pupa, or chrysalis (3). During this stage, it changes into an adult (4), which emerges from the pupa to dry and stiffen its wings before flying away.

Silken thread

Chrysalis skin

generally do not have such bright colors. However, some of the larger moth species possess a thick layer of scales, which may keep them warm when flying at night.

Most butterflies and moths (those belonging to the suborder Glossata) have a long, coiled feeding tube called a proboscis for ingesting liquid food such as nectar. However, a minority of species, belonging to the suborders Zeugloptera, Aglossata, and Heterobathmiina, have mandibles, grinding mouthparts, or bristles and spines, which they use to grind up pollen grains and fern spores.

All butterflies and moths have a mechanism to synchronize their wing beat, a feature essential for coordinated flight. With most species, a lobe of the forewing, called the jugum, overlaps with the hind wing. This lobe presses one set of wings against the other, ensuring a coordinated wingbeat. In other species, this is achieved with a set of stiff bristles (called the frenulum) on the hind wing, which interlock with the retinaculum, a series of hooked hairs on the underside of the forewing.

Life cycle

All butterflies and moths begin life as eggs. The female lays from a dozen to many thousands of eggs, and usually deposits them on or near a host plant. The eggs may be laid in clumps, or scattered on the host plant. In some species they may remain dormant for many months until suitable weather and food resources are available.

BUTTERFLY OR MOTH?

Butterflies

There is perhaps no more popular insect in the world than the butterfly. There are several reasons for this. Butterflies are generally harmless creatures: they do not bite or sting; they do not spread disease; they are silent and unobtrusive. Perhaps most important, they are often beautiful in appearance, and are sometimes referred to as "flying flowers."

Most butterflies are brightly colored. Their brilliant wing colors and intense patterns serve to attract members of their own species, as well as acting as a warning to predators in some species. Most species are diurnal (active in the day) when the light shows off their bright colors. When resting, butterflies hold their wings upright over their body instead of folding them flat against the abdomen, as is the case for most moth species. Recent studies have shown that in some species the wings are used to help warm the body. The wings are held at the correct angle and orientation to the sun to reflect light down against the dark, light-absorbing abdomen. Early in the morning, this behavior can speed up the warming of the body, so that butterflies, which are cold-blooded, can have as much time as possible to forage and look for mates.

Butterflies belong to two superfamilies: the Papilionoidea (the true butterflies) and the Hesperioidea (the skippers). Skippers look like a cross between butterflies and moths. They are rapid flying, and capable of tight maneuvers. Most species of skipper are not brightly colored and are small in size, with wings only 1¼ in (3 cm) from tip to tip. The wings are triangular, and are usually held upright over the body when the skipper is perched on vegetation or the ground. The

larvae build nests by sewing together a leaf of the host plant with silk that the larvae produce.

Butterflies are relatively slow moving compared to moths and skippers. This is because of their larger wing surface and slower wingbeat. The larger wings also result in a characteristic up and down movement of the body during flight and an erratic course.

Moths

Most species of moths are nocturnal or crepuscular (active at night or in the twilight hours). By contrast to the brightly colored butterflies, moths are generally drab browns and grays, with a mottled appearance that helps to keep them hidden when resting during the day. Daytime perches include tree trunks, lichens, or other irregular surfaces, where they can blend with the background and be camouflaged. In some species, the hind wings are brightly colored, usually in red. They are concealed under the forewing when the moth is at rest, but if it is disturbed, they are flashed in an attempt to frighten away attackers. In a few species, the hind wings also have eye spot patterns to deter attack.

Chemical communication is more important in moths than butterflies, because most moths are active at night when light levels are too low for visual communication. To enhance the detection of chemicals such as pheromones, most moth species have large feathering antennae, for detecting low pheromone levels. Experiments have shown that male Gypsy moths *(Porthetria (Lymantria) dispar)* can detect pheromones released by females around 2.5 miles (4 km) away.

MIGRATION

As resources are used up, or temperatures become less tolerable (or for other reasons not clear), butterflies and moths will either migrate from one region to another, or become dormant. Dormancy in insects is called diapause, and when it occurs the metabolic processes slow down significantly.

In butterfly and moth species that do migrate, individuals may spend their entire life only a few hundred yards from where they were born. Or they may travel as many as 1200 to 1900 miles (2000 to 3000 km) in one migration. Such is the case with the Monarch butterfly *Danaus plexippus* (see below), which migrates yearly southward across the United States to California, Florida, or the highlands of Mexico.

Scientists believe that butterflies use the position of the sun in the sky to orient their flight, while moths use the moon to orient their flight. This may be the reason why moths appear to be so abundant on full moon nights in the spring and summer. It also explains why moths fly to outdoor lights, mistaking the light for moonlight. When there is no moon, some moths will use the stars. Scientists also think that moths are able to use the Earth's magnetic field to orient their movements, much like a compass.

Occasionally the eggs are inserted into the plant tissue. The shape of the eggs varies greatly between species. They may be cylindrical, barrel-shaped, or flat and wafer-like. The surface of the eggs may be smooth, or sculpted with ribs, tubercules, or pits.

The larvae of both butterflies and moths are called caterpillars, and most are herbivores, though some species are scavengers (members of the families Tineidae and Oecophoridae), and a few are predators (members of the Lycaenidae and Noctuidae families). The herbivorous species eat roots, stalks, stems, leaves, flowers, and fruits.

Most larvae are solitary. One exception, the tent caterpillars in the family Lasiocampidae, are extremely gregarious, and live in large web tents on the host plant. Unfortunately, this gregarious behavior usually results in the defoliation of the host plant. The larvae are vulnerable to attack by a variety of predators, though many species are unpalatable as a form of protection. For protection, some species, such as tussock moths (from the family Lymantriidae) have inedible or stinging hairs, while others are completely furry.

All species of larvae produce silk from a pair of large glands situated along the digestive system. The ducts from each gland join together to form a spinneret in the caterpillar's mouth. The butterflies and moths use the silk, which is a protein, to construct cocoons or shelters.

Once the larvae have grown large enough, they enter the pupal stage. Pupation usually takes place on the host plant. In many species of moth, the pupae live in a silk cocoon prepared by the larvae. For most butterflies and ground-pupating moths, the pupae are naked and are formed either under the soil or hanging exposed from the host plant. The butterfly pupa is usually referred to as a chrysalis. This often has a glass-like appearance, and may be adorned with showy spots and patterns. Metamorphosis, or change, from the larval to the adult form occurs during the pupal stage.

These Monarch butterflies (Danaus plexippus) have massed on this Monterey palm tree in California. Every year, these butterflies migrate southward across the United States to California, Florida, and Mexico, where many winter in giant communal roosts, some of which have become tourist attractions.

Adult butterflies and moths emerge from their pupae fully formed. Most species are short-lived, surviving no longer than a week or two. In fact, the adults of a great number of species do not even have functional mouthparts and cannot feed. They must find their mates and lay their eggs before they run out of energy and nutrients.

The adult males and females of most species have functional wings. However, there are some species in which the females have shortened, atrophied wings (a condition called brachyptery), or no wings at all (a condition known as apterism). One reason for these conditions may be that they allow the energy saved by not producing large functional wings to be used in the development of a larger body and higher reproductive rate. Apterism may also be advantageous to species living in mountain habitats where the high winds and low temperatures increase the energetic cost of flight.

Communication by chemistry

Female butterflies and moths attract their mates with sex chemicals called pheromones. Recent studies of the African milkweed butterflies from the genera *Danaus*, *Tirumala*, and *Amauris*, have shown that these butterflies can produce more than 200 different chemicals to aid identification, some of which have never been discovered in nature before.

These pheromones, coupled with bright wing displays, provide a powerful signal for male butterflies and moths that are active during the day. In night-flying moths, the pheromones are particularly strong because the insects cannot use visual attractants to arouse their mates. The range over which pheromones are effective varies from only a few yards, to well over several hundred yards, as has been demonstrated in the Saturniids, a group of large and showy North American moths.

Chemical communication has been known for over 100 years. In fact, a popular way for collectors to obtain male specimens of otherwise elusive

PESTS VS. BENEFICIAL INSECTS

Adult butterflies and moths are not generally considered to be pests to humans. Most adults eat only nectar, or do not feed at all. It is quite a different matter for the larvae, however, a number of which are considered to be pests, eating agricultural crops, grains, and even wool sweaters! Two notorious species, the Gypsy moth (*Porthetria (Lymantria) dispar*) and the Brown-tail moth (*Nygmia (Euproctis) phaeorrhoea*) were introduced into North America from Europe and have now become destructive consumers of shade trees in the eastern United States. Cotton is a major crop in the United States that suffers from predation by caterpillars. Two main culprits are the Corn earworm (*Heliothis (Helicoverpa) zea*) and the Pink bollworm (*Pectinophora gossypiella*).

But not all butterflies and moths are troublesome to humans. Indeed, most are beneficial. They are effective pollinators, carrying pollen from plant to plant. One commercially valuable species is the Silkworm moth. The larvae is the source of natural silk, which it uses to create its cocoon. The harvesting of this silk, called sericulture, is an important industry in many parts of the world.

There are even cases where butterflies and moths have been used to control other pests (see BIOLOGICAL CONTROL). A cactus-eating moth, *Cactoblastis cactorum*, was used to help eradicate the invasive, nonnative Prickly pear cactus (*Opuntia* spp.) in Australia.

The larva of the Brown-tail moth (Nygmia (Euproctis) phaeorrhoea).

moths, was to entice them to their traps with the pheromones of females. Researchers today are investigating the potential uses of pheromones to control pest species. This research is concentrated on moth pests, and it is hoped that chemical analysis of female pheromone secretions will enable them to be synthesized on a large scale.

Male moths have an enhanced ability to detect pheromones. Male Silkworm moths have huge antennae, covered with thousands of sensory hairs. Most of the male's sensory receptors respond to only one kind of pheromone, bombykol, and are so sensitive that they can detect a single molecule of this chemical. This is far more sensitive than a human receptor, which needs millions of molecules

to detect any chemical. A female needs only to sit on a plant and release small quantities of bombykol in order to attract a male. A lone molecule of the pheromone lands on the antennae of the male and enters a tiny pore of the hair. The molecule then passes through the fluid that surrounds the receptor until it interacts with the receptor's outer membrane. The male becomes aroused and flies upwind until he locates the female. The female, by contrast, has small antennae, which are not as sensitive as those of the male. Whereas the male expends his energy finding his mate, the female saves hers for egg production, and mainly uses her antennae to find the best site for depositing her eggs.

Visual communication
The bright colors and beautiful patterns on the wings of many butterfly species are not just there for decoration. They have important functions. There are also a great number of white or lightly colored butterflies. The light color provides contrast with the green vegetation. In darker wooded habitats, these butterflies are very easily seen.

Most butterflies use visual communication between members of a species. The law of evolution by natural selection (see DARWINISM; NATURAL SELECTION) tells us that the benefits of being highly visible to a mate must be great enough to outweigh the cost of being easily detectable to predators.

In order to be able to communicate with color, butterflies must be able to see color. There is a lot of data to indicate that they can see a wider spectral range of color than humans. Tests have shown that butterflies can see the full range of color that humans can detect, as well as the ultraviolet. In fact, butterflies can see a wider range of

THE TALE OF THE MOTH TONGUE

The proboscis of butterflies and moths is a highly developed instrument, capable of collecting nectar and other nutritious liquids in an extremely efficient way. In some species, this "tongue" is adapted to collect nectar from certain kinds of flowers. For long, tubular flowers, a long tongue, like that of a hummingbird, is required, while a short tongue is sufficient for flowers lacking a tubular shape.

Charles Darwin made the observation that the long, tubular flower of the orchid *Angraceum sesquipedale* would need a pollinator with an equally long tongue. It was only later that the flower's specialized pollinator, the Hawk moth *Xanthopan morgani*, was discovered. This Hawk moth has a tongue-like proboscis just long enough to obtain the nectar at the base of the orchid flower. It is interesting to note that this moth also flies much like a hummingbird, as it moves from flower to flower. This moth-hummingbird similarity is cited as an example of convergent evolution (see EVOLUTION), in which similar ecological challenges (in this case, a long, tubular flower) need similar adaptive solutions (a long tongue).

A CLOSER LOOK

the color spectrum than any other animal in the animal kingdom, including all other insect species.

There are three kinds of color pattern on the wings of butterflies. The ultraviolet (UV) light components can only be seen by other organisms sensitive to this kind of light. Humans do not have this sensitivity, so they only see these patterns with the aid of special instruments. There is great variety in the ultraviolet patterns that exist, even between species that, to our eyes, look very much the same. For example, strikingly different ultraviolet patterns can be found in species in the genera *Colias* and *Gonepteryx*, though they look very much the same under normal light. Differences between males and females of a species are often most pronounced in the UV patterning of the wings.

Iridescence is another form of coloration of the wing, often described as a rainbow-like display of colors. This is due to a series of filters on the outer layer of the wing scales. Some of the most spectacular examples of butterflies, such as the Morpho butterfly (*Morpho peleides*), give an iridescent flash of intense blue to violet while flying. Many of these iridescent patterns are invisible to the human eye, as they are given off in the ultraviolet range.

Camouflage

The colors and patterns on butterfly wings are often a means of protection from predators. Camouflage is critical for moths, which must remain undetected while they are inactive in the daylight hours, and it is important for some butterflies, too. One species of butterfly, appropriately named the Leaf butterfly (*Kallima inachus*), looks like a dried leaf when its wings are folded up along its back.

The Glasswing butterflies (some species in the family Ithomiidae) of the New World tropics use a

The wings of butterflies and moths are composed of tiny overlapping scales. These scales, which are actually modified hairs, tend to rub off in a fine dust if the insects are handled. The color of the scales may be due to pigmentation or their physical structure, which causes only certain wavelengths of light to be reflected. This is a close-up of the wing scales of the Great purple hairstreak (Quercusia quercus).

slightly different means of camouflage. Instead of attempting to color match with their surroundings, the Glasswings have transparent wings, which allow the background to show through and make the butterflies very difficult to see in the low light conditions under the tropical forest canopy.

In some species of moth and butterfly, camouflage is coupled with various kinds of deception. The most common form of trickery is the eyespots, or ocelli, on the surface of the wings. Eyespots attempt to convince a potential predator that what it is looking at is a very large and threatening animal, rather than a butterfly or moth. The Bull's-eye moth (*Automeris io*) has eyespots on its hindwings, which it conceals with its forewings. When disturbed, it rapidly exposes its hindwings and displays an impressive pair of "eyes."

Many larvae also have eyespots. One remarkable example of caterpillar deception is found in the Hawk moth *Leucorampha omatus*. The caterpillar of this species is usually well camouflaged against leaves, as it has green skin. When disturbed, however, the caterpillar puffs up its head and thorax to look like a small poisonous snake, complete with a pair of large eyespots. To make this pretence even more convincing, it weaves back and forth, and hisses in a snake-like manner.

K. HOSOUME/J. KAUFMANN

See also: ANTENNAE; CAMOUFLAGE AND MIMICRY; ENTOMOLOGY; INSECTS; MIGRATION; PHEROMONES; POLLINATION.

Further reading:

Dennis, Roger L.H. *Butterflies and Climate Change.* New York: St. Martin's Press, 1993.
New, T.R. *Butterfly Conservation.* New York: Oxford, 1991.
Still, J. *Amazing Butterflies and Moths.* New York: Alfred A. Knopf Inc., 1991.
The Common Names of North American Butterflies. Edited by Jacqueline Miller. Washington: Smithsonian Institution Press, 1992.

CATERPILLAR CARETAKERS

Some families of butterflies (most notably the lycaenids and the riodinids) have a mutualistic relationship with ants – that is beneficial to both parties; see SYMBIOSIS AND COMMENSALISM.

The butterfly lays its eggs on its host vegetation, which is located near an ant colony. After hatching, the larvae begin to eat the host plant. Instead of devouring the caterpillars, the ants care for and protect them, making certain that predators are kept away. In return, the caterpillars secrete drops of honeydew from a nectary, or honey organ, located on the abdomen, which is eagerly harvested or drunk by the ants. Many species of caterpillar also have a pair of tentacles one segment back from the honey organ, which they raise whenever ants are close by. These tentacles release a cocktail of pheromones to excite and alarm the ants and make them draw near to the caterpillars. Then another secretion from pores along the body of the caterpillars pacifies the ants and helps them to begin "milking."

Lycenid pupae are also able to produce sounds by the use of organs situated on the top of their abdomens. Each species has a characteristic "song," and this singing becomes most apparent when the butterfly is about to emerge. It seems likely that these songs, as with the larval pheromones already mentioned, function to both alarm and pacify the ants, so that they congregate and protect the butterfly as it emerges from the chrysalis.

CACTI AND SUCCULENTS

Cacti and succulents are plants adapted to living in dry conditions by storing water in stems and leaves

Succulents, which include the cacti, are so-called because of their literally succulent nature – their juicy water-storing stems or leaves, which are efficient adaptations to the harsh, dry environments they inhabit. There are three major families of succulents, the Cactaceae (cacti), the Crassulaceae, and the Aizoaceae, which are among the most diverse of all plant groups.

Succulents are xerophytes, plants that are able to live in very dry habitats, where rainfall is low and infrequent. One of the main features of xerophytic plants is their ability to limit transpiration (loss of water vapor from the surface of a plant), or carefully control their water balance in other ways. Water storage is critical to the survival of succulents

– without this ability they would rapidly become dehydrated under the very dry conditions.

All succulents are able to store water in fleshy tissues. Cactaceae typically store water in their stems. It has been estimated that a barrel-shaped 8 ft (2.5 m) tall *Echinocactus* can store about 210 gal (800 l) of water. The Crassulaceae and Aizoaceae, on the other hand, store water in their leaves. Some cacti, such as *Sulcorebutia* spp. and *Lophophora* spp., store water in their large taproots as well as in their stems.

The water-storing cells of succulents contain large vacuoles filled with a watery mucilage (a glutinous carbohydrate). This creates a high osmotic potential (the high concentration of mucilage attracts water), which probably restricts evaporation from cell walls. All three families are also adaptated for dealing with water shortages by having a low transpiration rate, even when they have plenty of water. This is achieved as a result of a waxy cuticle covering the stem, a reduced leaf surface area, and stomata (microscopic pores in the leaves) that remain closed during sunshine hours (see box on crassulacean acid metabolism, page 220).

Cactaceae

There are over 2000 species of cacti, all occuring in the Americas, from Canada in the north to Argentina in the south, the largest variety being

CORE FACTS

■ The three major families of succulents are the Cactaceae, the Crassulaceae, and the Aizoaceae.

■ Succulents are characterized by fleshy stems or leaves, in which they store water as an aid to survival in arid conditions.

■ Succulents reduce their water loss from transpiration with waxy cuticles and a reduced leaf surface area.

■ All succulents also reduce water loss through transpiration by utilizing crassulacean acid metabolism, allowing their stomata to remain closed during daylight.

Flowering Hedgehog cactus (Echinocereus engelmanii) *displaying the swollen and spiny stems typical of most cacti. Cactus flowers are attached directly by the base without a stalk. They have many stamens, arranged spirally around a long central style.*

CRASSULACEAN ACID METABOLISM

Crassulacean acid metabolism (CAM) is an alternative to the usual method of photosynthesis; an adaptation that has evolved to allow plants to retain moisture in dry habitats. It was named after the Crassulaceae, the family of plants in which it was first observed. CAM occurs in most succulents.

Most plants open their stomata, small pores in the leaf, during the day to allow the entry of carbon dioxide (CO_2), which is converted to chemical energy by photosynthesis (see PHOTOSYNTHESIS), and close them at night. CAM allows the stomata to close during the day when heat from the sun causes most evaporation. The stomata open instead during the night and take in CO_2, which is stored until the next day when the sun's energy is used to drive photosynthesis while the stomata are closed.

By night, the incoming CO_2 is converted first into oxalacetic acid, and then into other acids of which malic acid is the most important. This process is called "dark CO_2 fixation," and is unusual in that it is most efficient at low temperatures (10-15°C). The malic and other acids are stored in large quantities in the vacuoles of the parenchyma (basic plant tissue cells) cells until the next day, when the process is reversed. Malic acid is broken down to release CO_2 and photosynthesis occurs as in other plants.

The function of carrying out photosynthesis is transferred to the stem, which has a green, photosynthetic outer layer. The cactus stem contains water storage tissue, which has developed from the cortex, or pith (the tissue between the outer epidermis and the xylem and phloem fibers). The stem may be ribbed, angled, or winged to deflect sunlight and reduce surface temperature. It is covered by a waxy cuticle, which further reduces any loss of water. Cacti can lose between one fifth to one quarter of their water without any permanent damage, but this ability slows metabolism and therefore growth.

An important characteristic feature of cacti, and the one that distinguishes them from similar, but unrelated, xerophytes such as *Euphorbia*, is the presence of growing points called areoles. These are made up of two parts, the upper part produces the flower buds and branches, and the lower one produces the spines.

All cacti are perennial dicotyledons (possessing two seed leaves) and range in size from the miniature *Blossfeldia minima*, which is about ½ in (1 cm) in diameter, to the gigantic Ball cactus (*Echinocactus ingens*), of which there has been one specimen reported with a diameter of 4 ft 1 in (1.25 m) and a height of 5 ft (1.5 m).

Cacti produce flowers each year on existing stems. Most cactus flowers are blue and their pollinators include bats, hummingbirds, bees, and hawk-moths. Cacti produce colorful fruits and berries, which are dispersed when they are eaten and excreted by birds.

Lithops *has a single pair of fused leaves and the typical daisy-like flower of the Aizoaceae.*

found in the dry mountainous regions on either side of the equator.

Cacti occupy a central role in desert ecosystems. Many animals rely on them as a source of food and water. For example, wild javelina (*Pecari angulatus*), a type of wild pig of the American Southwest subsists largely on the succulent pads of the beavertail cactus (*Opuntia basilaris*). Species such as the the lesser long-nosed bat (*Leptonycteris curasoae*), rely on the nectar and fruit of the Saguaro cactus (*Carnegiea gigantea*) as a critical food source during their yearly migrations between Mexico and the American Southwest.

Heavily spined cacti also provide defensible platforms for birds to roost and construct nests. The intensely branched and spined Silver cholla (*Opuntia echinocarpa*) of North America provides a highly protected site for the verdin (*Auriparus flaviceps*) and Cactus wren (*Campylorhynchus brunneicapillus*), despite the fact that the nests are not far above the ground. Some species, such as the Gila woodpecker (*Melanerpes uropygialis*), excavate nest cavities in the the thick succulent stem of large cacti, while the Cactus ferruginous pygmy owl (*Glaucidium brasilianum*) occupies abandoned Gila woodpecker sites. Large predatory bird species, such as hawks, construct their nests on the tall Saguaros.

All cacti, with the exception of *Pereskia*, have reduced or undeveloped leaves, which significantly reduce water loss from transpiration. The reduced leaves have usually developed into spines, which protect against predators seeking out the juicy stems!

Cacti are of special interest to evolutionists because of their unusual combination of primitive unspecialized flowers with advanced well-adapted stems. They also demonstrate a clear example of convergent evolution (in which plants and animals from different geographical regions have developed similar adaptations in response to similar environmental pressures) by their resemblance to some members of the *Euphorbia* family, which inhabit desert regions. The cacti and these euphorbs have evolved separately for millions of years but both have fleshy stems, protective spines, and tiny leaves.

Aizoaceae

Most of the Aizoaceae inhabit southern Africa, although some species also occur in the West Indies, North and South America, Australia, and New Zealand. The family contains more than 2000 species. It rivals the cacti as the largest completely succulent family.

Members of the Aizoaceae are remarkably varied in structure. They range from the least succulent species such as *Aptenia*, with its long stems and flat, only slightly fleshy leaves, to plants such as *Lithops*, and *Conophytum*, whose leaves are buried in the ground with only the tips visible. In *Fenestraria*, each leaf tip has a clear "window." Below the window, a specialized tissue rich in calcium oxalate crystals filters intense sunlight before it reaches the thin chlorophyll-containing layer below.

Members of this family are annual or perennial herbs, or small shrubs with fleshy leaves, which often have a central water storage tissue. In some species, the leaf epidermis (outer layer of cells) contains bladder-like water storage cells.

The flowers look like daisies and are composed of joined sepals with many stamens, the outermost of which are sterile and look like petals.

The seeds of the Aizoaceae are generally dispersed by the "splash cup" mechanism. Seed casings are hygroscopic (absorbing moisture from the air) capsules, which open out like a star when wet and close on drying out. The seeds disperse when hit by raindrops. This may catapault them several inches ensuring that seeds are shed, and germinate, only during rainy periods. Another means of dispersal involves the schizocarp (a dry fruit split internally into two halves), which falls into separate pieces, each bearing a seed. In *Carpobrotus*, the seeds are inside a fleshy fruit, which is eaten by animals.

Crassulaceae

The Crassulaceae are the widest ranging succulents, occuring from the Arctic to South West Africa, and in the Americas. Like the cacti, the Crassulaceae are generally perennial, but there are a few annual and biennial species (for example, *Mucizonia* spp.). Crassulaceae have succulent leaves, and members range from shrublets with fleshy leaves, such as *Kalanchoe*, to much more extreme xerophytic forms, such as *Crasssula deceptrix*, which has a thick waxy surface and very reduced leaves.

Wall-pepper stonecrop (Sedum acre), a member of the Crassulaceae.

Some Crassulaceae reproduce vegetatively as a fast, energy-efficient, means of exploiting periodic rainfall. In some, such as in certain species of *Sedum*, a leaf may fall off from the plant and lie on the soil surface. With rainfall, the leaf produces adventitious roots (roots that develop from organs other than roots) to form a new plant. In *Kalanchoe*, buds develop on notches in the leaves of the parent plant, and eventually drop off to form new plants.

Flowers in the Crassulaceae are small and shaped either like stars or tubes. They are almost always hermaphrodite (containing both male and female organs), and consequently do not need pollinators.

J. STIRLING

See also: DESERT BIOMES; FLOWER AND FLOWER STRUCTURE; LEAF AND LEAF STRUCTURE; PHOTOSYNTHESIS; STEMS AND STEM STRUCTURE.

Further reading:

Sajeva, M. and Costanzo, M. *Succulents: The Illustrated Dictionary*. Portland, Oregon: Timber Press, 1994.

HUMAN USES FOR SUCCULENTS

Many succulents are used for decorative purposes, in greenhouses or as house plants. Because of their diverse and interesting forms, cacti are particularly popular. This popularity has grown to such an extent that cactus rustling in Arizona has become both big business and a major ecological problem. Conviction for theft of the Saguaro cactus (*Carnegiea gigantea*) can result in a five year prison sentence or a $150,000 fine. The attraction of this cactus is its unusual candelabra shape, huge size – it can sometimes reach heights of 50 ft (15.2 m) – and its age, which may be up to 200 years. These plants are very slow growing: at 15 years they are only about 1 ft (30 cm) tall, and after 70 years they may reach 19.5 ft (6 m), when they begin to branch and flower. Two members of the Aizoaceae are eaten as vegetables. These are the New Zealand spinach, *Tetrasonia expansa*, and the iceplant, *Mesembryanthemum crystallinum*.

CAECILIANS

Caecilians are an unusual group of limbless amphibians in the order Gymnophiona (once called Apoda)

Caecilians are wormlike limbless amphibians that are found in warm, moist habitats. Many species live underground in burrows, making them extremely difficult to study. As a result, they are probably the least familiar group of living amphibians. So far, 162 species have been discovered. Most are found in tropical forests, some along the edges of rivers in savannas, and others are completely aquatic. They are fairly small animals, the majority ranging from 9 to 11½ in (24 to 30 cm) in length, although there are "giants" of over 59 in (150 cm) from head to tail. They are classified in the order Gymnophiona (formerly called the Apoda).

With little need of vision underground, caecilian eyes are reduced and often buried under a layer of pigmented skin, or even bone. Unusual paired tentacles originate from the sides of the brain and

CORE FACTS

- There are 162 described species of caecilian, divided into six families and classified within the order Gymnophiona.
- Caecilians are small, limbless amphibians, ranging from 9 to 11½ in (24 to 30 cm) in length.
- Unlike most other amphibians, caecilians have internal fertilization.
- Reproduction in caecilians may be viviparous (live-bearing), oviparous (egg-laying), or ovoviviparous (where eggs are retained and hatch inside the body).

protrude through the skin near each eye. These sensitive feelers, unique to caecilians, probably enhance the sense of smell by carrying chemical messages from the surroundings to the nasal cavity, and are used to determine the animals' location as well as to find food. Another unusual characteristic of these amphibians is that some species have dermal (bony) scales embedded in their skin.

Despite their many unusual characteristics, caecilians have some features in common with their close relatives the salamanders, newts, frogs, and toads. They have a moist skin, lacking in epidermal scales. Like other amphibians, caecilians' skin tends not to retain moisture, and so they must spend their lives in water or a damp environment.

Aquatic and subterranean life

There are generally two forms of locomotion in caecilians. Aquatic species swim much like water snakes, moving their bodies from side to side in an undulating movement. Terrestrial species move by ploughing their heads forward through dampened soil or through heavy leaf litter on the forest floor. To facilitate digging, their skulls are solid and heavily reinforced with bone. Their skin is arranged in folds so their long, thin bodies seem

CONNECTIONS

- Although caecilians and earthworms look very similar, and both play an important role in **SOIL ECOLOGY**, they are not related. Caecilians are **AMPHIBIANS**, which are classed as **VERTEBRATES**, and earthworms are **ANNELIDS**, which are classed as **INVERTEBRATES**.

- Caecilians are an unusual group of amphibians. Unlike most frogs, toads, and salamanders, their mode of **REPRODUCTION** involves internal, rather than external, **FERTILIZATION**.

to be divided into a series of rings. These rings make for easier movement through narrow underground burrows. Caecilians are so well adapted to their burrowing lifestyle that they have no trace of limbs or pectoral and pelvic girdles.

In terrestrial caecilians, burrowing increases the animals' chances of encountering their preferred diet of earthworms and other invertebrates such as termites, as well as providing a means of avoiding their most common predators, birds, and snakes. However, a variety of small tropical snakes hunt caecilians in their burrows. Aquatic species are preyed upon by fish, reptiles such as turtles, and amphibians such as frogs.

When feeding, most caecilians approach their prey slowly and seize it in their strong jaws. Caecilians have two rows of teeth in their upper jaw and one or two rows in their lower jaw. These teeth are sharp and curve inward to enable them to grab and bite their prey.

Caecilian families

There are six families of caecilians living today. The largest family is the Caeciliidae, with 24 genera and around 88 species. This group is also the most widespread, with species scattered throughout the tropical regions of South America, Asia, and Africa. The caeciliids are a diverse group, with several distinct subfamilies. However, in all members of this family, the adults are always terrestrial and the tail is almost completely absent. This family also contains the giants of the order, with the largest caecilian, *Caecilia thompsoni*, achieving a length of over 59 in (150 cm).

The family Ichthyophiidae includes two genera and 35 species, which are distributed throughout Southeast Asia, including Borneo, the Philippines, India, and Sumatra. These are moderate-sized caecilians, with an average length of around 19½ in

(50 cm), part of which consists of a tail. The Icthyophiids possess visible eyes, some dermal scales, and are gray to black in color. Some species have pale stripes along their sides.

The family Scolecomorphidae includes only one genus, with seven species scattered across sub-Saharan Africa. The caecilians in this group lack tails, dermal scales, and well-developed eyes. Also, unlike any other group of caecilians, they lack a stapes – a bone in the middle ear that is extremely important for hearing. As a possible compensation for a lack of sight and hearing, members of the Scolecomorphidae possess particularly large sensory tentacles. These caecilians are generally of average size for the order, although some species, such as *Scolecomorphus convexus*, reach a length of around 17½ in (45 cm).

The family Uraeotyphidae is a small group of caecilians from southern India, consisting of one genus and four species. These animals are small, with the larger species reaching a total length of only 11½ in (30 cm). Uraeotyphids possess scales, although these are restricted to the lower half of their bodies.

There are two genera and nine species in the family Rhinatrematidae, which are found in South America. Zoologists consider them the most primitive of the order, as their skulls are not as solid as those of other caecilians. They possess dermal scales and grow to a maximum length of 13 in (33 cm).

The family Typhlonectidae includes four genera and 19 species. This group is unusual even for caecilians, in that it consists largely of aquatic forms inhabiting streams and ponds in tropical South America. Skull features, such as the fusion of a number of separate bone elements, also distinguish this group from the other caecilian families. This solidifying of the skull suggests to some researchers that the aquatic Typhlonectids evolved from a burrowing ancestor. To facilitate swimming, the end of the body is flattened laterally like that of a fish. This streamlining makes it easier for the aquatic caecilian to move through the water.

Internal fertilization and fetal nutrition

One of the most unusual features of caecilians is their interesting and varied reproductive biology. The majority of amphibians display external fertilization, in which the males' sperm is exposed to the environment. By contrast, caecilians conduct internal fertilization, meaning that sperm is transferred directly from the body of the male to the body of the female during copulation. The male caecilian has an extendable cloaca (an intestinal, urinary, and reproductive cavity), which he inserts into that of the female. Reproduction can be viviparous (live-bearing), oviparous (egg-laying), or ovoviviparous (where eggs are retained and hatch inside the body), depending on the species. Viviparity is the most common form of caecilian reproduction.

A fascinating reproductive strategy develops between the female and her young in those caecilians practicing ovoviviparity. For example, a female Typhlonectid may give birth to as many as nine large young, each up to 7½ in (20 cm) long – as much as 60 percent of her own length. The initial growth of the embryo is supported by yolk in the egg at the time of fertilization. This yolk supply is exhausted long before birth, so the mother must then supply the necessary nutrition to the young in order for them to complete their development.

The developing fetuses acquire this nutrition through uterine milk, which is secreted from glands in their mother's oviducts. They can also scrape this substance from the walls of the oviducts with specialized embryonic teeth. These teeth, and the bone supporting them, develop well in advance of other skeletal structures to facilitate this mode of feeding. Repeated biting by the young appears to increase the rate of uterine milk production. This form of fetal maintenance is also known in sharks, lizards, some snakes, and two species of salamander.

K. HOSOUME/J. KAUFMANN

See also: AMPHIBIANS.

Further reading:
Reptiles and Amphibians. Edited by Harold Cogger and Richard Zweifel. New York: Smithmark, 1992.
Zug, George. *Herpetology: an Introductory Biology of Amphibians and Reptiles.* San Diego: Academic Press, 1993.

CAECILIAN RESEARCH

Caecilians are by far the least known of the amphibians. Their subterranean lifestyle makes them extremely difficult to study, as the collection of specimens involves hours of digging in search of them. For this reason, many species are known from only one or two specimens.

Despite their elusive nature, biologists have known of the existence of caecilians for many years. One of the first known published records of caecilians is by the naturalist Albertus Seba in 1735. The Swedish botanist Carl Linnaeus included two species of caecilian in his *Systema Natura*, published in 1758. However, he thought they were most closely related to snakes and classified them as reptiles. Scientists continued to think of them as reptiles until 1835, when Johannes Müller discovered that their larvae had gill slits, and on that basis concluded that they were amphibians. Nevertheless, caecilians did not become very well known to biologists until 1968, when Edward H. Taylor published his *Monograph of Caecilians*.

DISCOVERERS

CAECILIAN DIVERSITY

Only 162 species of living caecilians have been described, compared to over 350 species of salamander and over 3400 species of frog and toad. This low number of known caecilians is in part due to their secretive lifestyles, and also to the fact that they spend almost all their lives underground. It is almost certain that as biologists venture deeper into tropical regions, more species of amphibians, including caecilians, will be discovered.

CALCIUM

Calcium is a major mineral element in plants and animals, essential to many chemical reactions in cells

Calcium is an important mineral element in both animals and plants. It is the essential building block for your bones and teeth. It also enables your nerves to conduct messages, your heart to beat, and your muscles to contract.

In vertebrates – including humans – at least 95 percent of the calcium in the body is in the bones. As well as supporting the body, the bones of an animal serve as a storage area for calcium.

Bones are made up of an interlocking framework of calcium compounds and a protein called collagen. New calcium is constantly being laid down in bones while old calcium is removed. It is thought that this turnover helps to keep bones strong because new collagen fibers are formed at the same time calcium is deposited, while the old collagen, which has become brittle, is removed along with the old calcium.

Calcium is also important in plants. Most of the calcium in plants is found in the middle lamella of cell walls, where it forms part of substances called pectins that cement the cells to one another. Since calcium is required to form new cement between growing cells, plants that do not get enough calcium show deformities in areas of new growth. In calcium-deficient plants, the tips and edges of leaves often curl, and buds die. Plants obtain calcium through their roots from inorganic calcium salts naturally present in the soil.

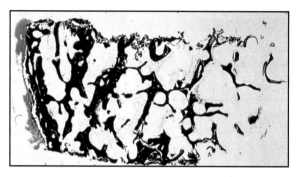

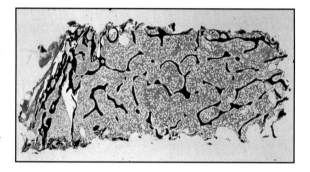

The black stained regions indicate areas containing deposits of calcium in healthy bone tissue (above) and that of an osteoporosis sufferer (below). Osteoporosis is an excessive loss of bone tissue. It is most common in elderly people and women after the menopause.

CORE FACTS

- In vertebrates, around 95 percent of calcium is in the bones.
- Calcium is the sixth most abundant element in most plants.
- In animal cells, calcium is an important part of chemical processes such as nerve impulse transmission, muscle contraction, and blood clotting.
- Calcium levels in the body are regulated by the thyroid and parathyroid glands.

Chemical reactions

Calcium is always present in the bloodstream and the fluid that surrounds most cells. By contrast, there is ordinarily very little calcium in the fluid of the cell's cytoplasm, although some is stored in organelles such as the mitochondria and the endoplasmic reticulum. There is usually 10,000 times as much calcium outside the cell as inside: this high concentration gradient is essential to maintain the cell's correct physiological state.

Through the process of diffusion, molecules naturally move from an area of high concentration to an area of low concentration, and so the calcium has to be constantly "pumped" out of the cell. This is done by a process called the calcium pump, in which calcium binds to the protein calmodulin and

is actively transported across the cell membrane. However, there are times when a higher concentration of calcium is needed in the cell in order to react with enzymes and trigger various chemical reactions. These reactions cover a variety of essential cell fuctions, such as hormone secretion, muscle contraction, and glycogenolysis (the breakdown of the energy store, glycogen). Then another process overrides the calcium pump.

When certain signaling chemicals, such as hormones, attach to receptor molecules on the outside of a cell they cause channels to open in the cell membrane. Then, because of the high concentration gradient, the calcium ions rush through the channels into the cytoplasm of the cell. As part of the same process, calcium is released into the cytoplasm from cell structures called mitochondria.

Once inside the cell, the calcium acts as a chemical messenger by attaching to various proteins such as enzymes in order to initiate other chemical processes. One of these proteins is calmodulin. With calcium attached the calmodulin molecule changes shape and is able to react more easily with enzymes in the cell to start further reactions. At the same time, the changed calmodulin initiates reactions that move calcium out through the cell membrane and back into the mitochondria. This halts the processes that were started when the calcium was first released.

A similar process takes place at nerve ends. When an electrical signal arrives it opens calcium channels in the membrane around the nerve ending. The calcium ions enter the cytoplasm and, by an unknown mechanism, cause chemicals called neurotransmitters to be released into the fluid sur-

---

CONNECTIONS

- Calcium is a soft, gray, metallic element belonging to Group II of the Periodic Table. The chemical symbol for calcium is Ca.

- Calcium is a major mineral element in animal **NUTRITION**. It is stored in the **BONES** and **TEETH**. In plants, calcium is stored in the middle lamella of **CELL** walls.

- Calcite ($CaCO_3$) is a common mineral containing calcium, carbon, and oxygen. It is very important in the formation of rocks such as limestones and marbles. Calcite is a soft mineral, third only in softness after talc and gypsum. Geologists number minerals using a scale of hardness called Mohs' scale.

rounding the nerve. It is believed that alcohol and some sedative drugs interfere with the opening of calcium channels in nerve endings, reducing the amount of neurotransmitters released and slowing down the nervous system.

In 1883 the British scientist Sydney Ringer discovered that if frog hearts were kept in a fluid that contained sodium and potassium but no calcium, the heart muscles quickly died. This was the first evidence of the vital role that calcium plays in muscle control. Calcium is stored in sacs in the muscle fiber, and is released when an electrical stimulus from a nerve reaches the fiber. It then combines with protein molecules in the muscle fiber. This converts the proteins into an enzyme that releases the energy needed to cause muscle fibers to contract. The calcium pump then works to pump the calcium from the cytoplasm back into the storage sacs, allowing the muscle fibers to relax.

Nowhere are these processes more important than in the muscles of the heart and the circulatory system. Although how they work is not perfectly understood, drugs called calcium antagonists or calcium-channel blockers are now used to correct disruptions in the rhythm of the heartbeat. They can also reduce spasms in the smooth muscle in the walls of arteries supplying blood to the heart muscle, improving blood flow to the heart. A shortage of calcium in the diet has been linked to hypertension (high blood pressure). This may be because of calcium's role in the contraction of muscles in blood vessels (see CIRCULATORY SYSTEMS).

Calcium also takes part in the chemical reactions that form blood clots. It converts proteins released at a wound site into the enzymes thromboplastin and thrombin. Thromboplastin stimulates the process of blood clotting and thrombin converts the protein fibrinogen into fibrin, the strong fibrous strands that make up the blood clot itself.

Calcium regulation in the body

These processes will not work if the concentration of calcium in the blood and the fluid surrounding cells is not carefully maintained. The thyroid and parathyroid glands regulate the amount of calcium in the blood.

When blood calcium falls too low, the parathyroid glands secrete parathyroid hormone. This, with the assistance of vitamin D, increases the activity of osteoclasts (cells that work to break down old bone and release calcium) and causes more calcium to be absorbed from the intestines. When there is too much calcium, the thyroid gland secretes the hormone calcitonin, which inhibits the activity of the osteoclasts, slowing calcium release from the bones and causing the kidneys to secrete more calcium in the urine.

If the regulatory mechanism fails to work, the body can become diseased. Too much parathyroid hormone and a deficiency of vitamin D or calcium can lead to a disease called rickets (softening of the bones), which occurs mainly in children. Too

---

ARE YOU GETTING ENOUGH CALCIUM?

We lose some calcium in urine every day, so we must regularly replace it by eating calcium-containing foods, such as milk and cheese. If we do not do this, our bodies will continue to remove calcium from our bones to maintain an adequate concentration in the bloodstream. The Federal Food and Nutrition Board, part of the National Academy of Science, lists these Recommended Daily Allowances (RDAs) for calcium:

Infants and children	
Birth to six months	400 mg
Six months to one year	600 mg
One year to ten years	800 mg
Adolescent and adult men and women	
11 to 24 years	1200 mg
24 and older	800 mg
Pregnant and breastfeeding women	1200 mg
Post-menopausal women	1500 mg

Our bodies also need vitamin D in order to absorb calcium from foods. Vitamin D is made in the skin during exposure to the sun – 15 to 30 minutes in the sun each day supplies enough. Vitamin D also occurs naturally in liver, fish-liver oil, egg yolk, butter, and margarine. Vitamin D is added to most milk in the United States.

A survey by the U.S. Department of Agriculture in 1990 found that most adult Americans do not get enough calcium in their diet. Women aged between 19 and 34 had an average of 665 mg per day, and men 975 mg per day. Women aged 35 and older averaged only 565 mg per day. The low figure for women is blamed on the fact that they are more likely to go on low-fat diets, and so avoid milk and milk products because of the fat content. Teenage girls are even more likely to diet, and often drink soft drinks containing large amounts of phosphorus, which tends to reduce calcium absorption. Teenagers and young adults seem to move away from drinking milk because of the mistaken idea that it is "childish."

It is extremely important to obtain adequate calcium to build bone mass at least up to age 25, and to continue to supply enough throughout life to discourage loss of bone mass. Intakes of calcium above the RDA have been shown to help reduce bone loss in patients with osteoporosis, and to reduce blood pressure.

Some good sources of calcium:

Milk (1 cup)	300 mg
Yogurt (1 cup)	275-400 mg
Canned salmon, with bones (3 oz)	285 mg
Swiss cheese (1 oz – about 1 slice)	272 mg
Cheddar cheese (1 oz)	200 mg
Low-fat cottage cheese (1 cup)	150 mg

A CLOSER LOOK

---

little parathyroid hormone can lead to a condition called tetany, in which the muscles twitch and spasm involuntarily.

It has been suggested that this regulatory mechanism — like other mechanisms of homeostasis (internal chemical regulation) — evolved when animals first moved out of the sea, in order to maintain inside their bodies an environment similar to the seawater that had formerly surrounded them.

W. STEELE

See also: BONE; CELLS; ENDOCRINE SYSTEMS; MUSCULAR SYSTEMS; NERVOUS SYSTEMS; NUTRITION.

Further reading:

A Practical Guide to the Study of Calcium in Living Cells. Edited by Richard Nuccitelli. San Diego: Academic Press, 1994.
Encyclopedia of Human Biology. Edited by Renato Dulbecco. San Diego: Academic Press, 1994.

CALORIE

A calorie is the amount of heat needed to raise the temperature of 1 g of water 1°C at 1 atmosphere of pressure

Most people count the calories in their food, but few know that the calorie is actually a unit of heat energy. One calorie (approximately 4.184 joules) is the amount of heat needed to raise the temperature of 1 g of water 1°C at 1 atmosphere (atm) of pressure. The amount of heat energy associated with food is the kilocalorie or Calorie. (The capital C in Calorie indicates the kilocalorie unit). The Calorie (abbreviated kcal or Cal) is the amount of heat needed to raise the temperature of 1 kg (1000 g) of water 1°C at 1 atm.

Direct calorimetry

Calorimetry is the measurement of the heat given off by a substance when it is completely burned or consumed in a chemical reaction. This process has been used to measure the caloric content of most of the foods we eat. Carbohydrates and fats are completely consumed by oxidation (combination with oxygen) to carbon dioxide and water. Although there are some differences in the caloric content of different types of carbohydrates and fats, the following average values are accepted for most

CORE FACTS

■ 1 calorie = 4.184 joules.
■ One calorie is the amount of heat needed to raise the temperature of 1 g of water 1°C at 1 atmosphere.
■ Food energy is measured in kilocalories (also called Calories).
■ The energy values of foods are measured by direct calorimetry.
■ A certain number of calories are needed each day for survival. The average recommended daily allowances are 2500 Cal for men and 2000 Cal for women.

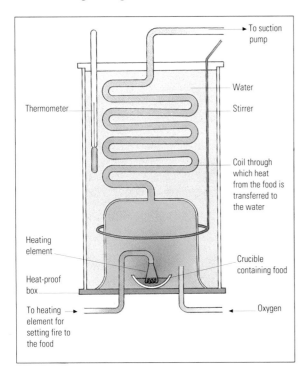

Thermometer
To suction pump
Water
Stirrer
Coil through which heat from the food is transferred to the water
Heating element
Heat-proof box
Crucible containing food
To heating element for setting fire to the food
Oxygen

The caloric content of a food can be determined by measuring the heat released by the complete combustion of the food in a strong metal device called a bomb calorimeter. A known mass of the food is placed in the calorimeter, where it is combusted. The resultant heat causes the temperature of the water to rise, and this is measured in calories.

by the body's metabolic processes. Proteins are broken down into carbon dioxide, water, and nitrogen-containing products, such as urea and ammonia, which are not completely oxidized by the body but contain caloric energy. These non-oxidized byproducts of protein breakdown are excreted in the urine. In addition, the amino acids that make up the proteins vary widely in their caloric content. However, because a normal diet contains many different types of protein, and the amount of calories excreted due to protein metabolism is relatively consistent, it is possible to use an average value of 4.1 Cal per gram of protein.

Indirect calorimetry

As well as knowing our calorie intake, we also need to know how much energy we expend. One way in which energy use in humans can be determined is to measure metabolic oxygen consumption – the amount of oxygen used to break down different food substances (carbohydrates, fats, and proteins) into usable energy in the form of ATP (adenosine triphosphate; see ENERGY) plus carbon dioxide and water. The amount of oxygen needed for the combustion of fat and carbohydrate is very different. Approximately twice as much oxygen is needed to oxidize fat (2.0 liters of oxygen per gram) as carbohydrate (0.8 liters of oxygen per gram). It is possible to determine the amount of oxygen a person uses for metabolism of a substance during rest or activity. This is done by measuring the amount of oxygen (and carbon dioxide) in the

purposes. The heat liberated by 1 g of carbohydrate is approximately 4.1 Cal, while the heat liberated by 1 g of fat is about 9.3 Cal. The energy content of fat is more than twice that of carbohydrate.

Since dietary carbohydrates and fats are completely oxidized by the body, the energy released during metabolism is the same as that measured by direct calorimetry. With proteins, there is a difference between the energies released in physico-chemical combustion in the bomb calorimeter and

BREAKDOWN OF FOOD IN THE BODY

	Carbohydrates	Fats	Proteins
Metabolic energy content (Cal/g)	4.1	9.3	4.1
O₂ consumed (l/g)	0.8	2.0	1.0
CO₂ produced (l/g)	0.8	1.4	0.8
Respiratory quotient	1.0	0.7	0.8
Cal burned/l of O₂ consumed	5.0	4.7	4.5

air breathed into and out of the lungs. It has been calculated that 1 liter of oxygen will metabolize 5.0 Cal of carbohydrates, 4.7 Cal of fat, or 4.5 Cal of protein. (Since protein metabolism accounts for so few of the calories burned in a normal person, it can be ignored as a major factor in food utilization.) Knowing the amount of oxygen a person uses during a given activity allows us to estimate the number of calories that are being used.

Respiratory quotient

The respiratory quotient (RQ) is a useful index for determining what substance is being used during any given activity. Your RQ will show whether you are burning calories mainly from fat or from carbohydrates (again, protein metabolism can be ignored). The RQ is the ratio of the volume of carbon dioxide produced to the volume of oxygen consumed due to the metabolism of foods during a given activity. When carbohydrate metabolism is the source of calories, the RQ is close to 1.0. During fat metabolism, the amount of carbon dioxide produced is less than that of oxygen consumed, and the ratio falls to about 0.7. The closer the RQ is to 1.0, the greater the contribution of carbohydrate breakdown; the closer to 0.7, the greater the fat metabolism. The RQ will always be between these values. A normal resting RQ is 0.82, with more fats being used than carbohydrates.

Under normal conditions, almost no proteins are being metabolized to supply your energy needs. Protein is generally used to synthesize enzymes and structural proteins. Protein is only used as an energy source when no carbohydrates or fats are available (under conditions of famine, for example) or when excess protein has been taken in. In this case, the protein is broken down into amino acids to generate energy and fat. The table on the previous page summarizes the relationship between calories (energy content), metabolic oxygen requirement, metabolic carbon dioxide production, and RQ for each food category.

Average daily requirements

Everyone needs a regular calorie intake in order to survive. Every individual has a basal metabolic rate (BMR): the number of calories needed to maintain normal resting maintenance of body function (see BASAL METABOLIC RATE). The BMR is a minimal value; total requirements are higher since many more calories are burned during daily activity. Average recommended daily amounts are 2500 Cal for men and 2000 Cal for women, but many factors influence a person's daily needs.

During childhood, metabolism is very high due to growth, and children need a high protein and total calorie intake. Daily needs peak around the late teens or in the twenties and then slowly decline. Very cold climates can cause metabolic increases in order to maintain a normal body temperature; BMR rises, as does daily caloric intake. In hot climates, lowered physical activity reduces

CALORIE CONTENT OF SELECTED MEALS

Meal	Item	Amount	Calories
Breakfast	Eggs (boiled)	2 large	150
	Bacon (grilled)	2 slices	70
	Butter	1 tablespoon	108
	Toast	1 slice	62
	Coffee (black)	1 cup	0
	Orange juice	180 ml	80
		Total calories	470
Lunch	Cheeseburger	195 g	510
	French fries	80 g	250
	Soft drink	355 ml	110
	Apple pie	⅛ section	282
		Total calories	1152
Dinner	Baked flounder	100 g	250
	Baked potato	1 medium	95
	Butter	2 tablespoons	216
	Green salad	180 g	50
	Salad dressing (blue)	3 tablespoons	250
	Broccoli	1 large stalk	18
	Iced tea	355 ml	0
		Total calories	879
Snack	Apple	1 medium	80
	Cheese	50 g	200
		Total calories	280
		Total daily calories	2781

caloric needs. Hormonal changes can also change caloric requirements. In pregnancy, a larger calorie intake is needed to boost the mother's metabolism and to support the developing fetus.

Daily physical activity is an important factor in deciding caloric needs. Total daily caloric expenditure is calculated as the 24 hour BMR plus the sum of the caloric costs of your daily activities. For example, a sedentary office worker will need far fewer calories than a very physically active laborer who may need more than 9000 Calories per day.

M. MAHALIK

See also: BASAL METABOLIC RATE; CARBOHYDRATES; ENERGY; FATS AND OILS; METABOLISM; NUTRITION; PROTEINS.

Further reading:

Frankle, R.T. *Nutrition in the Community*. St Louis: Mosby, 1993.

Today people are not just concerned about how many calories they consume, but where those calories come from. Nutritionists suggest that we should reduce our consumption of fat, and increase our consumption of carbohydrates such as whole-wheat bread, fruit, and vegetables.

CAMOUFLAGE AND MIMICRY

Camouflage and mimicry are methods of deception used by both animals and plants

Camouflage and mimicry are the twin arts of deception in the living world. In most cases, the desired outcome is the same – usually escape from predators or capture of prey – but the two methods work in very different ways. In camouflage, an animal or plant blends with its surroundings to avoid detection by other animals. Success results in predators being unable to see the animal or plant concerned. By contrast, mimicry is a way for a plant or animal to draw attention to itself.

CORE FACTS

- Cryptic coloration occurs when an organism's color closely matches that of the background.
- Disruptive coloration occurs in an organism with a strong pattern that breaks up its outline.
- Countershading occurs in an organism with shades of dark and light color on its body to counter the effects of light and shadow.
- Some animals and plants are camouflaged by their close resemblance to other objects within their habitat, such as leaves, flowers, stones, and bird droppings.
- Müllerian mimicry occurs in groups of unpalatable or toxic animals that have similar warning coloration.
- Batesian mimicry occurs in animals or plants that pretend to be other organisms in order to deter predators or attract prey.

This Epipristis nelearia *moth from the rainforests of Borneo demonstrates cryptic coloration. Its green and brown patterning camouflages it perfectly against the lichen-covered tree trunk while it rests during the day.*

Most harmless mimics use the warning coloration and pattern of a poisonous or distasteful organism to persuade predators to leave them alone. This employs what is known as a signal-response between predator and prey, in which the predator, having found several individuals distasteful, learns to avoid particular colors and patterns, regardless of which organism is displaying them.

FORMS OF CAMOUFLAGE

There are several different types of camouflage that occur in living things.

Cryptic coloration

The most common form of camouflage is cryptic coloration, in which the organism's color is the same or similar to that of its background. One obvious example is that of snow-dwelling animals such as the Snowshoe hare (*Lepus americanus*), whose coat changes from brown in the summer to white in the winter, when the ground is covered with snow.

In some animals, not only are the colors the same, but the pattern may be matched, too. For

CONNECTIONS

- Camouflage and mimicry are often used by **INSECTS.** Some **BUTTERFLIES AND MOTHS** use cryptic coloration, while **LEAF INSECTS AND WALKING STICKS** are masters of disguise.

- Many marine animals use camouflage. Countershading is common in **SHARKS** and other kinds of **FISH.**

- The military applies cryptic colors and patterns to its vehicles and buildings, as well as to its uniforms, in an attempt to blend in with the background.

example, the animal might have the same dappled pattern as is formed when light strikes the forest canopy, or the pattern of leaves in its habitat: the Gaboon viper (*Bitis gabonica*) from South Africa has a pattern and color that camouflages it perfectly among dead leaves on the forest floor.

Some animals use other animals as a background on which to camouflage themselves by cryptic coloration. This device is used by several species of crab that live among the corals of the Great Barrier Reef off the coast of Queensland in northern Australia. Examples include *Calthrop* crabs, which have color patterns that make them almost invisible against the background of the host sea urchins and feather stars on whose surfaces they live.

Other species, such as *Camposcia retusa*, cover themselves with debris, such as fragments of other animals in the surrounding habitat. The debris is all held together by masses of hooked bristles. The crabs' "decoration" masks their outlines. If their "dress" becomes inappropriate when they change locality, they simply discard it and replace it with more suitable fresh material.

Disruptive coloration

Another form of camouflage is called disruptive coloration. In this case, the animal is strongly patterned so that its outline is effectively broken up. The intense body pattern does not necessarily match the background pattern, but it does make it more difficult for predators or prey to recognize the creature, or focus on it.

There are many examples of disruptive coloration in nature. Tropical reef fishes, such as some butterfly fish from the genus *Chaetodon* and angelfish from the genus *Pomacanthus*, are vividly

REEF FISH

Many species of fish living on coral reefs use camouflage techniques to make themselves less conspicuous to predators and prey. The Coral blenny *(Exallias brevis)* is one of the few fish to mimic the coral reefs in which it lives, although many species, such as the sargassofish *(Histrio histrio)*, have imitation fronds that camouflage them against a background of seaweed. Flatfish, such as the Peacock flounder *(Bothus lunatus)*, use disruptive coloration to make them invisible against the sand as they settle on the seabed, even changing their color and pattern as they move from place to place. Other scorpion fish from the genus *Scorpaenopsis*, such as *Scorpaensis scrofa* shown below, are stealthy hunters. They lie hidden in coral, waiting for their prey to pass close enough for them to grab and suck them into their large mouths.

A CLOSER LOOK

Some species of cacti from the genera Fenestraria *and* Lithops *are perfect stone mimics. They are incredibly difficult to see against a background of rocks and stones when they are not in flower.*

CHAMELEONS

Chameleons are famous for their ability to color match with any background, and are often cited as examples of camouflage in action. In fact, some species can change color in a matter of seconds. This quick change is achieved by withdrawing or dispersing colored pigments throughout melanophores (pigment cells) found in varying levels of the skin. But despite their reputation for being masters of camouflage, studies of chameleons have shown that their changing color may have more to do with changes in the surrounding light and temperature, and the physiological and emotional state of the animal, than changes in the background itself. Skin color can change as a chameleon's body changes temperature, and this change may be very dramatic, from black to white. Other color changes are associated with emotions. Angry, territorial males facing one another, may change their color to intimidate their opponents.

A CLOSER LOOK

THE KILLDEER AND HER EGGS

A number of species of bird do not construct a nest in the traditional sense, but lay their eggs directly on the ground in a slight indentation called a scrape. Ground-nesting birds are most typically shorebirds and gulls, although other groups also show this behavior.

The killdeer *(Charadrius vociferus)* is a common shorebird species, which breeds in North America and produces eggs that are extremely well matched to the pebbled ground on which it nests. The young hatchlings are equally well camouflaged to their background. To enhance concealment, the young hold perfectly still if approached. So good is the camouflage of the killdeer, that many ornithologists have often searched for killdeer eggs and young, while they lay undetected at their feet.

A CLOSER LOOK

striped in an attempt to focus predators' attention on the colorful patterns, rather than on the fish themselves. Another classic example is the tiger (see the box on page 231).

Strong patterns can also be used to distract attention from parts of the body more vulnerable to attack by predators, such as the eyes and head. This is often seen in butterflies such as the Swallowtail *(Papilio machaon)*. This butterfly has false eye spots at the tail to confuse potential attackers into aiming for the lower part of the body instead of the more sensitive head.

Countershading

Many animals have shading on their bodies, which counters the effects of light and shadow that might otherwise make the creature visible to predators. Countershading, as this type of camouflage is known, is common in fishes. Many species of ocean fish are dark-colored on top and light below. This means that a predator looking down on the fish from above confuses the fish's back tones with the dark, deep waters, whereas the light underbelly allows the fish to blend in with the sky when the predator or prey looks up from below. These fish often have a silvery stripe along their sides, which covers the dense red muscle, heart, and liver that would otherwise be visible.

Disguise

Some organisms exploit their shape as well as color and pattern to fool predators or prey into thinking they are common objects within the surrounding environment. This ability is not restricted to animals: some plants, such as the African stone-plants *(Lithops* spp.), look very like small stones.

Many creatures attempt to mimic the shape and color of leaves and other plant parts, such as thorns and flowers.

In some leaf-mimicking species, such as the Leaf butterfly *(Kallima inachus)*, even the veins in the leaf are reproduced on the body of the insect. The Dead-leaf mantis *(Acanthops falcata)* resembles a dead, curled-up leaf; and there is even a species of toad called the Asian horned toad *(Megophrys nasuta)*, which has the appearance of dried leaves on the forest floor, where it lives and forages.

The famous walking stick insects, belonging to the family Phasmida, which occur in tropical and temperate habitats around the world, look just like sticks. Walking sticks occurring in the temperate desert, where most plant material is brown or otherwise drab, are themselves drab in appearance. Tropical species are much more brightly colored in reds and greens.

Another plant mimic is the thorn-imitating tree-hopper *(Umbonia spinosa)* that, when it remains motionless on the stem of a plant, looks remarkably like a thorn.

Yet other creatures escape detection by pretending to be something they are not. The larva of the Dagger moth *(Acronicta psi)* is covered in fine white hairs that, to a predatory bird, make it look like a tasteless spittle bug covered in froth; and the larva of the Swallowtail butterfly appears to

ALLIGATOR SNAPPING TURTLE

The Alligator snapping turtle *(Macroclemys temmincki)* is a slow-moving, bottom-dwelling reptile found in the southeastern United States, which uses a combination of camouflage and mimicry to ensnare prey. Its preferred diet, fish, would prove a difficult catch for such a slow, cold-blooded predator. So, instead of chasing its prey, it sits and waits for its victims to pass by. The turtle sits quietly at the bottom of a pond or lake, where the color of its skin and shell closely match those of the mud and vegetation, and it is well camouflaged. To attract its prey, the turtle holds its jaws wide open, exposing a worm-like, fleshy projection from the bottom of its large mouth. This moves like a worm, and acts as bait to unsuspecting fish. As a fish attempts to catch the "worm," the turtle quickly sucks it in, and closes its sharp beaklike bill, trapping its unlucky prey.

A CLOSER LOOK

ZEBRA STRIPES

Life on the open savanna can be a challenge for large herbivores that are the prey for predators such as lions *(Panthera leo)*. Surprisingly, the bold, black-and-white stripes of the zebra *(Equus* spp.*)* seem even to call attention to the animal, rather than help conceal it from enemies. Indeed, scientists are still unsure exactly what purpose this coloration serves.

However, if you consider a herd of zebra together, a possible explanation suggests itself. A lion is able to spot a lone zebra with relative ease; but, when disturbed and agitated, a herd of zebra becomes a mass of continuous black-and-white stripes. For the lion, an individual zebra becomes lost in this patterned backdrop, and the lion has difficulty locating and targeting one animal.

Another explanation is that lions are color blind, and so the black-and-white stripes are in fact an excellent camouflage against what appears to the lion as the vertical shades of black, white, and gray of the zebras' grassland environment. Yet another theory is that the stripes break up the zebras' outline and protect them from flies, which usually select distinct objects.

A CLOSER LOOK

be nothing more interesting than a bird dropping! Successful camouflage depends on the organisms behaving like the objects they mimic, as well as looking like them. For many plant mimics, this involves maintaining the correct posture and keeping absolutely still. However, this may sometimes draw attention to the mimic, if it is the only still object in a wind-buffeted scene.

Walking sticks and mantids will sometimes attempt to move with the rocking grass stalks or windblown leaves. These creatures must also ensure that they are against the relevant background – if a twig-like insect sits on a bright green leaf it is likely to be spotted very quickly.

One problem for many organisms attempting camouflage is symmetry. An animal's symmetric shape may distinguish it from its surroundings, since the background, with its random array of rocks, plants, or wind-blown leaves would not possess such symmetry. However, there are ways to solve this problem. One example is found in the moth *Hyperchiria nausica*. The moth produces an asymmetrical mid-vein by folding one forewing over the other. Other cryptic moths will extend one or two legs outward just on one side of the body, or twist the abdomen to one side to achieve the same effect.

Tests of camouflage

Examples of camouflage in nature are legion. However, considering this phenomenon is so widespread, there is a marked lack of scientific experiments designed to show that camouflage really does confer an advantage to the organism that uses it. Some studies have attempted to prove this point. In one study with Black-headed gulls (*Larus ridibundus*), various colored eggs were introduced into the ground nests. Equal numbers of white, khaki-colored, and natural spotted eggs were used in this test. The natural spotted eggs suffered less preda-

tion from herring gulls and carrion crows than the white or khaki eggs.

One way of measuring the degree of camouflage, or color matching, is to compare the amount of various wavelengths of light reflected from both the background and the organism itself. These data can then be used to plot graphs called reflectance curves, which can be compared to determine the effectiveness of the camouflage.

Many studies with reptiles and amphibians have demonstrated very similar reflectance curves for animals and background color. So precise is the matching in some species, that even small color irregularities in the background, such as unusually dark pebbles or leaf fragments, are matched.

The evolution of camouflage

As with other adaptations, the principle mechanism for the evolution of camouflage is natural selection (see ADAPTATION; NATURAL SELECTION). To take a hypothetical example, imagine a species of butterfly that feeds and mates in an open meadow bordering a forest. At this time, the butterflies rely on bright colors in order to recognize members of their population for mating purposes. Some time later, a new species of butterfly-eating bird finds its way to the meadow, and the birds begin to prey on the butterflies. The birds are visual hunters, seek-

CAMOUFLAGED CATS

Large predatory cats, such as leopards *(Panthera pardus)*, jaguars *(P. onca)*, and tigers *(P. tigris)*, use both traditional camouflage and disruptive coloration to outwit their prey. The leopard and jaguar, with their large spots, are well concealed in the dappled background of the forest floor, and the tiger's bold stripes match the streaked patterns of sunlight and shadow through the tall grasses and trees. The strong patterns help to break up the outlines of the cats, so concealing their form as they lie in wait for their prey.

A tiger well camouflaged against a grassy background by disruptive coloration.

A CLOSER LOOK

ing out the brightly colored wings of the tasty butterflies. In this scenario, all the butterflies would be lost if it were not for the fact that not all the butterflies in the population look exactly the same. Through a quirk of nature, some members of the population are slightly less colorful than others. When any of these "drab" butterflies move into the shady woodlands along the meadow's edge, they are less conspicuous to their predators and tend to survive longer – long enough to reproduce. If the variation in color is hereditary, the offspring of the drab butterflies will be drab, too.

As time progresses, and more predators arrive, there is additional pressure on the butterflies to become less conspicuous. Evolution is driven by the advent of mutations, or changes in character (see MUTATION). An advantageous mutation for the butterflies may result in the wings of the butterfly having a blotching pattern similar to the pattern of light and dark in the dappled woodland floor, or a color combination akin to that seen in the woodland flowers or mosses.

Every mutation that further conceals the butterflies spreads rapidly through the population, as butterflies with the mutation survive longer and produce more offspring, which then go on to reproduce, too. Every mutation that reduces the butterflies' chances of survival tends to get lost, as

those butterflies are eaten before they have time to reproduce. In this system of challenge and adaptive response, populations are driven into new forms and varieties, including camouflage, simply in order to survive.

The tale of the peppered moths

A much-cited example of camouflage as an adaptive response can be found in the peppered moths (*Biston betularia*) of Britain. There are two forms of this species: the "typica" form is pale and speckled, while the "carbonaria" form is black. In the early 18th century the most common form was the typica, as it was well camouflaged against the lichen-covered tree trunks in the forests where it lived. By contrast, the carbonaria form was uncommon to the point of being a rare prize for collectors, as these moths were conspicuous against the trees and usually eaten by predators before they had time to reproduce.

During Britain's industrial revolution, the burning of coal in the factories increased substantially. Soot from the smokestacks covered everything, including the once light-colored bark of the trees. The pale typica form was now conspicuous on the tree trunks, and eaten by predators such as birds. However, the black form of the moth was well camouflaged against the sooty bark. By the 1840s there were large numbers of the carbonaria form until these moths far outnumbered the typica form of the species. In Manchester, England's industrial center at the time, the carbonaria form of the peppered moth composed 98 percent of the total population. The typica form was now badly adapted in the sooty forest. However, in more rural areas, away from the factories, the pale form of the moth was still common. Today, pollution controls in Britain have lead to a cleaner environment, and the typica is the dominant form once again.

FORMS OF MIMICRY

There are two well-known forms of mimicry, Müllerian mimicry (named after the 19th-century German zoologist Fritz Müller) and Batesian mimicry (named after the British naturalist Henry Bates). There is also a lesser-known form of mimicry known as aggressive mimicry.

Müllerian mimicry

In Müllerian mimicry, groups of poisonous or unpleasant-tasting animals share similar colors and patterns, so that once a predator has learned to avoid one species, it will not attempt to catch and eat similarly marked species. One example is a group of bad-tasting butterflies, comprising four *Heliconius* species, which all resemble one another. This type of mimicry is beneficial for the predators, too, as it simplifies their learning process. Once they have learned to associate the relevant colors and patterns with a bad taste, they will keep away from every similar species, and so avoid another unpleasant encounter.

CORAL SNAKE MIMICS

The name coral snake covers a wide range of species found throughout North and South America, Europe, Asia, and Africa. Two species are found in the United States: *Micrurus fulvius* in the southeastern states, and the Arizona coral snake *(Microides euryxanthus)* in Arizona, New Mexico, and Mexico.

Many of these snakes are highly poisonous, and advertize the fact with bold bands of red, black, and yellow or white. As a result of their wide distribution, there are many harmless coral snake mimics, such as the Milk snake *(Lampropeltis triangulum)* and the Mountain Californian kingsnake *(Lampropeltis zonata pulchra)* below. It is possible to tell the difference between coral snakes and their mimics, as a coral snake's banding is usually continuous around the body, whereas that on a coral snake mimic usually stops short of the belly.

A CLOSER LOOK

BUTTERFLY AND MOTH MIMICS

There are many examples of Batesian mimicry in the order Lepidoptera (butterflies and moths). One example is the nontoxic butterfly *Dismorphia amphione (Pieridae)* from South America, which has a similar orange-and-yellow pattern to the poisonous *Heliconius isabella (Nymphalidae-Heliconiinae)*. Other examples include moths that have a remarkable resemblance to bees and wasps, such as this Hornet moth *(Sesia apiformis)*. Their wings are almost entirely scaleless so they look just like transparent wasp wings, and some of these mimics even make a buzzing noise when they fly! Although this strategy is very successful, some species of birds have developed the ability to distinguish between the impersonators and their models and will feed on the mimics.

A CLOSER LOOK

Batesian mimicry

In Batesian mimicry, a harmless animal uses color and form to pretend to be a species that is poisonous or distasteful; employing the same warning coloration ensures that predators keep well away. A classic example of Batesian mimicry is the harmless beetle *Clytus arietis* and hoverly *Helophilus hybridus,* which both closely resemble the wasp *Vespula vulgaris.*

Aggressive mimicry

Aggressive mimicry is the mimicry of a harmless animal by a predator or parasite in order to attract its prey or host.

A particularly striking example of this form of mimicry is the Orchid mantis (*Pseudocreobota ocellata*), found in the forests of Malaysia. This insect lies in wait for other insects that come to the elegant white orchid flower to gather nectar. It has shields on its body that exactly match the hue and surface texture of the orchid petals, creating such a complete disguise that not even the human eye is likely to detect it!

Other hunters and parasites go further and bait their targets. The Alligator snapping turtle (*Macroclemys temmincki*) pretends to be a tasty item of food that will encourage prey to come close enough to catch (see the box on page 230). And the Bee orchid (*Orphrys apifera*) pretends to be another bee to encourage mating. The orchid is a parasite of the bee, which it uses for pollination without offering any reward (see box below).

The Death adder (*Acanthophis antarcticus*) of the Australian desert is almost impossible to detect except by the movement of its tail, which is thin, pink, and very mobile. When the snake wriggles, the tail appears to be some kind of succulent worm. Interested birds often meet an unfortunate end as a meal for the snake!

K. HOSOUME/J. KAUFMANN

See also: ADAPTATION; BUTTERFLIES AND MOTHS; DARWINISM; DEFENSE; EVOLUTION; LEAF INSECTS AND WALKING STICKS; MUTATION; NATURAL SELECTION; PARASITES.

Further reading:
Martin, James. *Hiding Out: Camouflage in the Wild.* New York: Crown Publishers, 1993.
Powzyk, Joyce Ann. *Animal Camouflage: a Closer Look.* New York: Bradbury Press, 1990.
Sowler, Sandie. *Amazing Animal Disguises.* New York: Knopf; distributed by Random House, 1992.

BEE ORCHID

Orchids have developed a wide array of beautiful and fascinating forms, some of which involve mimicry. Examples of this are the Bee orchids (*Orphrys* spp.), such as this *Orphrys apifera*. The flower of this species closely resembles a female bumblebee (*Bombus* spp.). The male bumblebee, thinking the flower is in fact a female of his species, attempts to copulate with it. In his frenzy to mate, the male bee is tagged with the pollen sacs of the flower, which are then carried to the next Bee orchid, resulting in pollination. Similar strategies to entice pollinating wasps and flies are seen in other tropical orchid species.

A CLOSER LOOK

CANCER

Cancer is a disease in which altered cells grow and spread uncontrollably

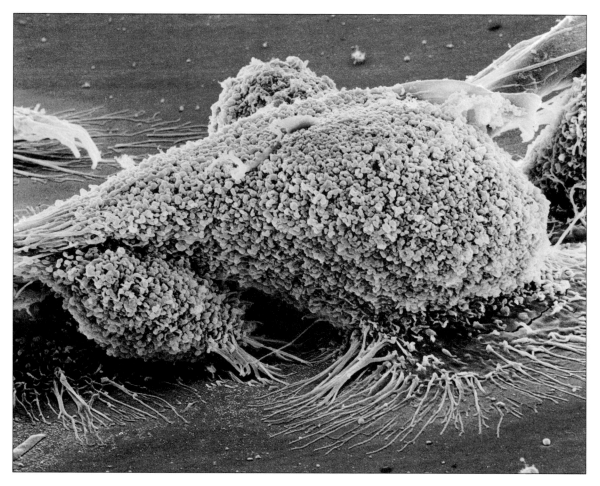

A human breast cancer cell (scanning electron microscope x 6000). Breast cancer is one of the biggest cancer killers of women in the West. Genetic factors often contribute to an increased risk of developing breast cancer.

As far back as the ape-like Java man, humans have been battling cancer. Early attempts to treat the disease date back to 2000 BC, when the ancient Egyptians cut tumors out with knives. Hippocrates, the Greek physician known as the father of medicine, tried to advance cancer treatment by burning tumors with a hot iron.

Although medicine has come a long way since then, cancer remains as humans' most dreaded disease. Every year, approximately 6 million people worldwide learn they have cancer. Another 4 million die from it. By the early 1990s, nearly one out of four people in the United States was expected to die from cancer. Some scientists predict that by the year 2000, cancer will surpass heart disease as the leading cause of death in the United States.

In spite of this high death rate, medicine has made huge advances in treating cancer. Consider the fact that in the 1930s, only one out of five cancer patients survived five or more years. Today, the rate has climbed to three out of eight. The jump in survival rates is credited to advanced diagnostic techniques, which detect cancer in its earliest, most treatable stages, and improved methods of treatment.

The future of cancer patients continues to improve as scientists begin to solve the complex mystery of how a healthy cell becomes cancerous. Until recently, it was not known why cigarette smoke, for example, would trigger the cells in one person's lung to become cancerous, while another smoker's lungs remained healthy. Now, researchers are learning that the answer lies in genetics. Just as genes determine hair and eye color, they may also determine susceptibility to cancer.

These discoveries have already led to gene therapy to treat cancer, and may someday pave the way toward a vaccine to prevent the disease.

CORE FACTS

- Over 8 million Americans alive in 1994 have had cancer and of these, 5 million can be considered "cured" (with no current evidence of disease).
- Deaths from cancer in the United States have risen from 143 per 100,000 population in 1930 to 174 in 1990, mainly due to an increase in lung cancer.
- In the 1930s, less than 20 percent of patients were alive five years after treatment; in the 1990s, 40 percent can expect to survive.
- The most common forms of cancer in the United States are lung cancer, breast cancer, bladder cancer, and cancer of the colon.

CONNECTIONS

● Various forms of radiation, such as **ULTRAVIOLET LIGHT** and **X-RAYS**, are known to increase the risk of cancer. However, radioactivity is not "unnatural," it occurs naturally in the environment. Uranium, a common element in the Earth's crust, is radioactive. Granite, an igneous rock produced from cooled lava from the Earth's core, also generates background radiation.

● The delicate **CELL** regulatory mechanisms, that can be thrown out of balance by carcinogens to cause cancer, can be described as **CYBERNETIC** systems – self-regulating systems of control in living things and machines.

Types of cancer

Cancer is cell growth gone haywire. Healthy cells multiply just fast enough to replace those that die or are damaged. Cancer cells, on the other hand, multiply out of control, building up to form a solid mass, or tumor.

Not all tumors are malignant (cancerous). Like cancer, these benign tumors are caused by abnormal cell growth, but lack cancer's unique ability to spread, or metastasize, to other organs. Cancer spreads when cells break away from the tumor and travel to distant organs through the bloodstream or lymph system. There the transplanted cells grow into new tumors, called metastases.

Some 30 percent of patients diagnosed with cancer for the first time already have metastases. Another 45 percent have undetectable metastases that eventually develop into tumors. It is these hidden metastases that eventually kill most victims.

Of the more than 100 types of cancer, the most common in the United States is skin cancer. Its incidence is also the fastest growing. Between 1973 and 1987, malignant melanoma, the deadliest form of skin cancer, increased by 83 percent. The more common, though less dangerous skin cancers, basal and squamous cell carcinomas, also skyrocketed.

Nearly all skin cancers are provoked by exposure to ultraviolet light from the sun. Researchers predict a growing incidence of skin cancer as pollution continues to deplete the ozone layer that shields the Earth from sunlight.

The second most prevalent cancers are breast cancer in women and prostate cancer in men. Both are also on the rise.

The deadliest form of cancer is lung cancer, killing more patients than any other type. Between 1973 and 1987, the incidence of lung cancer climbed by 32 percent. Scientists blame most cases on tobacco smoke.

All cancers fall into one of four groups – carcinomas; sarcomas; gliomas; and lymphomas, leukemias, and myelomas. Carcinomas arise from epithelial tissue, which includes the skin and most soft internal organs. Sarcomas affect bones, cartilage, and muscle. Gliomas are cancers of the brain and nervous system. Lymphomas arise in the lymph system, a network of vessels that collects fluid from the organs. Leukemias are characterized by uncontrolled growth of white blood cells, while myelomas arise from the bone marrow.

Cancers are further classified according to the organ where they originate. A kidney tumor, for example, is called renal cell carcinoma. Renal is an adjective that refers to the kidney. The prefix "osteo" refers to the bones. Hence, bone cancer is termed osteosarcoma.

Causes of cancer

Until the late 1980s, scientists believed that developing cancer was a matter of chance, although they knew factors such as cigarette smoking and alcohol consumption increased the risk. Today, scientists believe that cancer develops when genes controlling cell growth mutate, or change.

In a healthy organ, genes signal cells to multiply just fast enough to replace those that are dead or damaged. When one of these growth genes mutates, it becomes an oncogene. Oncogenes cause cell growth to accelerate. Researchers believe that everyone produces oncogenes throughout life, but they are usually kept in control by tumor-suppressor genes, which act as brakes to keep them from developing into cancer. Only when the the tumor-suppressor genes fail, do malignancies occur.

Researchers are now finding the specific genes that lead to cancer. By the mid-1990s, they had identified more than 100 of these genetic time bombs. Some are growth genes, while others are tumor suppressors. One, called p53, has been linked to 60 percent of all tumors. These new discoveries could someday lead to a blood test for cancer susceptibility.

Mutations that trigger malignancies may be caused by heredity, mistakes in the cell's duplication of DNA, or exposure to cancer-causing agents, called carcinogens. For many people, the term carcinogen evokes fears of a polluted environment beyond their control. In fact, environmental carcinogens are linked to relatively few cases of cancer.

ANTIOXIDANTS AND HEALTH

Antioxidants may be one of the most powerful weapons in our battle against cancer. Results of studies worldwide have indicated that antioxidants, such as the vitamins C and E, beta-carotene (see CAROTENES AND CAROTENOIDS), and the mineral selenium, can help reduce the risk of developing cancer and heart disease. Antioxidants are substances that protect the body from attack by free radicals, which may be circulating as the result of smoking, drinking, environmental pollution, prolonged exposure to the sun, certain drugs, and even some normal metabolic processes. Free radicals are molecules that contain a free, single electron seeking to attach itself to molecules in tissues and organs, causing damage to individual cells. Antioxidants protect against this damage by neutralizing the free radicals. Our best source of antioxidants is in fresh citrus fruits and leafy green or red and orange vegetables.

There is an undisputed link between smoking and lung cancer. Avoiding tobacco is the most important method of prevention. Since the early 1960s, when tobacco smoke was publicly linked to cancer, smoking in American men dropped by half. However, lung cancer in women is still rising, as they continue to smoke at the same rate.

The number one cause of cancer is completely natural and controllable. Between 30 and 50 percent of cancers worldwide are connected to poor diets, with the biggest culprit being fat. Fat contributes to colon and rectal cancer and has also been linked to breast, ovary, and prostate cancer. Other dietary carcinogens are alcoholic beverages, salt and pickling compounds, pesticides on fresh produce, and natural toxins produced by certain molds.

Some scientists have connected cancer to oxidants produced as a byproduct of metabolizing certain types of food. These oxidants are believed to cause mutations leading to cancer, heart disease, cataracts, and other diseases of aging. So while a poor diet may promote cancer, conversely, a healthy one may prevent it. Scientists recommend limiting fat, getting plenty of fiber, and feasting on fruits, nuts, vegetables and grains (see the box on page 235).

After diet, the most common carcinogen is tobacco, which accounts for 30 percent of all cancers. Recent data has shown that even exposure to tobacco in the immediate environment (passive smoking) is dangerous. Passive smoking is now taken so seriously that smoking is restricted in public places throughout the United States.

Viruses sometimes act as carcinogens, accounting for 10 to 15 percent of cancers. Although they do not cause cancer directly, they may lead to the disease after exposure to a co-factor such as alcohol or sunlight. One of the most widespread carcinogenic viruses is the human papillomavirus, which causes genital warts and is closely linked to cervical cancer. The AIDS virus, which weakens the immune system, has been associated with several forms of cancer.

Some benign growths can also be cancer risks. Malignant melanomas often arise from moles that were once benign. Benign growths in the stomach and colon, called polyps, are also linked to cancer.

Carcinogens are thought to cause cancer through a two-stage process. The first stage is exposure to the carcinogen. Damage to the cells' DNA may occur within a few hours or days. Cancer promotion begins when the damaged DNA is exposed to a second class of chemicals, called tumor promoters. Promoters do not damage DNA, but cause mutated cells to grow and suppress the cells' ability to repair damaged DNA. Promotion occurs in several steps and may take many years.

Who gets cancer?

Dinosaurs got cancer. Fish get cancer. Even trees get cancer. No human, it seems, is immune to the disease. Yet cancer does exhibit clear trends.

The strongest trend among nearly all forms of cancer is age. Consider the National Cancer Institute's statistics on breast cancer as one example. According to the NCI, a woman has a one in 19,608 chance of developing breast cancer by the age of 25. By the age of 85, however, her chances are one in eight.

Cancer also displays regional and cultural trends. Breast and prostate cancer are high in Western nations, where the diet is high in fat. In Japan and other Asian countries that consume less fat, the incidence of these cancers is low. When Asian natives immigrate to the United States, however, their risk rises, as they adopt a high-fat Western diet.

Some scientists believe that residents of smog-filled cities face a greater risk of lung cancer. This theory is difficult to prove, however, because so many victims of lung cancer also smoke cigarettes.

One of the most disturbing trends in the United States is the strong link between poverty and cancer. Poor people are not only more likely to develop cancer, but also more likely to die from it. Researchers tie their risk to habits of smoking, alcohol abuse, and a high-fat diet. Because they delay seeing a doctor, poor people are often diagnosed when their cancer is too advanced to cure.

THE AMES TEST

A lot of rats owe their lives to Bruce Ames. The Berkeley biologist in the early 1970s developed a method of testing the potential carcinogenicity of chemicals without using animals. His test is based on the theory that most chemicals capable of causing mutations could also cause cancer.

The Ames test, which is sometimes called the mutagenicity test, is performed by exposing *Salmonella* bacteria cultures on special plates to the chemical being studied. If the chemical is mutagenic, it will produce visible colonies on the plate within two or three days. The more colonies, the more mutagenic the chemical. Two decades after Ames introduced his test, it is still widely used. No substitutes are as quick, easy, and cheap.

Countless chemicals that failed the test have been banned. However, some scientists claim that the test is abused, needlessly discouraging the use of chemicals that pose little danger to humans. One of the biggest critics is Ames himself. He believes that the test is often over-interpreted, with users considering every mutagen as a carcinogen, even though the carcinogenicity of a substance can depend on the dose. A good example is coffee, which is full of carcinogens but is still widely drunk.

African Americans also fare poorly in the battle against cancer. Only 25 percent of black men survive five years after their diagnosis, compared with 40 percent of white men. The rate for women is 39 percent among African Americans and 55 percent among whites. Researchers are not certain whether this disparity is related to poverty – 36 percent of African Americans live in poverty compared with 10 percent of whites – or if race itself is a risk factor. Studies suggest that African Americans are more prone to lung cancer than whites of the same age and smoking habits.

Trends between the sexes are less clear. Skin cancer strikes slightly more men than women. Lung cancer was rare among women half a century ago, but has risen dramatically as more women have taken up smoking. Breast cancer is not restricted to women, although it is rare in men.

Although few cancers are tied to occupational exposure, workers handling coal, oil, certain chemicals, and other carcinogens do face elevated risks.

Cancer treatments

Through the last half of the 20th century, cancer treatment typically involved surgery, radiation therapy, and chemotherapy (drugs), alone or in combination. Around the early 1990s, immunotherapy gained acceptance as a fourth type of treatment. Today, doctors also place emphasis on prevention, by avoiding carcinogens and eating a healthy diet, and early detection. Cervical and breast cancer, in particular, can be prevented from developing by early detection.

Surgery has been and still is the backbone of cancer treatment. Dr William Halsted pioneered cancer surgery based on a firm set of principles in the early 1900s, when he performed radical mastectomies on women with breast cancer. He believed that the removal of the entire breast and nearby lymph nodes would prevent the cancer from spreading. Radical mastectomies are still performed today, although many women are now treated with lumpectomies if their tumors are small and localized. This breast-sparing treatment removes only the tumor. Remaining cancer cells are killed by combining surgery with radiation therapy or chemotherapy.

Radiation therapy uses x-rays to kill cancer cells. The radiation destroys the cells by attacking the DNA. A therapeutic dose is a half million times more than the average chest x-ray. Radiating only the tumor without damaging neighboring tissue is a delicate art. Early experiments in radiation therapy produced dangerous side effects, but by the 1920s, researchers had discovered that the best results came from several low-dose treatments.

Treatment was further refined in the 1970s and 1980s, as modern imaging techniques enabled radiologists to pinpoint tumors more accurately. A new and increasingly popular form of radiation therapy involves implanting tiny sources of radiation in the tumor. Advances in radiation therapy and surgery improved the cancer survival rate from 20 percent in the 1920s to 33 percent by 1950, when it leveled out. Scientists learned that most of the patients were dying from metastases too small to be detected when they were first treated. So they looked for a treatment that could destroy these hidden cells.

Most cancer drugs (chemotherapy) are cytotoxic, meaning that they kill only rapidly dividing cells. Unfortunately, as well as the cancerous ones, these drugs often affect other rapidly dividing cells in the body, such as the cells in the hair follicles and stomach lining. This can cause uncomfortable side effects, including hair loss and nausea.

Often two or more approaches are used in combination; for instance, chemotherapy is used after surgery to kill any cancer cells left behind and prevent metastasis. A more recent approach is to use chemotherapy before surgery to shrink the tumor and make it easier and safer to remove. Many forms of leukemia are treated with chemotherapy.

The young science of immunotherapy brings new hope to cancer patients. Immunotherapy attacks cancer cells without harming healthy tissue and works by stimulating the body's immune system to fight the cancer cells. One type of immunotherapy uses a cancer vaccine to introduce tumor antigens that stimulate the immune system. Another uses gene therapy. In this approach, doctors isolate immune-system cells from the patient's blood, transplant cancer-killing genes into the cells, then cultivate large numbers of these fighter cells before returning them to the patient.

C. WASHAM

See also: CELLS; CHEMOTHERAPY; DNA.

Further reading:

McAllister, R.M., Teich Horowitz, S., and Gilden, R.V. *Cancer*. New York: BasicBooks, 1992.
Rosenberg, S.A. and Barry, J.M. *The Transformed Cell*. New York: G.P. Putnam's Sons, 1992.

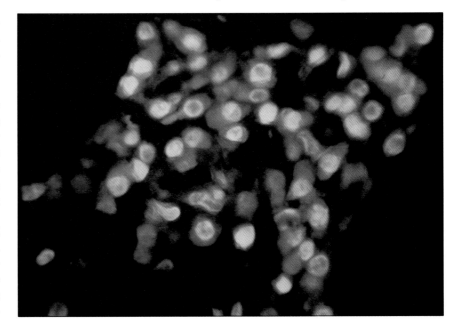

Immunofluorescence microscopy of cervical cancer cells. Regular cervical screening is essential in the prevention of cervical cancer, which can be treated successfully provided it is detected early in its development.

CARBOHYDRATES

Carbohydrates are important compounds consisting of carbon, hydrogen, and oxygen

Starch granules magnified x 50. Starch is the main food storage carbohydrate in plants.

Carbohydrates are a group of organic compounds consisting of carbon, hydrogen, and oxygen, that are extremely important to life. Some are used by both plants and animals to store and transport energy, others form part of the structure of living things. Carbohydrates include sugars, starches, cellulose, and other substances used in plant and animal structure.

In most carbohydrates the hydrogen and oxygen are present in the same proportions as in water (two atoms of hydrogen to one atom of oxygen). For this reason, chemists first thought of them as compounds of carbon and water, and named them "carbon hydrates."

Types of carbohydrate

Carbohydrates are classified as monosaccharides, oligosaccharides, and polysaccharides. Monosaccharides are simple sugars consisting of a short chain of carbon atoms (usually between three and seven), which have hydrogen and oxygen atoms attached. The most important monosaccharides are hexoses, built around a chain of six carbons. Although it is generally convenient to think of these as straight chains, known as stick formulas, they are usually arranged with the carbons linked in a ring. Both five-sided rings, called furanoses, and six-sided rings, called pyranoses, occur. However, a number of chemical variations are possible, with different atoms attached to one of the carbons in the chain or ring.

Three important monosaccharides are glucose, fructose, and galactose. (Chemists usually give sugars names ending in hose.) All have the same chemical formula, $C_6H_{12}O_6$, but different structures (see the diagram on page 239). Glucose, also called dextrose or grape sugar, is found in fruits and vegetables and is the primary energy source for almost all animal cells. Fructose, or fruit sugar, is also common in fruits and vegetables. Galactose is found in abundance in milk; hence its name, derived from the Greek word for milk, *gala*.

When two monosaccharides join together, the result is a disaccharide. Important disaccharides are sucrose (common table sugar), made by joining glucose and fructose; lactose (milk sugar), made by joining glucose and galactose; and maltose, which consists of two joined glucose molecules.

There are also trisaccharides made of three monosaccharides, tetrasaccharides made of four, and so on. Sugars combining up to ten monosaccharides are referred to as oligosaccharides. Combinations of more than ten monosaccharides are called polysaccharides. Polysaccharides are polymers in which simple saccharide molecules are linked in a repeating pattern. They may consist of chains as much as half a million molecules long. The most important polysaccharides are starch and glycogen; starch, because it is used to store energy in plants, and glycogen, because it is used to store energy in animals.

Storing energy

Starch is actually a mixture of two polysaccharides, amylose and amylopectin. Amylose consists of straight chains of several hundred glucose molecules, which curl into a helix, a coil with a spring-like shape. Amylopectin consists of glucose chains with many branches. It can be thought of as many amylose chains fastened together. These two polysaccharides are present in varying proportions in plant starches, creating starches with slightly different characteristics.

A small amount of starch in the form of tiny granules is found in plant leaves, where it is used as short-term storage; starch made in leaves during the day is probably mostly used up during the night. Other plant starches, such as those in seeds, are intended for long-term storage, and usually consist of large granules. Some plants also store energy in fructans, polysaccharides made of chains

CONNECTIONS

● Carbohydrates are examples of naturally occurring polymers. There are also many synthetic polymers, designed by chemists and produced industrially, including **FIBERS** such as nylon and polyester, and plastics such as polythene and polystyrene.

● Just as the body uses carbohydrates as fuel to produce **ENERGY**, so some car engines use the hydrocarbon compound gasoline, to provide energy to drive the car. The chemical reaction that occurs in the engine to produce the energy is called a combustion reaction.

CORE FACTS

- Carbohydrates are the most abundant class of biological molecules on Earth.
- Cellulose, one type of carbohydrate, makes up to 80 percent of a plant's dry weight.
- Starch is the main source of carbohydrate in the human diet.
- Glycogen is present in every animal cell, but in particularly large amounts in cells that make up the liver and skeletal muscle.
- One cellulose chain may consist of up to 15,000 glucose molecules.

of fructose molecules. The seeds of some legumes contain galactomannans, polysaccharides made up of galactose and mannose.

Glycogen is a branching chain of glucose molecules similar to amylopectin, but with more branches: a glycogen molecule may consist of up to 30,000 glucose molecules. The large numbers of branches of starch and glycogen make the molecules more accessible for quick breakdown into glucose when the plant or animal needs energy.

Cellulose molecules

Carbohydrates are also extremely important in the formation of the physical structure of plants. The rigid walls of plant cells are made of cellulose fibers mixed with substances called hemicelluloses and pectins. The structure is something like reinforced concrete: the cellulose fibers taking the role of iron rods, held together by the hemicelluloses and pectins, or "cement."

Cellulose molecules are straight chains of glucose units, ranging from 2500 to 15,000 molecules long. In many species of plants other sugars are found in the chains, creating different varieties of fiber. The chain molecules are arranged side-by-side, with links between the chains. It is this interlinking that gives cellulose fiber its strength.

Hemicelluloses are chains of various sugars, including many oligosaccharides. Pectins are gels. Cellulose, hemicelluloses, and pectins are not broken down by the acids and enzymes in the human digestive system and are classified as "dietary fiber" (see CELLULOSE).

Carbohydrates in animal tissues

As well as providing plants with their physical structure, carbohydrates also feature in the protective coverings of some animals, fungi, and bacteria. The hard exoskeleton of many insects is composed of alternate layers of proteins and chitins. Chitins are polysaccharides similar to cellulose, but made up of glucosamine molecules, which are derivatives of glucose containing nitrogen atoms. Chitins are also found in insect tendons and wing coverings, and in the cell walls of fungi.

The outer cell walls of bacteria contain a material called peptidoglycan, which is made of long chains of carbohydrates lying side by side, linked to one another by chains of amino acids. The crosslinks form a sort of molecular fabric that completely surrounds and protects the bacterium.

Polysaccharides are also found in a wide variety of tissues in higher animals. Connective tissue consists of fibers of a protein called collagen mixed with complex polysaccharides. Different polysaccharides form different types of connective tissue, ranging from the tough cartilage that holds joints together to the flexible walls of blood vessels. The vitreous humor of the eye (a jelly-like substance located between the lens and the retina in vertebrates, important in maintaining the shape of the eyeball) consists entirely of a polysaccharide called

hyaluronate. Chains of oligosaccharides join to proteins to form glycoproteins, and to lipids (fats) to form glycolipids. These substances are an important part of cell membranes and perform a variety of functions outside cells.

Glycoproteins have been under intensive study because they often act as receptors on the surfaces of cell membranes. Each receptor has a complicated shape onto which only certain molecules can attach; when the right molecule attaches, other events inside and outside the cell take place. This is the mechanism by which hormones deliver their signals to cells. It is also the mechanism by which viruses enter cells. The outer coat of the HIV virus that causes AIDS includes a glycoprotein called gp120, which attaches to a cell receptor on immune system cells as the first step in infecting them (see AIDS). Glycolipids are also found in cell membranes, especially in ganglion cells of the nervous system and in the myelin sheath that surrounds nerve fibers (see NERVOUS SYSTEMS).

Formation of carbohydrates

Almost all the energy used by living things comes from carbohydrates manufactured by plants. Through photosynthesis, plants (and some bacteria) use energy from the sun to make carbohydrates out of carbon dioxide and water (see PHOTOSYNTHESIS).

There are two stages in photosynthesis: the "light reaction" and the "dark reaction." In the light reaction, energy from sunlight is used to split water molecules into hydrogen and oxygen. The hydrogen is then carried by a molecule called a coenzyme. The dark reaction uses carbon atoms

This diagram shows the arrangement in two common simple sugar molecules. Carbohydrates are formed from chains of sugar molecules such as these.

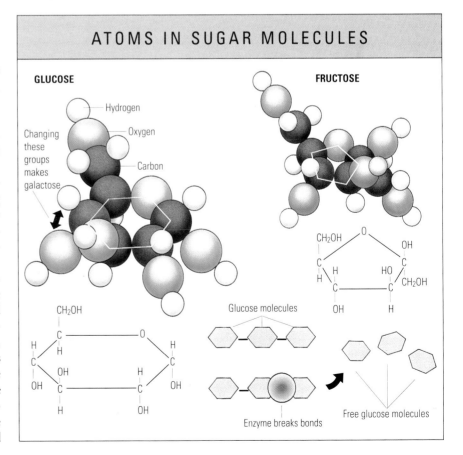

ATOMS IN SUGAR MOLECULES

GLUCOSE

FRUCTOSE

Hydrogen

Oxygen

Carbon

Changing these groups makes galactose

Glucose molecules

Enzyme breaks bonds

Free glucose molecules

CARBOHYDRATE LOADING

Heavy, continuous exercise, such as running a marathon or playing in a tennis match, can exhaust the body's supply of glycogen in two to three hours. After that, cells begin to convert fats to glucose as a source of energy, but the process is relatively slow. An athlete who is running on stored fat quickly becomes tired and slows down.

To overcome this, many athletes have adopted the practice of "carbohydrate loading." In its original form, the idea was to work to exhaustion in order to use up as much as possible of the stored glycogen, then eat a large quantity of carbohydrate-rich foods. This was supposed to encourage the body to replenish the glycogen supply at a higher rate. However, this produces unpleasant side effects such as tiredness, irritability, lack of concentration, and mental confusion. Instead, nutritionists recommend that athletes eat about 12 oz (350 g) of carbohydrate daily, beginning about a week before the event, and increasing to between 18½ and 19½ oz (525 and 550 g) per day during the last three days. (A "normal" diet includes about 7 to 9 oz (200 to 250 g) of carbohydrate each day.)

Small amounts of carbohydrates can be consumed during the last four hours prior to the event, and even up to five minutes before exercise begins. Continuing to take small amounts of carbohydrates during exercise – about ½ oz (24 g) every 30 minutes, usually in the form of sweet drinks – has been shown to delay fatigue by as much as an hour. However, carbohydrate loading will have no noticeable effect in events that last less than about 90 minutes. Nutritionists also recommend consuming more carbohydrates immediately after exercise, and again an hour later, to replenish glycogen stores.

Marathon runners practice carbohydrate loading before an event.

from carbon dioxide and hydrogen from the coenzyme to build hexoses. The carbon atoms are added one at a time, with an enzyme helping at each step. Later, other cells will break sugars down and release energy, in a process that is almost the reverse of the light reaction of photosynthesis.

The immediate product of photosynthesis is glucose, some of which is converted to more complex sugars. Plants use various sugars to transport energy, and they convert glucose to starch and fats (vegetable oils) to store energy.

Digestion of carbohydrates

The digestion of carbohydrates in humans and higher animals begins in the mouth, where chewing breaks down the walls of plant cells and mixes the contents with saliva. Enzymes in the saliva begin breaking starch down into the sugars maltose and isomaltose, which are disaccharides. Other enzymes in the small intestine break these, as well as lactose and sucrose from other foods, into the monosaccharides glucose, galactose, and fructose, which are absorbed through the wall of the small intestine into the bloodstream. As it passes through the intestinal wall, most of the fructose is converted to glucose.

Blood from the intestine then passes through the portal vein to the liver, where most of the galactose is also converted to glucose. The result is that almost all digested carbohydrates end up in the bloodstream as glucose. Although not exactly

digested, cellulose and other insoluble carbohydrates from the cell wall play an important role in the digestive system as dietary fiber. Fiber does not pass through the digestive system unchanged. It provides an environment for intestinal bacteria, which grow in and feed on the tiny bits of broken cell walls. In healthy mammals, feces will consist partly of undigested fiber and partly of bacteria that have fed and multiplied on the fiber.

A diet high in fiber seems to protect against colon cancer. One possible reason is that the fiber passes through the digestive system relatively quickly, allowing carcinogens (cancer-causing substances) less time to do damage.

Glucose and energy

The bloodstream carries glucose to every cell of the body, and for most cells glucose is the primary source of energy. Through many chemical steps, cells convert glucose to carbon dioxide and water. In the process, energy is released and stored in molecules called adenosine triphosphate, or ATP (see ENERGY).

Glucose may follow several pathways in its conversion to energy. The most common in animal cells is called glycolysis, which is a form of aerobic respiration (requiring oxygen). This begins in the cytosol of the cell. Through a series of reactions, glucose is broken down into a three-carbon compound called pyruvic acid, or pyruvate, producing energy in the process. Each step of this process is assisted by an enzyme. Although two molecules of ATP start off glycolysis, four are produced at the end, giving a net gain of two.

The pyruvic acid molecules produced in glycolysis then pass into the mitochondria of the cell. Here they are converted into a molecule called acetyl coenzyme A, or CoA, through a process called the link reaction. The rest of the conversion to energy is also carried on inside mitochondria, through a process called the citric acid cycle or Krebs cycle, named after the scientist Hans Krebs who first described it (see CITRIC ACID CYCLE). This takes eight steps to complete, each assisted by a specific enzyme. A simple description of this process is that the carbon atoms are removed from the CoA molecules one at a time and combined with oxygen to form carbon dioxide. This process creates 12 molecules of ATP for each molecule of CoA broken down.

If oxygen is lacking during this process, the pyruvic acid molecules are converted to lactic acid, or lactate, instead of CoA. If oxygen becomes available again in a short time, the lactic acid can be converted back to pyruvic acid and processed into energy by the mitochondria. This switch is important in muscles, which must sometimes contract quickly (during exercise, for example), using energy faster than the blood can supply oxygen. In these times of need, muscle cells obtain energy by converting stored glycogen into lactic acid. The

CARBOHYDRATES WON'T MAKE YOU FAT

Every few years a new reducing diet appears, based on the idea of avoiding almost all carbohydrates. These diets have tremendous appeal to many people, because their proponents claim you can eat all you want, including bacon, eggs, steak, and other appealing foods, as long as you skip the carbohydrates. The result, they claim, is that your body will start to burn fat at a higher than normal rate.

People who try these diets do lose some weight, for several reasons. Although the foods the diets allow have a lot of fat in them, the total calorie content of the recommended meals is fairly low. The foods you are allowed to eat are usually high in fat, and most people get sick of eating fat fairly quickly. It is also true that if very little glucose is available from carbohydrates, the body will burn fat for energy. When this happens, fats are broken down into acetyl CoA faster than it can be processed by the cells' mitochondria. The excess acetyl CoA is converted to chemicals called ketones,

and too many ketones in the bloodstream is called ketosis. The effects of ketosis are mild at first: it causes nausea, which might actually help you eat less. But in the long run it increases the amount of uric acid in the blood, which can lead to gout – a disease that causes excruciating pain in the joints – or kidney failure.

Meanwhile, a diet deficient in carbohydrates is also deficient in vitamins, minerals, and fiber, while a high-fat diet increases the risks of many types of cancer. Many recent studies suggest that the best reducing diet is exactly the opposite of the low-carbohydrate plan: eat a large amount of complex carbohydrates – including fruit and vegetables – and as little fat as possible, and use the energy provided by the carbohydrates to exercise regularly. Some studies show that people who sharply reduce their fat intake – getting as little as ten percent of their calories from fat – will lose weight even though they eat a normal amount of calories for their weight.

CARBOHYDRATE CATABOLISM

The catabolism, or breakdown, of glucose follows several pathways, but most often moves through glycolysis, the link reaction, and the citric acid cycle.

amount of oxygen then needed to convert the lactic acid into pyruvic acid is called the oxygen debt. It is the lactic acid present in the muscles that produces the feeling of stiffness after strenuous exercise. The conversion of glucose to lactic acid also provides energy in some cells that do not contain mitochondria, for example in the retina of the eye.

Lactic acid that is not converted back into pyruvic acid eventually diffuses from the cells back into the bloodstream. When it reaches the liver, it is converted back into glucose, which is returned to the bloodstream to serve as an energy source again.

In animal cells, if the precursor to pyruvic acid (a compound called glucose-6-phosphate) is not immediately used as an energy source, it may be converted to glycogen, which is stored in the cell and converted back into glucose-6-phosphate when needed. Excess glucose-6-phosphate may also be converted into more complex sugars that are used to build other chemicals, such as ribose and deoxyribose, which form the basis of ribonucleic acid (RNA) and deoxyribonucleic acid (DNA), the molecules responsible for carrying the genetic code in every cell (see DNA).

Small amounts of fructose are usually left in the bloodstream after digestion. Cells can also convert fructose to energy. There are several other less-used pathways that cells can use to convert glucose to energy, including some that do not require oxygen. Pathways that do not use oxygen are called anaerobic, meaning "without air."

CARBOHYDRATE CONTENT OF SOME COMMON FOODS

Bread, one slice	13 g
Dry breakfast cereal, one cup	24 g
Flour, 2 tablespoons	11 g
Navy beans, ½ cup	20 g
Green beans, ½ cup	4 g
Spaghetti or macaroni, ½ cup cooked	16 g
Peanuts, ¼ cup	7 g
Pie crust, one ⅙ slice	13 g
White potato	18 g
Rice, ½ cup cooked	25 g
Chocolate chip cookie	6 g
Cola, 12 oz	36 g
Chocolate bar, 1 oz	16 g
Apple	18 g
Ice-cream cone	14 g
Milk, 12 oz	12 g
Sugar, 1 tablespoon	11 g
Honey, 1 tablespoon	13 g

Many bacteria use anaerobic respiration, as do yeasts. In yeasts the process is called fermentation, and the end product is alcohol. The alcohol in wine is made by the fermentation of sugars in grape juice. Other alcoholic beverages are made by the fermentation of sugars in grains. In addition to alcohol, fermentation produces carbon dioxide gas (see BIOTECHNOLOGY; FERMENTATION).

Carbohydrates in the diet

"Starchy foods," such as potatoes, bread, and pasta, were once thought inadequate as a large part of the diet. But the picture emerging from current research in nutrition is that they should make up a major part of almost every meal, while fat consumption should be reduced. The U.S. Food and Drug Administration recommends that carbohydrates provide at least 55 percent of the calories in the diet. Thirty percent, or preferably less, should be fat, and the rest should be protein. This means that in a typical 1800 calorie per day diet, about 1000 calories should come from carbohydrates. One gram of carbohydrate yields four calories; therefore a "normal" diet should contain 7 to 9 oz (200 to 250 g) per day. Ideally, most of the carbohydrates should be complex carbohydrates (polysaccharides). These are available from grains, such as wheat, corn, brown rice, oats, and barley; from grain products, including breakfast cereals, breads, and pastas, such as macaroni and spaghetti; and fruits and vegetables. These foods also supply vitamins, minerals, protein, and fiber.

Glucose regulation

The amount of glucose in the human bloodstream is carefully regulated by the body (see HOMEOSTASIS). After a meal rich in carbohydrates, the amount of glucose in blood flowing through the portal vein from the intestines to the liver almost doubles, but the liver removes about two-thirds of the excess and stores it as glycogen. A high blood glucose level causes the pancreas to secrete the hormone insulin. This causes glucose to enter cells rapidly, reducing the amount in the blood (see INSULIN).

By contrast, when the glucose level in the bloodstream falls, the pancreas secretes a hormone called glucagon, and the adrenal glands secrete the hormones epinephrine and norepinephrine (see EPINEPHRINE). These signal the liver to convert glycogen back into glucose and release it into the blood (see LIVER).

The human liver stores a maximum of about 10½ oz (300 g) of glycogen, and the muscles about twice as much. This is enough to supply glucose for around 24 hours of normal activity, but only three hours of strenuous exercise. After that, the liver can convert fats and amino acids into glucose. Most

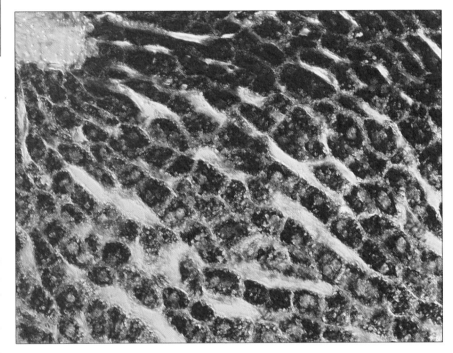

cells can also convert fats directly into energy. The fats are first converted to CoA, which is then processed by the mitochondria. However, some cells, including neurons in the brain, cannot use fats and must have a supply of glucose to function.

W. STEELE

Low magnification micrograph of liver cells, packed with glycogen granules.

See also: CELLULOSE; CITRIC ACID CYCLE; DIGESTIVE SYSTEMS; ENERGY; GRAINS; METABOLISM; NUTRITION; PHOTOSYNTHESIS.

Further reading:

Appetite and Body Weight Regulation: Sugar, Fat, and Macronutrient Substitutes. Edited by John D. Fernstrom and Gregory D. Miller. Boca Raton, Florida: CRC Press, 1994.
Cell Surface Carbohydrates and Cell Development. Edited by M. Fukuda. Boca Raton, Florida: CRC Press, 1992.
Haron, N. and Halina, L. "Carbohydrates and Cell Recognition." *Scientific American*, **268**, pp 82-89, Jan. 1993.

CARBON CYCLE

The carbon cycle is the process in which carbon atoms are recycled over and over again

The planet Earth can be thought of as a sealed capsule. The only substance that enters from outside is energy from the sun. All other materials have to be constantly recycled (see BIOSPHERE). The carbon cycle is the process by which carbon moves through living things, the atmosphere, oceans, soils, sediments, and rocks. Tracing the flow of carbon gives scientists an insight into how living creatures interact with their environment.

Carbon is a basic building block of life. It is the cornerstone of the huge family of chemical substances called organic compounds, which include carbohydrates, proteins, lipids, and nucleic acids, that make up living organisms.

Although the amount of carbon on Earth always remains the same, the carbon changes its form from time to time. A carbon atom in your fingernail might have been part of a dinosaur millions of years ago. Since the dinosaur died, the carbon atom has probably been in many forms and places: perhaps in a molecule of carbon dioxide in the air, as part of a seashell, in the body of a plant or animal, or locked away in limestone rock. The continual recycling of carbon ensures that it will be available for use by future generations of living organisms.

CORE FACTS

- The carbon cycle is one of the biogeochemical cycles that cause materials in the environment to be naturally recycled. Other biogeochemical cycles are the nitrogen cycle and the phosporus cycle.
- Carbon is cycled between living things and the nonliving environment.
- Technological development and human activities, such as burning fossil fuels and cutting down forests, disturb the balance of the carbon cycle and cause a buildup of carbon dioxide in the atmosphere.
- A continual supply of carbon is essential for living organisms. The compounds that build our bodies – carbohydrates, proteins, lipids, and nucleic acids – all contain carbon.

The carbon cycle can be represented as a diagram showing the different processes that move the carbon from one form to another. These processes include photosynthesis, respiration, decomposition, the natural weathering of rocks, and the combustion of fossil fuels. The cycle is made up of "sources" and "sinks." A source in the carbon cycle is something that puts carbon into the environment, such as

CONNECTIONS

- The three common forms of carbon are: graphite, which is soft and flaky, diamond, the hardest naturally occurring substance, and charcoal.

- The carbon cycle is contained within the boundaries of the Earth's BIOSPHERE.

- The amount of carbon dioxide in the ATMOSPHERE, along with other "greenhouse gases," is one of the determining factors of climates.

- Carbon is a non-metallic element in Group IV of the Periodic Table. It forms more than one million chemical compounds.

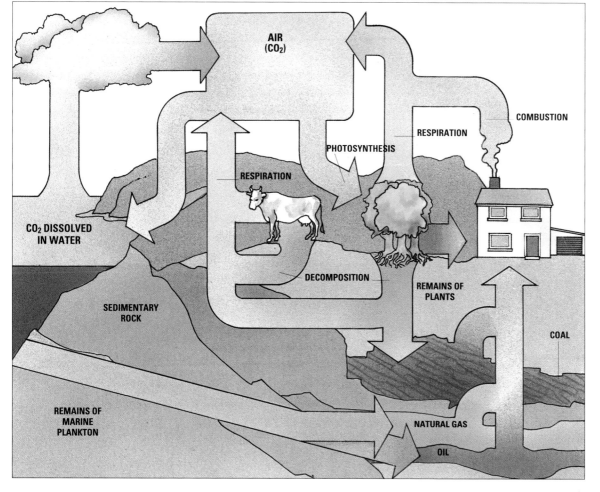

Diagram of the carbon cycle showing the processes that move carbon around the Earth. Carbon as carbon dioxide is removed from the atmosphere by plants in photosynthesis and returned to the atmosphere through respiration and decomposition. The remains of ancient organisms form deposits of sedimentary rocks and fossil fuels, which remove carbon from the cycle for a long time. The carbon is released again by the natural weathering of the rocks or when the fuel is burned.

burning carbon-containing fuels. A sink is something that absorbs carbon from the environment and locks it away in the soil or in rocks. A plant that uses carbon dioxide in photosynthesis is a sink.

The amount of carbon in the environment is enormous, although scientists can only guess at the total quantity. For example, all the Earth's living creatures contain between 660 billion and 1100 billion tons (600 billion and 1000 billion metric tons) of carbon in their bodies. The atmosphere contains about 770 billion tons (700 billion metric tons), mostly in the form of carbon dioxide gas. Carbon dioxide gas makes up approximately 0.03 percent of the atmosphere. Several hundred trillion (10^{12}) tons of carbon are also present in a dissolved form in the ocean, and locked away in rocks and sediments.

Photosynthesis

Photosynthesis is the process by which green plants, algae, and bacteria use the energy of the sun to make food (see PHOTOSYNTHESIS). During photosynthesis, the plant takes carbon dioxide from the air and combines it with the hydrogen in water to produce glucose (a simple carbohydrate), which the plant uses for energy. Plants absorb around 77 billion tons (70 billion metric tons) of carbon dioxide from the atmosphere each year. Aquatic plants photosynthesize using dissolved carbon dioxide from the water.

Animals cannot photosynthesize because they lack chloroplasts: structures filled with chlorophyll, the green pigment that absorbs sunlight. Animals get their energy, and absorb carbon, by eating plants directly or by eating animals that have themselves consumed plants (see FOOD WEBS).

Respiration

In respiration, carbohydrates are oxidized (they react with oxygen) to release energy (see RESPIRATION). Unlike photosynthesis, this process takes place in both plants and animals. Plants obtain chemical energy using the carbohydrates they have made themselves through photosynthesis. Animals use carbohydrates they have obtained by either eating plants or by eating other animals that have eaten plants. In either case, the process of respiration returns carbon to the atmosphere as carbon dioxide.

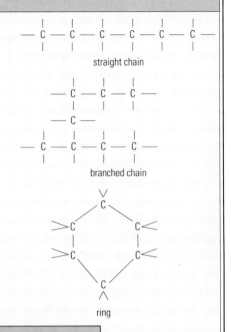
Decomposition

Most of the carbon dioxide that is returned to the atmosphere comes not from the respiration of plants and higher animals but from the activities of decomposers. Decomposers are organisms, mostly soil and water microorganisms, that feed on the decaying remains of dead plant and animal material. For example, mushrooms, toadstools, and bracket fungi live and feed on dying tree trunks. They use the carbon in the dying plant material to respire. This respiration then returns the carbon to the atmosphere in the form of carbon dioxide gas. Decomposers are also active in the oceans, breaking down the bodies of dead plants and animals.

Other processes

Sometimes the carbon in plant or animal material is not recycled for some time. Most of the carbon that leaves the cycle for millions of years is contained in the shells of marine plankton. The hard shells of many species of marine animals are made from calcium carbonate. When these animals die, their shells sink to the bottom of the ocean and eventually form a sedimentary rock called limestone. Over millions of years, the seafloor may rise above sea level to form land surfaces. Once the rock is exposed, the process of weathering gradually releases the carbon and it continues on its journey through the carbon cycle. The eruption of volcanoes also releases small quantities of carbon into the atmosphere from deep inside the Earth.

Carbon dioxide is not the only naturally occurring, carbon-containing gas in the atmosphere. Methane gas (chemical formula CH_4) is produced when organic material is broken down in an anaerobic (oxygen-free) environment. One major source

PHOTOSYNTHESIS AND RESPIRATION

PROCESS OF PHOTOSYNTHESIS

Carbon Dioxide + Water + Light Energy $\longrightarrow$ Glucose + Oxygen

$6CO_2$ + $6H_2O$ $\qquad$ $C_6H_{12}O_6 + 6O_2$

PROCESS OF RESPIRATION

Glucose + Oxygen $\longrightarrow$ Carbon Dioxide + Water + Energy

$C_6H_{12}O_6$ + $6O_2$ $\qquad$ $6CO_2$ + $6H_2O$ + ATP

of methane is the decomposition of organic material by bacteria in waterlogged soil, such as marshes and rice paddy fields. Methane is also produced by ruminants, such as cows and sheep, and by anaerobic microorganisms in the guts of termites.

Human activities disturb the balance

Left to themselves, the natural processes of photosynthesis, respiration, and decomposition are in balance. For tens of thousands of years, humans lived in harmony with nature. But in the modern world, this balance has been disrupted by two relatively recent human activities: the burning of fossil fuels and mass deforestation.

The combustion of carbon-containing fuels, such as coal and oil, produces gases, including carbon dioxide, which escape into the atmosphere. Altogether, fossil fuel reserves contain more than 5500 billion tons (5000 billion metric tons) of coal. Combustion of fossil fuel releases about 6 billion tons (5.4 billion metric tons) of carbon into the atmosphere each year.

Since the industrial revolution during the 19th century, factories, automobiles, and other fuel-burning devices have become widespread. As a result, carbon dioxide levels in the atmosphere have been rising. At first, the extra carbon dioxide released into the atmosphere was probably absorbed by the oceans. But as the rate of the release increased, the oceans were no longer able to take in all the additional carbon dioxide.

Carbon dioxide is a greenhouse gas, which means that, in the atmosphere, it traps heat and prevents it escaping from the Earth. Many scientists believe that this is causing the Earth's temperature to rise. This could have dramatic effects on the global climate, shifting rainfall patterns, destroying the agriculture of many regions, and killing thousands of plant and animal species. Rising temperatures could melt the polar ice caps, which would raise the levels of the oceans and flood many low-lying coastal regions (see GLOBAL WARMING).

Deforestation is the clearing of forests and woodlands to provide land for farming, grazing, or building. This decreases soil fertility and increases soil erosion. It has led to the extinction of many plant and animal species by destroying their habitats. Burning the cut trees, or just allowing them to decay, releases carbon to the atmosphere as carbon dioxide gas. Ploughing the soil increases the amount of oxygen in it. This speeds up the decay of organic matter in the soil, releasing yet more carbon dioxide to the atmosphere. Deforestation also reduces carbon dioxide absorption by removing trees that would use the gas in photosynthesis.

Carbon in the ocean

The carbon cycle does not only operate on the land. The oceans also have a constant recycling of carbon. There is a slow exchange between the atmosphere and the oceans as carbon dioxide gas from the air dissolves in the water to form bicarbonate and carbonate ions. This reaction also happens the other way around, and carbon dioxide is constantly being released back into the air.

The open ocean has two main parts. The top (approximately the first 330 ft to 660 ft or 100 m to 200 m) allows enough sunlight to penetrate so that algae and other plants can photosynthesize. The deep ocean is darker and colder: most of the ocean below 330 ft (100 m) is at a constant temperature of 37.5°F (3°C).

Rainforests are being cut down at the rate of up to 58,000 sq miles (15 million hectares) per year. As well as reducing the number of trees available to absorb carbon dioxide through photosynthesis, carbon is added to the atmosphere when the trees are burned or left to decay.

CARBON FROM FOSSIL FUELS

By far the greatest reservoir of carbon is in the floors of oceans, lakes, and other bodies of water. As much as 110,000,000 billion tons (100,000,000 billion metric tons) of carbon are locked away in sediments at the bottom of oceans and other bodies of water, greatly outweighing the 770 billion tons (700 billion metric tons) found in the atmosphere. But how did the carbon get there? Bear in mind that the carbon cycle is just that: a cycle. The carbon in the sediments must have come from somewhere and will eventually move on to another place and form.

During the Coal Age, about 300 million years ago, much of the Earth was covered by shallow swamps and seas. The warm wet environment allowed plants to grow all year round. The land was covered with giant relatives of today's club mosses, horsetails, and ferns. Some were more than 65 ft (20 m) tall.

As the plants died, they were shielded from the decomposing action of microorganisms by a covering of mud and soil. As more and more sediments piled on top, the dead plants were gradually transformed by high temperature and pressure into deposits of fossil fuel, mostly coal, oil, and gas. Today these deposits are mined and used as fuel. When the fossil fuels are burned, the carbon stored in them is released as carbon dioxide.

A CLOSER LOOK

MISSING CARBON DIOXIDE

When scientists calculate the amount of fossil fuels that humans have burned through history, they find that there is less carbon dioxide in the atmosphere than they would expect. Some would have been absorbed by the oceans, but this does not account for all the missing carbon dioxide.

The problem boils down to simple mathematics. Burning gasoline and other fossil fuels adds 6 billion tons (5.4 billion metric tons) of carbon to the atmosphere each year. Deforestation of tropical rainforests and other changes in how land is used adds another 1.8 billion tons (1.6 billion metric tons) annually. That adds up to about 7.7 billion tons (7 billion metric tons) of carbon being pumped into the atmosphere each year. But the levels of carbon dioxide in the air, which scientists can measure quite accurately, is actually only growing at the rate of 3.5 billion tons (3.2 billion metric tons) each year. Using computer programs that simulate how the ocean behaves, scientists estimate that about 2.2 billion tons (2 billion metric tons) of carbon dioxide are absorbed by the ocean.

That leaves 2 billion tons (1.8 billion metric tons) that are mysteriously being removed from the air every year. Scientists are focusing on three possible explanations. One is that their computer programs are underestimating the amount of carbon dioxide that the oceans absorb. To check whether this is the case, scientists from several nations are cooperating on the Joint Ocean Global Flux Study, in which scientists at sea will precisely measure the rate at which different oceans absorb carbon dioxide from the air. A second, somewhat similar, possible solution to the mystery of the missing carbon is that it may have been absorbed by the Earth's soil.

The third explanation for the missing carbon is that scientists have underestimated the amount of carbon dioxide that plants on dry land are removing from the air. Until now, scientists have assumed that the amount of photosynthesis taking place on Earth has remained approximately constant (apart from the effect of deforestation of tropical rainforests). But since plants need carbon dioxide to grow, it is possible that the extra carbon dioxide in the atmosphere from combustion may have spurred plants to photosynthesize faster than before. If so, that would convert more carbon dioxide to oxygen and might account for the missing carbon.

The flow of carbon within the ocean is not all from the upper layers to the lower layers. Significant amounts of carbon also move from the deep ocean back to the surface layers through currents, known as upwellings, that carry waters rich in nutrients from the ocean floor up toward the surface.

V. KIERNAN/M. MAHALIK

See also: ATMOSPHERE; BIOMES AND HABITATS; CARBON DIOXIDE; ECOLOGY AND ECOSYSTEMS; GLOBAL WARMING; PHOTOSYNTHESIS; RESPIRATORY SYSTEMS.

Further reading:
The Global Carbon Cycle. Edited by M. Heimann. New York: Springer-Verlag, 1993.
Gore, A. *Earth in the Balance.* Boston: Houghton Mifflin, 1992.

RADIOCARBON TESTING

When archaeologists unearth an ancient wooden object, they are able to calculate its age using a technique called radiometric dating. This is based on nuclear half-lives, the time taken for half the atoms in a given sample of radioactive material to decay and for the sample's radioactivity to halve. Radiocarbon dating is one of the best known radiometric techniques. Carbon exists in two forms: the normal carbon-12 and the radioactive carbon-14, which has a half-life of 5730 years. When plants take carbon dioxide from the atmosphere, this contains a known percentage of carbon-14, which is then incorporated into the living tissue. When the plant dies, the carbon-14 starts to disintegrate. By comparing the radioactivity of a modern piece of wood with that of a wooden object of an unknown age, it is possible to work out how much time has passed since the older wood was living.

SCIENCE AND SOCIETY

Most of the carbon processing takes place within the top zone. Microscopic phytoplankton, which live within 660 ft (200 m) of the surface, photosynthesize using the carbon dioxide dissolved in the water. They are eaten by zooplankton, other microscopic organisms, whose fecal waste is then consumed by other organisms, including bacteria.

About three quarters of all water in the ocean lies below 3280 ft (1000 m). Until recently, scientists thought that there would be very little life on the ocean floor because it is too dark for photosynthesis, but this is not so. The ocean floor is home to vibrant communities of animals and bacteria, which feed on dead plants and animals, and on the feces that pour down from the upper ocean.

The sea floor is also home to a form of bacteria that can take advantage of the enormous heat produced when the sea floor is broken, allowing molten rock from deep inside the Earth to well up into the water. The heat produces a chemical reaction, converting dissolved sulphate in the seawater into sulphite. Certain bacteria, known as chemosynthetic baacteria, obtain energy by converting the sulphite back into sulphate. They use the energy released by this chemical process to take dissolved carbon dioxide from the seawater and convert the carbon into simple sugars.

The oceans cover over two thirds of the Earth's surface and are major sinks, absorbing carbon dioxide from the atmosphere. They contain thousands of billions of tons of carbon, as carbon dioxide dissolved in water, and in rocks and sediments.

CARBON DIOXIDE

Carbon dioxide is an atmospheric gas, which plays an important role in living systems

Carbon dioxide (CO_2) is one of the major atmospheric gases, along with nitrogen and oxygen, making up 0.03 percent of the atmosphere. It plays a vital role in living organisms and in the carbon cycle, the process in which carbon is moved around the Earth from one form to another. Carbon dioxide gas is both colorless and odorless. Each molecule is made up of a central carbon atom joined to two oxygen atoms.

Carbon dioxide and the carbon cycle

In the carbon cycle (see CARBON CYCLE), carbon dioxide is constantly moving between the atmosphere and living things. Plants take in carbon dioxide gas during photosynthesis and use it to produce sugar and oxygen. Carbon dioxide gas is released by plants and animals during respiration, when the sugars are broken down to release energy. It is also released when decomposers, such as bacteria and fungi, break down organic material. Today, significant amounts of carbon dioxide are being produced by factories, power plants, and cars, which burn fossil fuels such as oil, natural gas, and coal.

Carbon dioxide and the environment

The amount of carbon dioxide in the atmosphere is one of the factors that affects the climate. Carbon dioxide is known as a "greenhouse gas," because it acts like the glass in a greenhouse, trapping the heat escaping from the Earth and reflecting it back to the Earth's surface. A normal concentration of carbon dioxide in the atmosphere has the beneficial effect of warming the planet. However, too much carbon dioxide could lead to overheating. Atmospheric levels of carbon dioxide have been rising over the past hundred years. This is a result of the destruction of massive regions of the rainforests, which would have used up much of the carbon dioxide in photosynthesis, and because of an increase in the burning of fossil fuels, which releases carbon dioxide as a byproduct. Scientists have calculated that global levels of carbon dioxide will have doubled by the middle of the 21st century unless we take steps to check these activities. If the global carbon dioxide level does double, this could raise the Earth's temperature by between 2.7 and 8°F (1.5 and 4.4°C).

Carbon dioxide in the human body

Carbon dioxide is generated by the cells in the body as a waste product of cellular respiration. It is removed from the body by the lungs, and is transported from the cells to the lungs in the bloodstream. Carbon dioxide is carried in the blood in three ways. A small proportion (7 to 8 percent) is dissolved in the plasma, the liquid part of the

In 1986 a cloud of carbon dioxide gas, which was emitted from Lake Nios in Cameroon, Africa, killed nearly 2000 people. Atmospheric conditions probably caused the water in the lake to turn over. The colder water at the bottom of the lake contained a large amount of carbon dioxide, which was released into the air as this water was brought to the surface. Animals and humans in the area quickly suffocated.

blood. Between 15 and 20 percent is bound to hemoglobin in the red blood cells. The rest is transported in the form of bicarbonate ions.

The amount of carbon dioxide in the blood affects the rate of breathing. The carbon dioxide level is monitored by carbon dioxide receptors in certain arteries, including the aorta and the carotid arteries, which carry blood to the brain. A rise in the level of carbon dioxide stimulates these receptors and increases the rate of breathing, while a drop in the carbon dioxide level lowers the breathing rate. An increase in the amount of carbon dioxide in the air raises the level in the blood and causes animals to breathe faster. At a concentration of 3 percent, human breathing becomes difficult. By 5 to 6 percent, panting starts. If the amount of carbon dioxide goes above 10 percent, people lose consciousness. A level of 18 percent is enough to cause suffocation.

M. MAHALIK

See also: ATMOSPHERE; CARBON CYCLE; GLOBAL WARMING; PHOTOSYNTHESIS; RESPIRATORY SYSTEMS.

Further reading:
Manahan, S.E. *Environmental Chemistry*. 5th Edition. Chelsea, Michigan: Lewis Publishers, 1991.

CONNECTIONS

● Most substances have three stages: gas, liquid, and solid. Carbon dioxide changes directly from a gas to a solid without passing through a liquid stage. Solid carbon dioxide is called "dry ice" and is used to preserve frozen foods.

● **YEASTS** convert sugar (glucose) into alcohol and carbon dioxide through the process of **FERMENTATION.**

● Part of the biochemical process that produces carbon dioxide during respiration is known as the **CITRIC ACID CYCLE.**

● Carbon dioxide is heavier than air. It does not support burning and is used in fire extinguishers.

CARNIVORES

Carnivores are mainly meat-eating animals in the mammalian order Carnivora

The word carnivore usually brings to mind ferocious hunters, such as lions, Grizzly bears, and wolves. Or we may just think of any meat-eating animal, such as a bird of prey. However, when biologists use the term carnivore they mean members of the mammalian order Carnivora. There are around 236 species of carnivores, including the familiar cats and dogs that share our homes.

CORE FACTS

- There are eight families of terrestrial carnivores. The Canidae, Ursidae, Procyonidae, and Mustelidae are derived from the dog branch of the carnivores. The Felidae, Hyaenidae, Viverridae, and Herpestidae are derived from the cat branch.
- Aquatic carnivores – seals, sea lions, fur seals, and the walrus – are known as pinnipeds.
- Carnivores are characterized by a keen sense of smell, forceful jaws, and canine and carnassial teeth.
- Carnivores are largely meat eaters, although some, such as the bears, are omnivorous.

The anatomy of the carnivore

Carnivores can be found all over the world in habitats as diverse as tundra, rainforests, and deserts. Despite their great variation in size and ecology, carnivores have many characteristic features, due to their common need to capture and subdue prey.

Carnivores typically have a keen sense of smell, which they use to find and stalk their prey. The carnivore brain is large and complex, allowing these animals to develop flexible behavior adapted to hunting and rearing young. In some carnivores, such as wolves, these include social behavior such as pack hunting and sharing food among the group.

Most of the terrestrial carnivores are fast and efficient runners. The cheetah (*Acinonyx jubatus*), for example, is the fastest land animal on Earth, capable of bursts of speeds of up to 75 mph (121 km/h). African wild dogs (*Lycaon pictus*) can cover distances of more than 3 miles (5 km) at about 37 mph (60 km/h). Similarly, most of the aquatic carnivores are fast and maneuverable swimmers.

Carnivores have forceful jaws to kill and dismember their prey. The lower jaw is strong enough to cut through thick bones and tough hides. The biting power comes from the large temporal muscles, which stretch from the top of the lower jaw to the side of the braincase behind the eye. This arrangement gives the carnivores a wide and powerful gape, although it prevents the side to side grinding motion of the lower jaw typical of her-

Carnivore teeth are specialized for tearing and crushing the flesh and bones of animal prey.

bivorous animals such as cows. Carnivore teeth are highly specialized. The canines are large and curved. These formidable teeth are used mainly for grabbing and puncturing prey. Most carnivores also have a unique set of shearing teeth called carnassials, usually formed by the upper premolars and the first set of lower molars. These razor-sharp teeth slide past each other like scissor blades. Carnivores use their carnassials to slice tough flesh, skin, and gristle into pieces small enough to swallow. The family dog may use its carnassials to shred its owner's shoes.

Once a carnivore has caught, killed, and eaten its prey, it has to digest the meat. Meat is easier and quicker to digest than plant material, since the cells are not surrounded by a tough cellulose wall. Consequently, carnivore intestines tend to be shorter than a herbivore's (see DIGESTIVE SYSTEMS).

However, not all carnivores depend on meat as their main type of food. Most species of bear, for example, have a very mixed diet and will eat large amounts of plant material as well as meat. In these animals, the carnassial teeth may be modified for grinding plant matter.

The major groups of living carnivores

There are two suborders of carnivores, known as the Fissipedia and the Pinnipedia. The Fissipedia are essentially terrestrial, or land-dwelling, while the Pinnipedia have adapted to a marine (sea-dwelling) lifestyle. However, some scientists consider the Carnivora and the Pinnipedia to be two separate orders.

CONNECTIONS

- Many carnivores are **ENDANGERED SPECIES** as a result of human activities, such as hunting and destruction of habitat.

- One of the most important features of carnivores is their **TEETH.** All carnivores have carnassials, although in some species they have lost their slicing abilities.

- Aquatic carnivores have **ADAPTATIONS** that allow them to dive to great depths. Other animals, such as humans, are less well adapted. Deep-sea divers who surface too quickly may experience breathing difficulties, joint and muscle pain, and cramps, a condition known as the bends.

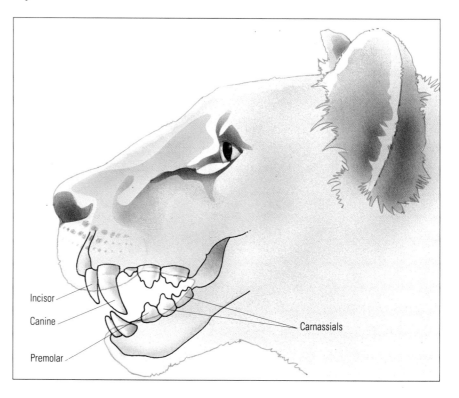

Incisor

Canine

Premolar

Carnassials

The Fissipedia is the older of the two carnivore groups, and is divided into three large and distinctive infraorders. The infraorder Aeluroidea contains a wide variety of extinct and living species, such as the cats and their relatives, including civets, mongooses, and hyenas. This infraorder is sometimes referred to as the Feloidea. The second group, the infraorder Arctoidea, is represented by dogs and their relatives, including weasels, skunks, otters, raccoons, and bears. This infraorder is sometimes called the Canoidea. The extinct infraorder Miacoidea is the third group represented in the Fissipedia. As a group, the Fissipedia represent the most diverse terrestrial predators on Earth since the dinosaurs.

The second major group of living carnivores, the suborder Pinnipedia, represents extinct and living marine carnivorous mammals. Living forms include the seals, seal lions, and the walrus.

SURVEY OF THE CARNIVORES
Suborder: Fissipedia
Eight famies comprise the suborder Fissipedia, the terrestrial carnivores:

Family Mustelidae
The Mustelidae family is very large, with 23 genera and 65 living species. The group comprises weasels, skunks, badgers, otters, and ferrets. Mustelids are found on every continent except Antarctica and Australia. They live in a range of habitats, from the Arctic to the tropical rainforests, on land, in trees, and in rivers. There is even a marine form, the Sea otter (*Enhydra lutris*), which lives in the kelp beds off the California coast. Mustelids are the most recently evolved carnivores. Their fossils date back to the early Oligocene Epoch (30 to 36 million years ago) in North America and Asia.

Mustelidae are small carnivores with short limbs and long bodies. This sleek body shape allows mustelids to crawl down narrow burrows, squeeze through crevices, wiggle under dense vegetation, and search for prey in other hard-to-reach places. They are aggressive hunters, sometimes attacking prey much larger than themselves.

Most mustelids are swift and graceful runners, able to pursue and overcome their prey, and to escape their enemies. Rather than speed, some rely on another mustelid characteristic, well-developed scent glands, for defense. Skunks, for example, produce a foul-smelling liquid that they spray from special anal scent glands to ward off enemies. They can shoot this liquid to a distance of more than 33 ft (10 m). Zorilles, polecats, and stink badgers are other mustelids that spray scent as a defense.

Mustelids have a large range of body sizes, from the Sea otter, which can be as large as 90 lb (40 kg), to the Least weasel (*Mustela nivalis*), which rarely weighs heavier than 2½ oz (70 g). The Least weasel is the smallest of all the carnivores.

NONMAMMALIAN CARNIVORES

Besides its special use referring to a specific family of mammals, the term carnivore can be applied more generally to meat-eating organisms. Many reptiles, including all snakes, crocodiles, alligators, and certain types of lizard are carnivorous. Raptors (birds of prey), including eagles, hawks, ospreys, falcons, and owls are fierce hunters. Many fish are carnivorous, including sharks, piranha, and barracudas. Certain invertebrates, including sea anemones and jellyfish, are just as carnivorous as mammalian carnivores. There are even some plants that live on a meat diet, mainly of insects (see CARNIVOROUS PLANTS).

Family Ursidae
The Ursidae, or bear family, contains just seven species: the Polar bear (*Ursus maritimus*), the American black bear (*Ursus americanus*), the Asian black bear (*Ursus thibetanus*), the Sun bear (*Ursus malayanus*), the Sloth bear (*Ursus ursinus*), the Spectacled bear (*Tremarctos ornatus*), and the Grizzly or Brown bear (*Ursus arctos*). There are also several subspecies of Brown bear, some of which are highly endangered.

Some scientists include the Giant panda (*Ailuropoda melanoleuca*) in the bear family. However, others believe that the Giant panda is more closely related to the Red panda (*Ailurus fulgens*), and they place both these animals in the Raccoon family (see the box on page 250 for more information on this controversy). Living bears are widely dispersed throughout the world. They are

The Sea otter (Enhydra lutris) *lives at sea and only rarely comes ashore. It is one of the few tool-using mammals, and uses stones to dislodge shellfish from rocks. After diving to catch its prey, the Sea otter returns to the surface to eat. Floating on its back, the otter holds a stone on its chest and uses it to crack open the shells of clams, mussels, and other shell-covered prey.*

WHEN IS A BEAR NOT A BEAR?

Ever since the Giant panda was first "discovered" in 1869, scientists have been unable to agree on how it should be classified. The first European to learn of its existence was Père David, a French missionary and naturalist. He placed it with the bears. But one year later, Alphonse Milne-Edwards decided that the Giant panda was more like the raccoons and moved it into that family. From that day on, the arguments have contined to rage.

Although the Giant panda looks like a bear, it shares many characteristics with the Red panda, a member of the Raccoon family. Both have similar skulls, teeth, and forepaws for processing and eating bamboo. Giant pandas and Red pandas have similar scent glands and reproductive organs. But similarities such as these do not necessarily mean that the animals are closely related. These adaptations could have evolved independently in the two species as a result of similar habitats, lifestyles, and feeding habits (see ADAPTATION; EVOLUTION).

Fossils often hold clues about how species evolved, but in the case of the pandas the fossil record has large gaps. The advent of molecular biology offered some hope for ending the debate, but again the results have been contradictory. Scientists using DNA studies have found evidence to support the view that the Giant panda is a bear and the Red panda is a raccoon. But other molecular research suggests that the Giant and Red pandas are more closely related to each other than is the Giant panda to the bears, and the Red panda to the raccoons. The view currently held by most experts is that the Giant panda is, in fact, a bear.

A CLOSER LOOK

found in most of North America, Eurasia, the Malay Peninsula, the South American Andes, and the Arctic Circle. Bears also occupy a wide range of habitats, from Arctic ice flows to tropical forests.

Bears, or ursids, first appeared about 20 million years ago in the form of the Dawn bear (*Ursavus elmensis*), which was the size of a small dog, measuring around 30 in (75 cm) at the shoulder. As the family evolved, more species appeared, and the animals gradually became larger. The most recent species is the Polar bear, which probably appeared 70,000 years ago.

Bears have large bodies and short, powerful limbs. They have a long snout and an excellent sense of smell. Sight and hearing are less well developed, and the eyes and ears are small compared to the size of the head. Bears walk and run on the soles of their feet (this is known as a plantigrade gait). They may look clumsy, but they can still outrun most humans!

Bears are among the most omnivorous (eating both meat and vegetation) carnivores, eating a wide range of meat, fish, insects, fruits, berries, grasses, and nuts. This diet is reflected in their teeth: the carnassials are more triangular and lack the shearing capabilities of other carnivores. The molars are square with rounded cusps to crush different types of food. The Polar bear is the only species in the bear family that is mainly flesh-eating. Polar bears are very active hunters. Their main food source is seals, which they pursue in the open ocean up to 40 miles (60 km) from the nearest coast. They are very strong swimmers and can swim steadily at speeds of up to 4 mph (6.5 km/h).

Raccoons (Procyon lotor) make their dens in hollow trees, rock crevices, barns and other farm buildings, and even in the attics of houses. They often live in communal dens with more than 20 individuals.

In colder climates, where food is seasonally available, bears spend the winter in deep sleep or semihibernation. This saves energy but is not considered to be true hibernation because the animal will occasionally wake up to forage. The Polar bear is particularly well adapted to its cold, hostile environment. It has thick fur and an insulating layer of fat to protect against the cold air and water.

Family Canidae

The canid family is a diverse group of dog-like carnivores, made up of wolves, jackals, foxes, and dogs. The canids are equally diverse in their distribution, which stretches from Arctic regions to the tropics. They seemed to have first evolved sometime in the late Eocene Epoch, between 35 to 40 million years ago.

Canids first evolved in open grasslands, but have become adapted to a wide range of habitats. They were among the first animals to be domesticated, and dogs of various breeds have since been introduced throughout the world.

Regardless of their overall size, which ranges from 2 to 165 lb (1 to 75 kg), all canids have the body shape of a general carnivore. They have a long snout, with a large nasal chamber that gives them an excellent sense of smell.

The canid is a running animal with long limb bones and a digitrade foot. This means that, like a sprinter, the animal walks and runs on its toes, which adds extra length to each stride.

Some canids, including the Gray wolf (*Canis lupis*), the African wild dog (*Lycaon pictus*), and the Asian dhole (*Cuon alpinus*), hunt in packs. This allows them to overwhelm much larger prey than they would be capable of killing alone. Group living

CARNIVORE EVOLUTION

Over 65 million years ago a small, squirrel-sized, insectivorous creature called *Cimolestes* scurried through the forests, trying to avoid being stepped on by dinosaurs. Many scientists now believe that this animal, or one very like it, was the ancestor of today's modern carnivores. As well as insects, *Cimolestes* also fed occasionally on small vertebrates, killing them with rapid, jabbing bites much like those of the modern civets and genets. Indeed, its teeth give us the clue to its carnivorous descendents: it had flattened cheek teeth that were beginning to develop the "scissor-action" of the carnassials. By 58 million years ago, *Cimolestes* had given rise to two separate groups, the creodonts and the miacids.

To begin with, the creodonts (in the order Creodonta) dominated the miacids, and they flourished between 55 and 35 million years ago. These early mammals were small and sluggish by contemporary standards, as they had relatively small brains and short limbs compared with today's carnivores. They also lacked their ossified

auditory bullae of the skull, paired structures that protect the sensitive middle ear from damage. However, they had the specialized cutting molar teeth, called carnassials, which are typical of modern carnivores. Creodonts died out at least eight million years ago.

By 30 to 20 million years ago the miacids, in the order Miacoidea, had become the top predators. These small mammals may have been largely arboreal (tree-dwelling). They shared some features with the creodonts and some with the more advanced carnivores. For example, although they had the carnassial molar teeth and large brains of modern carnivores, they lacked the ossifed auditory bullae, suggesting a creodont pattern. No Miacoidea survive today. About 55 million years ago, the miacids gave rise to two main branches of carnivores: the cat branch (the viverravines) and the dog branch (the vulpavines). The dog branch diversified to produce the modern dogs, bears, raccoons, and weasels, while the cat branch gave rise to cats, civets, hyenas, and mongooses.

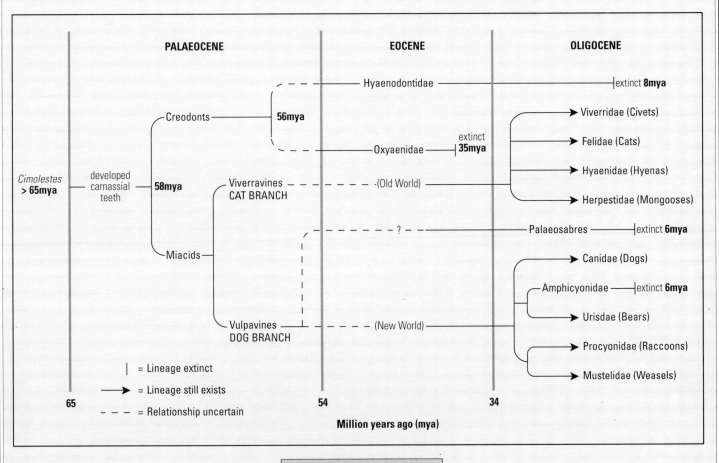

EVOLUTION

gives the animals other advantages, such as defense of territories and nurturing their young.

Family Procyonidae

The Procyonidae family includes the raccoons, the coatimundis or coatis, the olingos, the kinkajous, the cacomistles, and the Red panda (also known as the Lesser panda). Altogether, seven genera and 19 species are known, ranging in size from 2 to 26 lb (1 to 12 kg). As with the bears, this group is largely omnivorous.

Procyonids are found in woodland areas throughout the temperate and tropical regions of the Western Hemisphere. Exceptions are the ringtail (*Bassariscus astutus*) and the coatis (*Nasua* and *Nasuella* spp.), found in the mountains of desert and semidesert regions. Procyonids are descended from the dog branch of the carnivores. The earliest fossils date back to the late Oligocene Epoch (23 to 30 million years ago).

In diet, the procyonids are the least carnivore-like of the carnivores. Raccoons (*Procyon* spp.) eat fish, frogs, birds, eggs, small rodents, insects, fruit, and nuts. Coatis live on insects and fruit, while the kinkajou (*Potos flavus*) eats fruit and nectar, which it collects from flowers with its long tongue.

The omnivorous diet is reflected in the procyonid's teeth. The carnassials have almost completely lost their shearing ability and instead have the grinding surfaces typical of molars. The most carnivorous species are the cacomistles (*Bassariscus* spp.). These have dog-like teeth, and prey on lizards and small mammals, most of which they catch in trees. However, even these species will also eat insects, fruit, and nuts.

The procyonids are slow runners but excellent climbers. The kinkajou has a prehensile (grasping) tail, which it wraps around branches as it moves among the trees. Procyonids also have dextrous forepaws. The raccoon, for example, can manipulate items of food with considerable ease. When collecting food along the edge of a stream, raccoons often "wash" it in the water before eating it. This may be an attempt to remove mud, though some more fastidious pet raccoons have been known to wash everything before eating it.

Coatis are the only procyonids that are active during the day (all the other species are nocturnal). They have an interesting social arrangement: the males live alone while the females form tribes of five to twenty animals. The females forage for food as a group, groom one another, and often care for each other's young.

Family Viverridae

The family Viverridae (the civets and genets) contains 35 species, distributed in the Old World, mostly in tropical regions. The group first appeared in Europe in the late Eocene (over 38 million years ago) and apparently did not reach Africa until the Miocene, about 20 million years ago.

Viverrids resemble the ancestors of the carnivores, the Miacoidea, very closely. Modern viverrid fossils are almost identical to those of their early miacoid relatives. This is probably because they are still living in habitats once occupied by these primitive carnivores, and so display similar adaptations.

Today's viverrids are small carnivores, ranging from the Spotted linsang (*Prionodon pardicolor*), which weighs just over 1 lb (600 g), to the fossa (*Cryptoprocta ferox*), which weighs 44 lb (20 kg). They have roughly the general shape of a weasel, with a long body, short legs, long tail, and well-developed scent glands. They possess a long snout, and have well-developed carnassials. Many viverrids are almost exclusively carnivorous, although they may occasionally feed on insects, eggs, and fruit.

Civets are most well known for their scent pouches, called perineal glands, which produce a thick secretion called musk or civet. For many years, humans have used this substance in perfumes and skin lotions and as an aphrodisiac. Today, synthetic alternatives are more likely to be used, although there is still a flourishing trade in some countries in East Africa and the Far East.

Family Hyaenidae

The hyaenids are an unusual group that have adapted to eat carrion as the major part of their diet. (Other carnivores only occasionally eat carrion.) They are a small group with only three genera and four species: the Spotted hyena (*Crocuta crocuta*), the Brown hyena (*Hyaena brunnea*), the

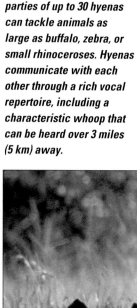

*Spotted hyenas (*Crocuta crocuta*) are skilled hunters. Hunting alone, a hyena can bring down an adult wildebeest. Hunting parties of up to 30 hyenas can tackle animals as large as buffalo, zebra, or small rhinoceroses. Hyenas communicate with each other through a rich vocal repertoire, including a characteristic whoop that can be heard over 3 miles (5 km) away.*

Striped hyena (*Hyaena hyaena*), and the aardwolf (*Proteles cristatus*), the smallest of the hyaenids. Their distribution is strictly Old World, in Africa, southwestern Asia, and India. (There are fossils of a North American species from the Pleistocene Epoch.) The hyaenids first appeared in Eurasia in the Miocene Epoch, about 22 million years ago.

Hyaenids have heavy bodies: the larger species weigh more than 175 lb (80 kg), or the weight of a Saint Bernard dog. The skulls are strongly built, with heavy and powerful teeth, including well-developed carnassials. The cheek teeth are broad and heavily crowned to crush bone, a favorite food.

With its forelimbs longer than its hind limbs, the hyena has a distinctive crouching posture. The hyena's unusual appearance becomes even more striking when the animal is threatened: the long hair on its mane and tail stands straight up. The aardwolf releases a foul odor from anal scent glands when threatened. These defensive behaviors are often seen when the hyaenid is scavenging in the presence of a large predator such as a lion.

Hyaenids are also known for their aggressiveness, and can drive a cheetah from its kill. Some larger species, such as the spotted hyena, hunt in large packs of up to 30 or more. These hunting packs can bring down animals as big as a zebra or a water buffalo.

Family Felidae

The Felidae family contains some of the most familiar and proficient carnivores, the cats. A wide variety of feline species are native to Europe, Africa, Asia, and North and South America. Humans have also introduced domesticated cats to Australia and New Zealand.

The first true cat, *Pseudaelurus*, lived during the Miocene about 20 million years ago. The most familiar prehistoric cat is the Saber toothed tiger (*Smilodon*) which appeared about two million years ago and died out 9000 years ago.

Although all cats have a similar shape, scientists have divided them into two main groups: big cats and small cats. There are seven species of big cats, including lions, tigers, leopards, jaguars, and cheetahs, and 30 species of small cats, including the bobcat, lynx, puma, ocelot, and the familiar domestic cat. One of the main differences between the two divisions is that big cats can roar but cannot purr, while small cats can purr but cannot roar (see CATS).

Cats range in size from the Black-footed cat (*Felis nigripes*) at just over 2 lb (1 kg) to the male Siberian tiger (*Panthera tigris altaica*) at around 750 lb (360 kg). They all share a reduced number of back teeth and a shortened snout, which provides a powerful bite. They have large ears and eyes, giving them excellent hearing and sight. However, their sense of smell is not as keen as that of canids and other long-nosed carnivores.

All cats have large pointed canine teeth, which they use to catch and kill their prey. The carnassials are very well developed to help with shearing. Molars are absent, so cats swallow their food in relatively large chunks.

The felid body is well adapted for hunting, with strongly built forelimbs. The forepaws can be supinated (bent inward at the wrist) so that the felid can grab and swipe at prey. The paws have long curved claws, which are used for climbing as well as for killing. The claws can be retracted, allowing the cat to expose them when they are needed and, when necessary, to pull them back to protect them, keeping them sharp, and to prevent unnecessary noise as the animal stalks its prey.

An exception to this is the cheetah, which has lost the retractile ability in favor of an extremely fast running speed. The cheetah's claws are permanently exposed. Just like the spikes on a sprinter's running shoes, the claws give the cheetah extra grip as it sprints after its prey. Apart from the lion, most cats hunt alone.

Color patterns on the body include stripes and spots that are effective in concealing the animals as they stalk or ambush their prey. However, cats have few natural enemies. The greatest threat to their survival comes from humans, who destroy their habitats and hunt them for their skins.

Family Herpestidae

The 36 species of mongoose were originally classified in the family Viverridae, along with the civets and genets. However, scientists now group them in a family of their own, the Herpestidae, and some even think that mongooses are more closely related to hyenas than any other carnivore group. The

Leopard (Panthera pardus) *chasing a gazelle. Leopards hunt alone. They leap on their prey after stalking them closely or ambushing them. Leopards often drag their kills up trees where they can eat them or store them away from scavengers such as jackals and hyenas.*

mongooses are descended from the cat branch of the carnivores. Fossils dating back 18 to 22 million years have been found in both Europe and East Africa, so it is uncertain from which of these continents the family originated. Today mongooses are found only in Asia, the Near East, southwest Europe, most of Africa, and Madagascar.

Most mongooses, including the Slender mongoose (*Herpestes sanguineus*) and the Cape gray mongoose (*H. pulverulentus*), live alone or in pairs. However, the eight species in the subfamily Mungotinae live in large social groups. For example, communities of Banded mongooses (*Mungos mungo*) may contain up to 30 individuals, and groups of around a dozen Dwarf mongooses (*Helogale parvula*) live together in termite mounds.

Most social mongooses are diurnal (active in the daytime) and insectivorous. One of the most familiar social species of mongoose is the Gray meerkat, or suricate (*Suricata suricatta*). Like other group species, these mongooses have a complex social organization, in which individuals take on specific roles, such as hunting for food, sentry duty, and care of the young.

The solitary mongooses are mainly nocturnal forest dwellers, hunting small vertebrates and insects and stealing eggs. Some species have very specialized diets. For example, the Ruddy mongoose (*Herpestes smithi*) restricts its diet to large snails, and the Water mongoose (*Atilax paludinosus*) eats mainly crocodile eggs.

Suborder: Pinnipedia

Three families make up the suborder Pinnipedia. These are the earless seals (family Phocidae) comprising fur seals and sea lions, the eared seals (family Otariidae), and the walrus (*Odobenus rosmarus*). Although at first glance eared and earless seals look to be closely related, the Phocidae seems to have evolved from a mustelid-like ancestor, whereas the Otariidae and the Odobenidae evolved from bear-like ancestors. Pinnipeds are generally larger than their terrestrial counterparts, ranging from 77 to 7940 lb (35 to 3660 kg).

All pinnipeds reproduce on land. However, some species, including the Elephant seals (*Mirounga* spp.), spend months at sea without ever climbing out on land. These and other pinnipeds have many adaptations for life in the oceans. They have a compact body shape and an insulating layer of fur or blubber (or both) to help prevent loss of body heat in cold water. Their limbs are modified into strong flippers and fins, which they use to propel themselves through the water. They are able to dive to great depths and stay under water for a long time.

Before they dive, pinnipeds take a deep breath and close their nostrils, as if they were nature's answer to a Scuba diver. The earless seals hold the record for the longest dive of any mammal. For example, Elephant seals can dive to depths of more than 2920 ft (890 m) and make repeated dives of over an hour with only a few minutes in between.

Seals and sea lions hunt active prey and have large eyes that give good vision under water. The walrus, which feeds on the ocean floor, does not have as good a sense of vision. Instead it has very sensitive vibrissae (whiskers) to find its prey by touch. Many pinniped species have highly developed hearing, and some are believed to use echolocation in a similar manner to bats.

The 33 species of pinniped are distributed in seas worldwide and in two landlocked areas, Lake Baikal and the Caspian sea. Some species are very numerous: there are an estimated 30 million Crabeater seals (*Lobodon carcinophagus*), which makes this species the most numerous large mammal apart from humans.

Some species of seal, including the Hawaiian monk seal (*Monachus schauinslandi*), the Mediterranean monk seal (*M. monachus*), and the Saimaa ringed seal (*Phoca hispida saimensis*), are highly endangered from direct hunting and degradation of their environments. Fortunately the area off the western Hawaiian islands, where the Hawaiian monk seal lives and breeds, was named a Research Natural Area in 1967. Government and environmental groups are monitoring the remaining seals and devising plans to increase their numbers.

K. HOSOUME/J. KAUFMANN/R. LEAPER

See also: ANIMAL KINGDOM; CATS; DOGS; MAMMALS.

Further reading:
Estes, R. *The Behavior Guide to African Mammals: Including Hoofed Mammals, Carnivores, Primates.* Berkely: University of California Press, 1991.
Macdonald, David. *The Velvet Claw.* New York: Parkwest Publications, 1993.
Reeves, R., Stewart, B., and Leatherwood, S. *The Sierra Club Handbook of Seals and Sirenians.* San Francisco: Sierra Club, 1992.

The California sea lion (Zalophus californianus) is an eared seal. It is found along the west coast of North America, off California and Mexico. Eared seals are social animals and tend to live in groups. They are more agile on land than the other pinnipeds, turning their hind flippers under their bodies to "walk." Although they look awkward, they can climb stairs. A wild sea lion was once found wandering the streets of San Francisco!

CARNIVOROUS PLANTS

Carnivorous plants are plants that gain at least part of their nourishment by digesting animals

This carnivorous sundew (Drosera rotundifolia) has trapped a midge in its sticky leaves.

Carnivorous plants have the ability, unique among plants, to capture and digest animals (mostly small insects) for nourishment. When they were first discovered, and for a long time afterward, the suggestion that plants could feed on animals was considered very shocking. People refused to believe it. The idea was not widely accepted until the 1870s when Charles Darwin experimented with sundews, bladderworts, and the Venus flytrap and proved the carnivorous nature of these plants. Since then people continue to be fascinated by them. They have provided inspiration for scientists and science fiction writers alike.

Carnivorous plants are arranged in 17 genera and nine families. The size varies according to species, from about ¼ in (6 mm) to over 22 ft (20 m). The plants catch their prey by tricking them into entering traps made from the leaves of the plant. Once a victim has been caught, the trap begins to work like a stomach; digestive enzymes break the victim down into a form that the plant can absorb. Most carnivorous plants trap various kinds of insects, and so they are sometimes described as insectivorous. However, some of the larger species trap and digest reptiles, frogs, birds, and even small mammals, so the term carnivorous is a more accurate description.

These plants grow mainly in boggy habitats where the soil is nutrient-poor. Whereas normal plants gain nutrients from the soil through their roots, carnivorous plants have had to find another way of getting nourishment. They do this by trapping and digesting animals, and are so successful at this that they can survive in places where normal plants would die from lack of nutrients.

Carnivorous plants kill their prey in different ways, depending on the type of trap.

Hinged traps

The Venus flytrap (*Dionaea muscipula*) captures its prey with a hinged trap similar to a steel trap. The trap snaps shut on the prey, and the victim is slowly digested (see the box on page 257).

The Venus flytrap has a little-known underwater cousin: the Waterwheel plant (*Aldrovanda vesiculosa*), which is found in ponds across Europe, Africa, Asia, and Australia. It has tiny underwater traps, which take only a few hundredths of a second to snap shut on the aquatic prey.

Suction traps

Unlike the Venus flytrap, bladderworts (*Utricularia* spp.) trap their victims by sucking them inside tiny underwater bladders. The bladders are formed from the leaves. They are hollow bags with a door at one end. Trigger hairs guide the insect prey toward the door. There are around 214 species of bladderworts worldwide, including terrestrial, epiphytic (an epiphyte is a plant that grows on the surface of another plant), and aquatic forms. Although the bladders are only a few hundredths of an inch long, they are highly effective deathtraps. The aquatic species, found in lakes, swamps, slow-moving rivers, and bog pools, trap fast-swimming water fleas (*Daphnia* spp.), protozoa, small worms, small crustaceans, and the aquatic larvae of small insects. In parts of the tropics, the plants play an important role in the control of mosquitoes by eating mosquito larvae.

Sticky traps

Some carnivorous plants catch their prey with a sticky liquid. The leaves of sundews (*Drosera* spp.) are covered with small tentacles, each tipped with a drop of shiny glutinous liquid. The liquid glistens in the sunlight, attracting small insects, which stick in it. As the victim struggles, it touches other tentacles and becomes more and more entrapped. In some sundews, the tentacles are touch-sensitive and bend toward their victim, so it is surrounded

---

CORE FACTS

- There are between 400 and 500 species of carnivorous plant, and new species are still being discovered.
- They are arranged in 17 genera and 9 families.
- They have the unique ability among plants to trap and digest animals.
- These plants are mainly found in boggy, aquatic, and other nutrient-poor habitats worldwide.
- Many species are popular in cultivation. Several species have medicinal properties, and butterworts can be used in cheese-making.

CONNECTIONS

- Parts from *Nepenthes* pitcher plants are used in **HOMEOPATHY**. The liquid from young unopened pitchers is thought to soothe skin and eye disorders, sore throats, and inflammations.

- The leaves of the butterwort are highly acidic. They are sometimes used to curdle milk to make cheese.

- The Venus flytrap captures its prey in a similar way to the steel traps used by hunters to catch animals. In these traps, the steel jaws are activated by a spring.

THE BLADDERWORT

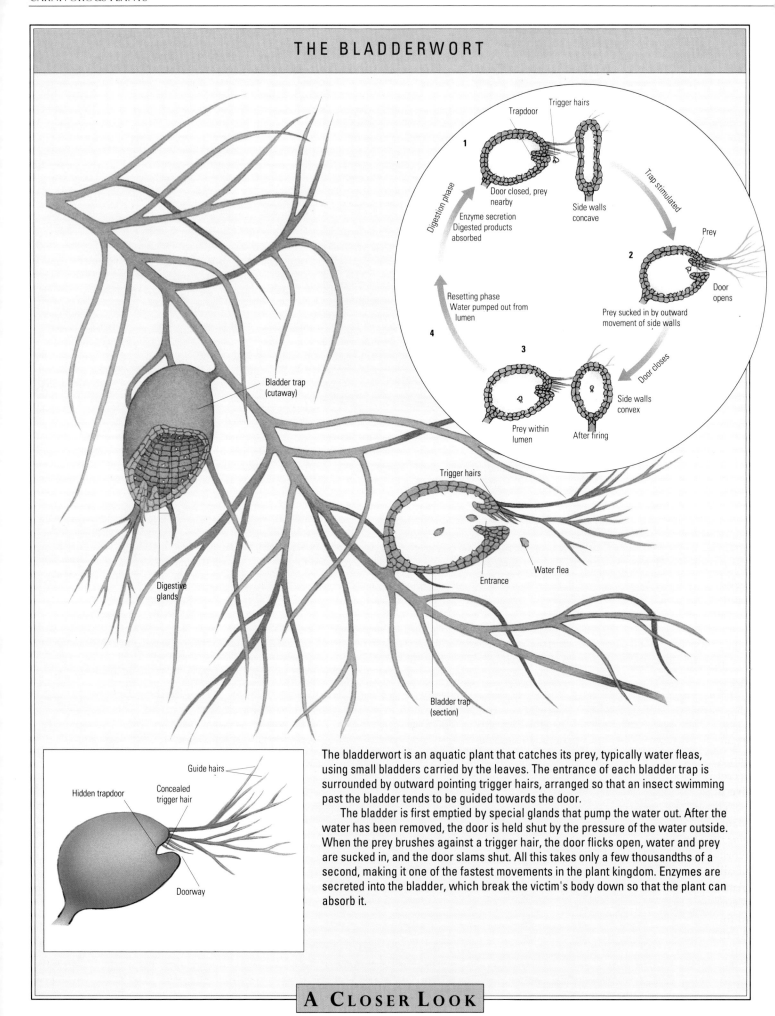

Bladder trap (cutaway)

Digestive glands

Trigger hairs

Entrance

Water flea

Bladder trap (section)

The cycle diagram:

Trapdoor

Trigger hairs

1 Door closed, prey nearby

Side walls concave

Digestion phase

Enzyme secretion Digested products absorbed

Trap stimulated

2 Prey

Door opens

Prey sucked in by outward movement of side walls

Resetting phase Water pumped out from lumen

Door closes

4

Side walls convex

3 Prey within lumen

After firing

Bottom-left diagram:

Guide hairs

Hidden trapdoor

Concealed trigger hair

Doorway

The bladderwort is an aquatic plant that catches its prey, typically water fleas, using small bladders carried by the leaves. The entrance of each bladder trap is surrounded by outward pointing trigger hairs, arranged so that an insect swimming past the bladder tends to be guided towards the door.

The bladder is first emptied by special glands that pump the water out. After the water has been removed, the door is held shut by the pressure of the water outside. When the prey brushes against a trigger hair, the door flicks open, water and prey are sucked in, and the door slams shut. All this takes only a few thousandths of a second, making it one of the fastest movements in the plant kingdom. Enzymes are secreted into the bladder, which break the victim's body down so that the plant can absorb it.

A CLOSER LOOK

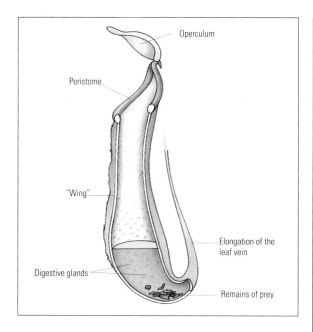

Operculum

Peristome

"Wing"

Digestive glands

Elongation of the leaf vein

Remains of prey

Pitcher plants attract their prey using bright colors and by secreting nectar. After the victim has fallen into the pitcher, downward-pointing hairs stop it from climbing out.

by many tentacles. As the insect thrashes around, glands in the tentacles secrete digestive enzymes. Digestion usually takes several days; the tentacles then straighten out, ready for the next victim. In butterworts (*Pinguicula* spp.) the leaves are covered with sticky glands. They catch insects as fly-paper catches flies.

Pitcher traps

Pitcher plants drown their victims. The leaves are shaped like a pitcher with a lid at the top and a pool of digestive fluid in the base. The pitchers are often brightly colored in reds, greens, yellows, and browns. Unsuspecting prey, mainly insects and other invertebrates, are attracted by the bright colors and by nectar secreted from around the rim of the pitcher or on the lid. Victims crawl in through the opening at the top of the trap, slide down the slippery inside wall, and are prevented from climbing out by a covering of downward-pointing hairs. They fall into the pool of liquid at the bottom of the pitcher and eventually drown. Enzymes, secreted from glands in the leaf or by bacteria that live in the liquid, digest the insect's body.

The most common North American pitcher plant is the Purple pitcher plant (*Sarracenia purpurea*), which is found on the Atlantic coast from Florida to Labrador. Among the most spectacular of all the carnivorous plants are the giant pitcher plants from tropical Asia belonging to the genus *Nepenthes*. The central vein of each leaf is extended to form a long tendril, enabling the plant to climb. At the end of the tendril most leaves develop a pitcher-shaped trap. In *Nepenthes rajah*, from Borneo, the pitchers can reach 1 ft (30 cm) in length and hold up to 0.5 gal (2 l) of water – large enough to hold a rat – and they often catch frogs and lizards.

THE VENUS FLYTRAP

The Venus flytrap is named after Venus, the Roman goddess of beauty. It was the first species of carnivorous plant to attract attention and it remains the best known carnivorous plant. It occurs naturally in sandy bogs on the coastal plains of North and South Carolina.

Each leaf has a wedge-shaped stalk ending with two hinged lobes, which form the trap. The lobes are fringed with numerous pointed teeth. The trap size varies with the age of the plant and ranges from $\frac{1}{2}$ to 1 in (1 to 3 cm) long. The plant's main prey are insects such as cockroaches, butterflies, and flies. There are three trigger hairs arranged in a triangle on the inside face of each lobe. The hairs are surrounded by a reddish area of digestive glands. Nectar cells around the edge of each lobe attract the insect prey. When an insect touches the internal trigger hairs, the trap snaps shut and the teeth become tightly interlocked. Closure takes only $\frac{1}{30}$ second, so even the quickest insects get caught. As the victim thrashes around it stimulates the lobes to squeeze tighter, and digestive juices ooze from the glands. After about a week the insect is digested and the leaf reopens, ready to trap a new victim. The lobes only squeeze together if there is prey in the trap. If a person triggers the mechanism by touching the hairs, and the trap is empty, the lobes open again after a few hours.

The trigger mechanism can "count." The trap only responds when two hairs are touched or if one hair is touched twice in quick succession. This may guard against false alarms so the plant does not waste energy by closing the trap on raindrops or specks of dirt.

A CLOSER LOOK

Relationship with humans

Carnivorous plants have become very popular in cultivation. They are grown in botanic gardens and in private collections. Unfortunately many of their natural habitats are fragile and under threat.

Carnivorous plants also have valuable medicinal properties. The juices from butterworts (*Pinguicula* spp.) are antiseptic and have been used for centuries to treat wounds. Extracts from the sundew's sticky liquid are used to treat coughs.

K. McCallum

See also: DIGESTIVE SYSTEMS; EPIPHYTES; HERBAL MEDICINE.

Further reading:
Cheers, G. *Guide to Carnivorous Plants of the World.* New York: Harper Collins, 1992.

PITCHER PLANT MOSQUITOES

Surprisingly, the larvae of some insects can survive in the pitcher fluid. The mosquito *Wyeomyia smithii* lays its eggs in the fluid of the *Sarracenia* pitchers and apparently nowhere else. The eggs hatch into larvae, which are not digested by the plant but which feed on bacteria, protists, and other organic debris inside the pitcher. These insects are found in eastern North America, ranging from Labrador in the north east, west to northern Manitoba, and south to the Gulf of Mexico. In Canada, the larvae can live through the winter frozen solid inside the pitchers of *Sarracenia purpurea*. Further south, in the United States, they are found in other pitcher plant species such as *S. flava*, *S. leucophylla*, and *S. rubra*. The larvae benefit from the arrangement by being kept safe from predators in their enclosed and protected homes.

CAROTENES AND CAROTENOIDS

Carotenes are yellow and orange pigments found in the chloroplasts of many plant cells

Carotenes are yellow and orange pigments manufactured by plants and present in flowers, leaves, roots, and stems. They were first discovered in carrots, hence the name carotene. Later, chemists discovered several hundred other yellow, orange, and red pigments in the chloroplasts and other plastids of plants, fungi, and some bacteria. These molecules, known as xanthophylls, are very similar in structure to carotenes. Collectively, carotenes and xanthophylls are classed as carotenoids, meaning "similar to carotenes."

Carotenoids absorb particular wavelengths of light in the blue-violet range (from 460 to 550 nm), and reflect light from the red end of the spectrum, so appearing red, orange, and yellow. They are responsible for the color of many flowers and also of ripening fruits such as tomatoes.

Carotenoids assist in the process of photosynthesis (see PHOTOSYNTHESIS). In fact, these pigments probably evolved to make photosynthesis more efficient. The main source of energy for photosynthesis is sunlight, which is absorbed by a green pigment called chlorophyll. This pigment absorbs light mainly from the red end of the spectrum and reflects wavelengths within the green part. As carotenoids absorb light from the blue-violet range, they can provide more light energy for the plant than it would have received from chlorophyll alone.

Only plants manufacture carotenoids, but animals and some microorganisms take the pigments into their bodies when they eat plants, or when they eat the tissues of other organisms. For example, flamingos' feathers derive their pinkness from the birds' diet of tiny, aquatic, carotenoid-containing animals.

Carotenoids and vitamin A
When humans and other animals eat carotenoids, these pigments are broken down and converted into vitamin A, also known as retinol. About half the vitamin A in the human diet comes from the carotenoids in plants.

Food manufacturers sometimes add carotenes to their products to improve their color or to fortify them with vitamin A. For example, beta carotene, or β-carotene, is added to margarine for both these reasons. It may also be added to butter, which can vary widely in carotene content, and thus in color, depending on the diet of the cows that produced the milk used to make the butter. Carotenoids are also used as colorings in such products as orange drinks, processed cheese, and snack foods. They may slightly enrich the vitamin content of these foods.

Recent population studies have shown that people who eat large amounts of certain green, yellow, and red fruits or vegetables, including carrots, sweet potatoes, melons, broccoli, spinach, red pep-

In leaves, carotenoids are usually masked by green chlorophyll. As the chlorophyll disintegrates in the fall, the carotenoids are unmasked and show through as golden and fiery red, just before the leaves fall to the ground.

CONNECTIONS

● Scientists believe that β-carotene, along with the **VITAMINS** C and E, protects against **CANCER** because it is an antioxidant, which shields the body from the effects of oxidation reactions.

● Oxidation is a chemical reaction in which an atom loses electrons, oxygen is added to a substance, or hydrogen is removed. When oxygen in the atmosphere reacts with iron, it produces a compound called rust, or iron (III) oxide (Fe_2O_3).

pers, and tomatoes, are less likely to develop lung cancer, skin cancer, and cancers of the digestive system. All these foods contain large amounts of β-carotene. β-carotene may help prevent these diseases because it is an antioxidant, a substance that protects the body from free radicals. Free radicals are atoms or molecules that contain single electrons, which easily attach to molecules in or on body cells. They can cause harmful changes in cell structure, which may lead to the development of disease. Antioxidants may also play a role in preventing heart disease, arthritis, and cataracts.

W. STEELE

See also: CANCER; PHOTOSYNTHESIS; VITAMINS.

Further reading:
Gershoff, S. and Whitney, C. *The Tufts University Guide to Total Nutrition.* New York: Harper and Row, 1990.

CAROTENEMIA

Once ingested, animals store some carotenoids in their skeleton, feathers, skin, or fatty tissue, giving it a characteristic color. In humans, an excessive intake of foods containing carotenes (especially carrots) can result in a disorder called carotenemia, in which the skin turns a dark yellow – particularly on the soles of the feet and palms of the hands. This abnormal color soon disappears if the person stops consuming the carotene-containing foods.

A CLOSER LOOK

CARTILAGE

Cartilage is a tough, flexible substance, one of the most important structural tissues in vertebrates

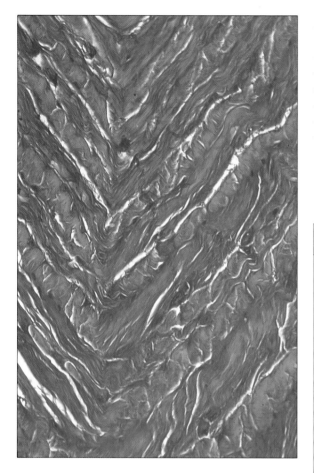

Cartilage is a connective tissue, made up of a collection of connective fibers embedded in a stiff gel-like matrix or ground substance. It has the strength and flexibility of plastic and plays an important part in the vertebrate skeleton, where one of its roles is to act as a shock absorber in the joints and the backbone. One way it does this is by compressing during activity. It then expands again during long periods of inactivity, sleep for example. This means that the spine can actually alter in length between night and day.

Cartilage forms the entire skeleton of the fetus before birth. At birth, the cartilage skeleton is flexible and strong enough to pass safely through the birth canal. In land animals, cartilage is not strong enough to support a heavy moving body. As a land animal matures, the cartilage is gradually reinforced by mineral salts. Most of it eventually turns into

Fibrocartilage is the rarest type of cartilage. It is also the densest, containing many bundles of fibers and few cells. It is found in the intervertebral disks that lie between the bones of the spine.

CONNECTIONS

● The fibrocartilage of the backbone in **VERTEBRATES** fulfills a function similar to the shock absorbers of a car, protecting the **SKELETAL SYSTEM** from damage by jolting.

● Like many plastics such as polythene, hyaline cartilage is made up of long complex chains of carbohydrates, making it extremely strong and flexible.

bone. Certain aquatic vertebrates never develop bone and retain a cartilaginous skeleton as adults. These include the Condrichthyes (sharks and rays), the Cyclostomes (lampreys and hagfish), and a few members of the Osteichthyes (bony fish). However, the cartilage in a shark's skeleton contains calcium salts. This makes it much stronger and more rigid than the cartilage found in other vertebrates.

In most adult vertebrates cartilage is still found in certain parts of the body. The outer ear (pinna) of mammals is an irregularly shaped piece of cartilage covered by skin. It acts like an antenna to pick up soundwaves. The human nose is also made of cartilage. Both the ear and nose need a definite shape as well as a certain amount of flexibility. Cartilage is also found in the joints, or articulation points, which need a smooth surface to stop the bones from wearing against each other.

Formation of cartilage

As the embryo develops, the cells that will eventually form cartilage divide in a process called mitosis. This division produces cells known as chondroblasts. The chondroblasts mature into cells called chondrocytes, which secrete a matrix, called chondrin, around themselves. The matrix is the substance in which the cartilage cells are suspended. It is mainly made up of the fibrous protein collagen and various complex glycoproteins (proteins with carbohydrates attached).

In the embryo, the cartilage continues to grow in two ways. First, the cartilage can expand from within as the chondrocytes go through a series of cell divisions. This is called interstitial growth.

CORE FACTS

■ There are three types of cartilage: hyaline, elastic, and fibrocartilage.

■ In adult vertebrates cartilage is found in the joints, the ear, and in the human nose.

■ Cartilage forms the entire skeleton in developing embryos and in some groups of fish, including sharks and rays.

FROM CARTILAGE TO BONE

Cartilage forms the basis of the vertebrate skeleton. The skeleton of the developing embryo is formed entirely from cartilage and provides the floorplan for the eventual size and shape of the bones that in adults replace cartilage. This process of bone development is known as endochondral ossification. During this process, cells from the center of the hyaline cartilage enlarge, while the material between the cells becomes compressed. Crystals of calcium are deposited on this extracellular material. A thin layer of bone is deposited around this region of cartilage, which is known as the primary center of ossification.

The interior of the slightly calcified cartilage is invaded by blood vessels that carry with them cells that will later produce red blood cells, white blood cells, platelets, and the bone-forming cells called osteoblasts.

Once the osteoblasts have been deposited, they multiply on the calcified cartilage and begin to secrete collagen fibers on which more calcium is deposited to produce spongy bone. When the bone is completely formed, all that is left of the cartilage are two narrow bands, called the epiphyseal plates, which lie between the shaft of the bone and its ends. These bands of cartilage contain cells that divide actively, allowing the bone to elongate as the animal grows. Once the bones have stopped growing, however, the epiphyseal plates also become ossified (converted to bone).

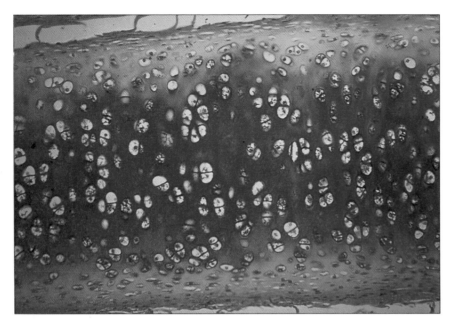

Hyaline cartilage is the commonest of the three types of cartilage. It is found on the ends of many bones, in the larynx, and where the ribs attach to the breastbone.

Second, the growth can occur on the surface of the cartilage, a process known as appositional growth. This also involves cell division, but here it consists of the production of new cells from the perichondrium, the layer of dense irregularly packed connective tissue that surrounds most types of cartilage. This form of cartilage growth can continue into adulthood, so that it grows as our bodies grow and can be repaired when damaged. However, repair is usually slow because cartilage cells receive nourishment only by diffusion from outlying blood capillaries. Damaged cartilage in a joint, for example, may take years to repair.

Types of cartilage

There are three types of cartilage: hyaline, elastic, and fibrocartilage. They are classified according to the shape and density of the fiber elements.

The most common type of cartilage is hyaline cartilage (from Latin, *hyalinus*, and Greek, *hualinos*, meaning glass). It is a tough elastic material with a translucent, glass-like appearance. The matrix of this cartilage is made of a sulfated polysaccharide (a complex carbohydrate), which is also

known as chondromucoprotein. It has the consistency of a stiffened gel. The cartilage gets its flexibility from a network of collagenous and elastic fibers within the intercellular matrix. As well as fibers, there are also scattered spaces, called lacunae, which contain cartilage cells, or chondrocytes. The chondrocytes, which have a rounded shape, produce and secrete the cartilage matrix. As they do so, they become increasingly isolated from each other. Only the very largest regions of cartilage have blood vessels, so the nutrients for the chondrocytes must diffuse through the matrix.

The outer layer of cartilage, called the perichondrium, is made up of a dense layer of connective tissue. The inner cells of the perichondrium contain chondrocytes, which continue to secrete cartilage matrix, adding to the diameter and overall size of the cartilage.

Hyaline cartilage is found in the long bones during development and remains on the articulation surfaces in the joints of the adult animal. It provides a smooth lining over the bony parts of the joint. Hyaline cartilage also makes up the flexible part of the nose, and it supports the larynx, or voice box, in the trachea. The trachea is much like a vacuum cleaner hose, with the flexible parts of the hose supported by the embedded coil. The ring-like supports for the trachea are made of hyaline cartilage. Without them the trachea would collapse when an animal breathes in.

The other two types of cartilage both develop from hyaline cartilage. Elastic cartilage is soft and rubbery. It contains many wavy elastic fibers embedded in the matrix, which give it much greater flexibility. It is found in regions where a combination of support and flexibility are needed, for example the external ear, epiglottis, the walls of the external auditory canal, and the eustachian tubes (the passages that connect the inner ear to the back of the nose).

Fibrocartilage is solid and very strong. It has many bundles of collagen fibers and fewer cells than other types of cartilage. Fibrocartilage is found in regions that need some stiffness. It makes up the shock absorbing pads of tissue that are found in joints.

The flat circular disks that lie between the individual vertebrae in the backbone of mammals are composed of fibrocartilage. They act as shock absorbers, cushioning the vertebrae during movement. No one knows more about their importance than people who have damaged their disks and now live with severe back pain.

K. HOSOUME/J. KAUFMANN

See also: BONE; CELLS; CONNECTIVE TISSUE; EARS; EMBRYO; FISH; SHARKS; SKELETAL SYSTEMS.

Further reading:
Hall, Brian and Newman, Stuart. *Cartilage: Molecular Aspects.* Boca Raton, Florida: CRC Press, 1991.

WHAT CAME FIRST — BONE OR CARTILAGE?

Scientists now think that sharks, rays, and other cartilaginous fishes, traditionally considered as more primitive than vertebrates with skeletons made of bone, are as highly evolved as their bony relatives. The "primitive" status of the cartilaginous fishes resulted from the work of Ernst Haeckel (the late 19th-century German biologist), which was based on the fact that the skeletons of all vertebrates pass through a cartilaginous phase during the early stages of development. Haeckel proposed his "recapitulation" theory in which he suggested that the stages in development seen in an embryo represented the past stages in the evolution of an organism. Today, evidence for both types of material occurring in the most primitive fishes in the Devonian Period, over 400 million years ago, suggests that cartilage and bone evolved at the same time. Some scientists believe that sharks and rays may, in fact, have evolved from more bony ancestors.

CATS

Cats are highly developed predatory mammals belonging to the order Carnivora and the family Felidae

Cats are carnivorous mammals with strong predatory instincts. In fact, there are probably no more perfect predators on Earth than cats. From mighty jungle beasts to the domestic house pet, all cats share traits that make them silent, patient hunters and efficient killing machines. Cats are members of the family Felidae, which belongs to the order Carnivora. There are 35 species, which fall into four genera.

All cats have long, sharp fangs, which they use to puncture and tear their prey; although these are called "canine teeth," they are usually better developed in cats than in dogs. Cats are master killers, able to kill their prey with one well-aimed bite. The canines of small cats act like long sharp daggers and are stabbed into a victim's neck, severing the spinal cord.

CORE FACTS

- Cats vary widely in size, from the male Siberian tiger *(Panthera tigris altaica)*, which weighs 750 lb (360 kg), to the Black-footed cat *(Felis nigripes)*, weighing just over 2 lb (1 kg).
- There are 35 species of cat in the family Felidae, which falls into the order Carnivora.
- Lions are the only big cats that live in social groups.
- It is likely that cats were first domesticated in Egypt around 5000 BC.
- *Pseudaelurus* was the first true cat. It lived in the Miocene epoch about 20 million years ago.

Each species of cat (and often even each sex within a species) will hunt a specific size of prey, and their canine teeth fit this prey exactly. The canines are exactly the right width to avoid the vertebrae of the victim and to fit into the gaps between them. This allows the cat to pry the bones apart, and sever the spinal cord. Big cats, such as lions and tigers, which feed on larger prey, usually kill their victim by a bite to the throat, once it has been brought to the ground.

The premolars in most cats, called carnassials, do not meet but rather slide past one another like the blades of a pair of scissors, and the molars are not flat on top. For these reasons, cats slice up their food, rather than chewing or grinding it. To cope with a diet consisting mainly of meat, cats have a short intestinal tract, which is designed to digest meat protein rather than vegetables.

The sense of smell

The cat's sense of smell is not as acute as that of a dog, and is less used in hunting, although cats do depend on it to recognize their environment. When it comes to food, the smell is more impor-

A tiger (Panthera tigris) *snarling – this is a typical example of a "roaring cat." In these cats, the tongue and larynx are arranged differently from the rest of the cats, which are only able to purr.*

tant than looks in telling a cat whether or not it is edible, so a cat whose nasal passages are clogged due to illness usually will not eat. Smell is also very important in communication: cats may mark their territories with urine, feces, and pungent or fatty secretions that are released from glands under the chin, along the sides of the mouth, on each side of the forehead, at the base of the tail, and along the tail itself. When a domestic cat rubs its head against your legs, or a favorite piece of furniture, it is actually scent marking.

The shape of a cat's head is related to the use of its senses. Dogs have long snouts and jaws, to make

CONNECTIONS

- Like a fast sports car, the cheetah is well adapted for speed. It has a long, light, streamlined body, and is able to accelerate up to 75 mph (121 km/h) in less than ten seconds. Its paws are also like the best designed sprint shoes, with long "anti-skid" ridges on the pads and short straight claws like spikes.

room for a highly developed nose used in hunting. However, most cats hunt in twilight, using sight and hearing far more than smell, so cats' heads have evolved to be short and fairly rounded. This shape allows cats to use sight and hearing effectively. It is not really a coincidence that the head and face of most cats are similar in shape to those of an owl, another night hunter.

Hearing and sight

Cats have an acute sense of hearing. Domestic cats can hear sounds up to a frequency of about 65 kHz (65,000 cycles per second), which allows them to hear the high-pitched squeaks made by rodents and the mews of their own kittens. (Human hearing cuts off at about 20 kHz.) A cat's ears are surrounded by moveable flaps that help to capture sound and determine its direction.

Behind the retina of a cat's eye is a reflective layer called the tapetum, which amplifies light and allows the cat to see in low light conditions. When a cat looks toward a light from a darkened area (as when looking from the forest toward a campfire), the tapetum reflects light, giving the impression that the cat's eyes glow in the dark. In poor light, a cat can see about five or six times as well as a human.

Like humans, cats have binocular vision. The eyes are forward-facing and the fields of vision of the two eyes overlap, allowing depth perception. This is useful for judging distance when leaping among branches or pouncing on prey. (In contrast, most of the animals that serve as prey, from small rodents to large herbivores like the antelope and zebra, have eyes on the sides of their heads, allowing them to watch in all directions for predators.) Cats also have a translucent covering, called the third eyelid, which they can draw over their eyes during a "cat nap," so reducing their sensory input while still remaining alert (see picture on page 263).

The cat's whiskers, growing out of the cheeks and the forehead above the eyes, are very useful in night hunting. They help the cat feel its way through thick brush in almost total darkness, without pushing branches around and making sounds that would alert wary prey. The whiskers can also be used to detect prey by sensing air currents caused by slight movements.

Cats also have additional tufts of long hair on the underside of their forelegs, just above the paws, which are attached to touch receptors in the skin. These receptors send signals to the brain whenever any of the hairs are bent, and so a cat can use them to gauge its footfall without having to look at the ground when stalking prey.

The feline body

Nearly all cats, large and small, have long, lean bodies with fairly short legs and powerful muscles. The muscles are attached in ways that give a great deal of leverage, so the cat can accelerate rapidly from a standing start and quickly reach very high running speeds, or make great leaps. The champion runner among cats is the cheetah, clocked at over 75 mph (121 km/h) in pursuit of its prey. When walking, cats walk on their toes rather than on the soles of their feet. To go a little faster, a cat trots like a horse, but at maximum speed it puts both hind legs forward and pushes off from them at almost the same time, moving in long bounds.

The bones in the cat's backbone are held together by muscles, rather than by ligaments as in most animals. This makes the backbone extremely flexible; the cat can twist in midair when leaping from one tree limb to another. The domestic cat in particular is legendary for its ability to land on its feet when falling. Slow-motion films show that the cat does this by first twisting the front end of its body parallel to the ground, then bringing the back end around to match. Cats have been known to survive falls of several stories from apartment windows with only minor injuries. It is believed that they do this by spreading their bodies out like skydivers to create the maximum air resistance and slow the fall. Obviously this is a useful talent in a creature that first evolved to hunt in the trees.

A cat can extend its claws, which causes the paw to spread, making a dangerous weapon. It can also rotate its forelegs from the shoulders, allowing them to move not only forward and back, but also sideways, in order to climb trees, encircle prey, or slash at an enemy. In all cats but cheetahs, the

A female lion (Panthera leo) *sharpening its claws on a tree trunk and clearly displaying the powerful, flexible body possessed by most cats.*

long curved claws are retracted when not in use for fighting or climbing. Retracting their claws allows cats to move silently on padded paws.

Most cats hunt by stalking, quietly moving as close to their prey as possible before the final charge or pounce. A cat can remain motionless for long periods of time, waiting for its prey to come closer. Some cats hunt in the trees, and almost all cats climb, although lions seldom climb above the low branches.

The tail is used for balance in the trees and for communication. Among lions it may serve to help members of a group locate each other, so it may be no accident that the lion's tail has a highly visible tuft on the end. However, lions are the only wild breed with a tuft. They are also the only social cat, living and hunting in groups of up to about two dozen animals, called prides. By contrast, other cats are solitary hunters.

Cats and civilization

Sometime in prehistory, when human beings invented agriculture and began to live in villages, small cats probably began their relationship with human civilization. The large central food storage of the village would attract hordes of small rodents, and cats would find this gathering of prey irresistible. The villagers would quickly see that the cats were useful, and would encourage them to stay. Perhaps part of that encouragement would include a scratch behind the ears, and the cats that responded most warmly would be accepted as friends as well as business partners. Natural selection bred a smaller, friendlier cat.

Scientists think that this happened around 5000 BC in Egypt. (For comparison, the dog was probably domesticated around 12,000 BC.) The cat first

A Snow leopard (Panthera uncia)*, showing the third eyelid, characteristic of all cats, in the inside corners of its eyes.*

appears in recorded history in the records of ancient Egypt from around 1500 BC.

Exactly how domestic cats spread around the world is not known, but it is likely that soldiers, explorers, and especially sailors carried them on their travels. Wherever they went, domestic cats probably interbred with their wild relatives, producing a wide range of sizes, shapes, and colors. However, many of the so-called breeds of cat we now know have been produced by deliberate breeding, especially by breeders in England in the late 19th century.

In the latter half of the 20th century the domestic cat has become the most popular pet in the United States, pulling ahead of the dog for the first time. This is probably because a greater proportion of the population now lives in large cities, where living space is limited. Wild cats, however, are less fortunate, as civilization cuts into their habitats.

THE DIFFERENT KINDS OF CATS

Below the level of the family Felidae, there is considerable debate between scientists as to how cats should be classified. Generally four genera are recognized: *Panthera* (the big cats), *Felis* (the small cats), *Neofelis* (the Clouded Leopard), and *Acinonyx* (the cheetah).

Panthera: This genus contains five species: the lion (*Panthera leo*), found mainly in Africa from south of the Sahara to South Africa, with a small

ENDANGERED CATS

Most of the great cats and many smaller wild cats are in danger of extinction. Their numbers have been greatly reduced by hunting, by the demand for their furs, and by the destruction of their habitats as human civilization expands.

In the United States, the Eastern cougar *(Felis concolor cougar)*, the ocelot *(F. pardalis)*, and the Florida panther *(F.c. coryi)* were placed on the endangered species list in 1993. The Florida panther, actually one of about eight subspecies of the American cougar, may be in most danger. Once living throughout Florida, Arkansas, Louisiana, and South Carolina, it is now found only in a small swampy area of southern Florida less than 100 miles square. Some of this area is in protected wildlife refuges, but much more is private land, which could be opened to commercial development in the future. Only about 50 Florida panthers remain, and inbreeding has led to infertility and birth defects. A computer model predicts that the species could die out in 20 to 25 years.

The U.S. Fish and Wildlife Service has begun a captive breeding program, in which kittens are captured in the wild and raised and bred in zoos. The program is controversial: some conservationists say that removing animals from the wild reduces the chance for the wild population to recover. The Fish and Wildlife Service believes that half the kittens born in the wild die anyway, and that removing some of them gives the rest a better chance to survive. There are many such programs in zoos throughout the world. In the United States, members of the American Zoo and Aquarium Association are conducting a series of Species Survival Plans, covering the Asiatic lion, three subspecies of tiger, and the Snow leopard, among others

Worldwide, the endangered species list also includes the Mexican bobcat *(Felis rufus)* and the cheetah *(Acinonyx jubatus)*. Efforts to save most endangered species concentrate on protecting their habitats and preventing illegal hunting.

AT RISK

population in northwest India; the tiger (*P. tigris*), found in India, Manchuria, China, and Indonesia; the leopard (*P. pardus*), found mainly in South Asia and Africa south of the Sahara, with a few scattered populations in north Africa, Arabia, and the Far East; the jaguar (*P. onca*), found in Central and South America; and the Snow leopard (*P. uncia*), found in the mountainous regions of Central Asia.

Of these, the Asiatic lion (*P.l. persica*), the tiger, and the Snow leopard are endangered throughout their range, the leopard is endangered in some parts of its range and threatened in others, and the jaguar is endangered in regions south of Mexico.

The most important difference between the genus *Panthera* and the other groups of cats is the arrangement of the tongue and larynx, which allows the *Panthera* to roar but not purr. For this reason, the *Panthera* are sometimes referred to as the "roaring cats." Another difference is that the pupils of the eyes of all *Panthera* are round, while those of almost all other cats contract to vertical slits in bright light.

Felis: This genus contains around twenty eight species, including the lynx (*Felis lynx*) found throughout western Europe to Siberia, Spain and Portugal, Alaska, Canada, and the northern United States; the bobcat (*F. rufus*), found from southern Canada down to southern Mexico; the puma or cougar (*F. concolor*), found in eastern North America and from southern Canada down to Patagonia; and the ocelot (*F. pardalis*), found from Arizona down to northern Argentina. This genus also contains the wildcat (*F. silvestris*), of which the domestic cat (*F.s. catus*) is a subspecies. Of the species in this genus, around 16 are threatened. These include the Asiatic golden cat (*F. temminicki*), the Little spotted cat (*F. tigrina*), the Marbled cat (*F. marmorata*), and the Flat-headed cat (*F. planiceps*).

Neofelis: This species contains only one species, the Clouded leopard (*Neofelis nebulosa*), which is found in much of Southeast Asia. It is endangered

CAT EVOLUTION

The first true cat, *Pseudaelurus*, is known from the Miocene epoch about 20 million years ago. *Pseudaelurus* was the ancestor of both the modern cats and the saber-toothed cats, which were dominant around five to six million years ago, only becoming extinct about 9000 years ago.

The most famous saber-toothed cat was *Smilodon*, which was about the size of a lion and lived in North America two million years ago. *Smilodon* had massively enlarged canine teeth (up to 7 in or 18 cm long) known as sabers. It was first thought that *Smilodon* used these teeth in the same way as modern cats do, plunging them into the neck of their prey. However, biologists have discovered that, in fact, the sabers would not have been strong enough to do this and would have shattered on impact. It is more likely that the prey was attacked from below, the sabers biting into the soft tissues of the throat or belly. The creature would have been aided in this action by its enormously wide gape: it could open its jaw to a gape of 90 degrees compared with 70 degrees in modern cats.

The oldest surviving cat lineage is that of the ocelots, which branched off 12 million years ago. The wildcats were the next to appear, about two million years later. Today's domestic cat may be descended mainly from *Felis libyca*, the African wildcat, and also from *F. silvestris*, the European wildcat. Domestic cats and these wildcats really belong to the same species, and can interbreed. However, cats that live in civilization have been bred over thousands of years to be smaller and friendlier.

The larger modern cats are a much more recent development, with the cheetah branching off 2.5 million years ago, and the jaguar, leopard, and Snow leopard branching off around 10,000 years ago. Lion-like cats emerged 1.8 million years ago, and the true lions 600,000 years ago in the form of a species called *Panthera atrox*.

EVOLUTION

There are over a hundred breeds of domestic cat. The gene that codes for coat color in Siamese cats (like those below) is controlled by temperature: warmth produces a light coat and cold produces a darker coat. This is why the extremities – the ears, tail, legs, and face – are darker than the rest of the body.

throughout its entire range. This cat has characteristics in common with the big cats and the small cats, without belonging completely to either genus. Like the other big cats, it is large and heavily built and rests by lying with its forelegs outstretched and its tail straight behind (small cats tuck their forepaws beneath their bodies and wrap their tails around them). However, like the small cats, the Clouded leopard lacks a hyoid bone in its vocal apparatus. It can purr but is unable to roar.

Acinonyx: This genus also contains only one species, the endangered cheetah (*Acinonyx jubatus*), found in much of Africa, the Middle East, and parts of South Asia. This cat is the fastest animal on land, and the only cat whose claws are not completely retractable.

W. STEELE

See also: ANIMAL KINGDOM; CARNIVORES; DOMESTICATION; MAMMALS; PREDATION.

Further reading:

Kitchener, A. *The Natural History of the Wild Cats*. New York: Comstock Publishing Associates, 1991.
Macdonald, David. *The Velvet Claw*. New York: Parkwest Publications, 1993.
Morris, Desmond. *Catwatching* (1987) and *Catlore* (1988). New York: Crown Publishing.
Simon, Seymour. *Big Cats*. New York: HarperCollins, 1991.

CAVE HABITATS

A cave is a habitat with low levels of light and relatively constant environmental conditions

Caves are naturally-formed cavities that exist below the surface of the Earth, often extending under the ground as interconnected spaces. They vary from enormous "people-sized" caverns to tiny tunnels less than $1/25$ in (1 mm) in diameter. Caves are habitats for a variety of species that have adapted to the challenges of life underground. These unique cave-dwelling species show marked differences from their surface relatives. Collectively called troglodytes or cavernicoles, cave-dwelling organisms have been studied with great interest by many biologists. Their adaptations to the cave habitat give clear evidence of evolutionary pressures and processes experienced, often in less obvious forms, by all organisms.

CORE FACTS

- Cave habitats have relatively constant environmental conditions.
- Caves can be classified as microcavernous, mesocavernous, and macrocavernous, depending on the size of their inhabitants.
- The largest known cave is the 150-mile (240-km) system of the Mammoth Cave in Kentucky.
- Many cave inhabitants have adaptations to darkness.

The cave habitat

Compared to habitats above ground, the cave habitat is relatively simple. The physical factors that influence and define habitats, such as light, temperature, and water, vary greatly on the surface with the time of day and the season. Inside a cave, conditions are far more stable. There is little variation in light, temperature, and moisture from day to day or from season to season, although variations in environmental conditions are found among different caves.

An important common characteristic is that, with the exception of areas near their openings, caves are essentially devoid of light. Organisms that live in caves must therefore survive in total darkness. Green plants, which rely on sunlight to carry out photosynthesis, cannot grow in caves. Consequently, many cave ecosystems employ other organisms to supply energy for the base of their food chains. These include bacteria that produce energy by the process of chemosynthesis. In this process, the bacteria break down chemicals, such as hydrogen sulfide, to produce energy that they then use to make carbohydrates. These bacteria rely on the introduction of organic material, often from outside the cave, to supply hydrogen sulfide. Other cave-dwelling organisms also need organic material from outside the cave as a source of nutrients. Fungi can grow in the dark, feeding on seeds and

The Greater horseshoe bat (Rhinolophus ferrumequinum) is one of many cave-dwelling bat species.

CONNECTIONS

- The science of caves is called speleology. Basic work consists of recording physical, biological, and archaeological data about caves.

- Most caves form in limestone rock as the result of a chemical reaction. **CARBON DIOXIDE** from the air dissolves in rainwater to form a weak acid, carbonic acid. Over thousands of years, as the rainwater seeps into the earth, the acid dissolves the limestone.

branches brought into the cave from outside, and in turn provide food for other cave inhabitants.

Organic materials enter caves in several ways. Decaying plant and animal materials can flow into the cave through streams or rivers or be washed down through vertical shafts in the cave roof. Water that percolates through the rock itself also carries organic material into caves. Animals may leave behind feces, a concentrated source of organic material. In North America, cave crickets of the family Rhaphidophoridae provide the major source of organic material for the cave community. At night, these insects feed on plant materials ouside the cave. They return to the cave by day and defecate, providing a rich supply of organic material. Organic material can also enter caves in more unusual ways. In some Hawaiian caves, the tree roots that grow into caves form a path for percolating water carrying organic material. Regardless of the source, the amount of organic material is relatively small compared with that available in other ecosystems. This scarcity limits the number of cave inhabitants.

Temperature and water

The cave environment maintains a fairly constant temperature, lacking the extremes of the surface. The temperature deep inside a cave is generally the average annual temperature of the region.

CAVE PAINTINGS

The earliest examples of human art are cave paintings from the Pleistocene epoch (35,000 years ago). Most of the paintings are of wild animals, especially those that our early ancestors hunted for food. These include reindeer, bison, wild horses, and mammoths.

The painters were probably trying to produce some sort of magical control over the animals: by painting them, they gained power over them, and could catch and kill them more easily. The paintings may also be an attempt to increase the animals' fertility, so that more were available for the early humans to hunt. The cave painters used charcoal for the outline of the figures, and a mixture of vegetable dyes, burnt bone, and metal oxides to fill them in.

In the most remote regions of a cave, the temperature hardly varies at all. For example, in the Flint Ridge Mammoth Cave system in Kentucky, air temperature varies between 56.5°F and 57°F (13.6°C and 13.9°C) during the course of a year, while on the surface, temperatures may vary from as low as 11°F (-14°C) in winter, to over 95°F (35°C) in summer.

The degree to which temperature varies is dependent on the distance from the mouth of the cave. In the Sainte-Catherine cave in Ariege, France, seasonal temperatures can vary from almost 35.6°F to 55.4°F (2°C to 13°C) approximately 66 ft (20 m) into the cave, but at over 475 ft (145 m) inside the cave, temperatures remain at a constant 50.9°F (10.5°C).

This constancy of temperature may seem an optimal condition for life, but in many caves temperatures are low, rarely exceeding 50°F to 53.6°F (10°C to 12°C). For cold-blooded species, including amphibians, fish, and many invertebrates, this means a lowered metabolism and reduced levels of activity.

The amount of cave water also tends to be constant compared with that on the surface, although water levels vary far more between caves than either light or temperature do. Some caves are

This cave fish is blind. Many cave species have adapted to the darkness by losing their sight.

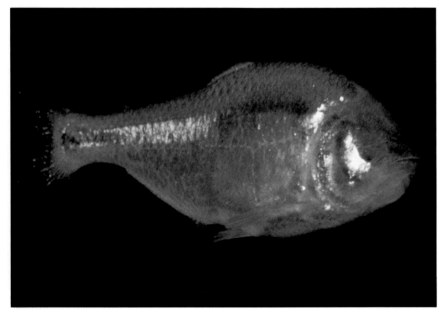

under water at all times. Others experience periodic inundation from heavy rainfall, changes in the water table, or changes in the tides where the cave is located in a rocky coastline. Even exclusively terrestrial caves may have air that is completely saturated with water. For this reason, many cave-dwelling animals have particular adaptations to help them cope with excess water.

Not all caves are damp. In a cave that has more than one opening and is sufficiently exposed to wind from the surface, warmer dry air may move through the cave passageways and reduce the moisture content of the cave's air. This can be potentially lethal to cave species adapted to the more typically moist cave conditions. The general pattern is that, the more variable the water pattern, the lower the diversity and abundance of the organisms that live in the cave. However, open dry caves are accessible to vertebrates as a daily refuge and support a variety of birds, bats, and other small mammals. This type of cave user rarely shows any of the special adaptations to cave dwelling.

Cave sizes

The size of the cave determines the size of the cave dweller. The entomologist Frank Howarth, working with the fauna of Hawaiian caves, proposed a size-based classification system for caves based on the size of different kinds of cave fauna.

The smallest caves, termed microcavernous, have a diameter of less than $\frac{1}{25}$ in (1 mm). The inhabitants include thin bodied invertebrates, such as specialized nematodes (roundworms) and rotifers (microscopic worms).

The second category, known as mesocavernous caves, have a diameter from $\frac{1}{25}$ to 8 in (1 to 200 mm). These miniature caves represent a much more common subterranean habitat than the larger, more familiar caves and caverns. The inhabitants include amphibians, and a wide range of invertebrates, such as insects and crustaceans.

Macrocavernous caves are larger than 8 in (200 mm) in diameter and include the typical "people-sized" cave. The inhabitants of these large caves depend on whether a cave is dry, wet, or filled with water. Dry caves will attract creatures such as bats, while the wet Hawiian caves, with almost 100 percent humidity, are home to an endemic cricket of the genus *Thaumatogyllus*. Wet caves will be inhabited by cave fish and invertebrates, including the Kentucky cave shrimp (*Palaemonias ganteri*).

More is known about larger caves simply because they are accessible to human investigators, although tiny caverns can now be explored with miniaturized cameras and fiber optics.

Adaptations to cave life

The most striking characteristic shared by many cave-dwelling organisms involves adaptation of the sensory apparatus. These sensory structures help cave dwellers assess their immediate surroundings when light is limited or absent. The general evolutionary pattern in the adaptation to darkness involves an increase in the size or density of sensory organs that respond to stimuli other than light. This is sometimes accompanied by a degeneration of the eyes (which are not particularly useful in the dark), which has evolved from a regression of all or some parts of the optical system, depending on the type of animal.

A classic example of the modification of sensory organs of cave-dwelling species involves crayfish of the genus *Orconectes*. The antennae of the cave-dwelling form are twice the length of those of its close relative living on the surface. The cave dweller's antennae also possess more chemoreceptors (receptors which respond to chemical aspects of the environment). The antennae provide tactile information about the animal's surroundings, while the chemoreceptors help to locate food.

Cave fish

Cave fish also show an interesting range of sensory compensation as adaptations to the cave environment. The family Amblyopsidae contains four genera, which include swamp and spring dwellers, part-time cave dwellers, and an obligate cave-dwelling species (meaning it can live nowhere else). The variation in habitat allows scientists to observe adaptive trends in this group of related fish. These include adaptations in the structure of the brain. In Amblyopsidae, the optic lobe, which is associated with vision, is smaller in cave forms. However, the cave-dwelling species show an increase in the size of those portions of the brain associated with obstacle avoidance and spatial memory. (Spatial memory enables an animal to recall physical features and dimensions in its immediate surroundings.)

The most striking adaptive trend of fish toward the cave-dwelling form involves the hypertrophy, or enlargement, of the lateral line system. The lateral line system consists of arrays of special sensory cells on the surface of the fish, which are stimulated by turbulence in the water. In the cave-dwelling forms, the lateral line system is far more developed than it is in those fish living on the surface. Tests have shown that fish with an enhanced lateral line system are better able to detect food when there is little or no light.

Other adaptations

Some cave-dwelling animals show a loss in skin pigment. Cave fish and salamanders lack almost all their skin pigment and have a white porcelain-like appearance. The loss of pigments is probably an adaptation to low light levels. The production of pigments requires large amounts of energy. For cave-dwelling species, such an energy use would be a waste, since the pigments would be impossible to detect in the cave environment. Therefore cave-dwelling fish and salamanders conserve the limited food energy by cutting out pigment production.

Insects that live in caves have particular adapta-

tions to help them survive in this very humid environment. Insects take in oxygen through holes, called spiracles, in their outer body covering, or cuticle. Water, in the form of water vapor, can also enter the cuticle through these spiracles, upsetting the chemical balance in the insect's blood. To avoid this problem, cave-dwelling insects have developed a cuticle that allows water to be emitted more easily. However, a more water-permeable cuticle has the dangerous potential for causing the insect to become dehydrated if it enters a dry area. Some cave beetles have sensory structures on their antennae that can detect slight variations in humidity, permitting the insect to avoid drier areas. Similar adaptations are seen in other cave-dwelling arthropods.

A number of cave-dwelling organisms display an interesting phenomenon called paedomorphosis. In paedomorphosis, juvenile characteristics are retained in the sexually mature adult. Cave-dwelling salamanders (all members of the lungless family of salamanders, Plethodontidae) maintain many larval characteristics, such as external gills, even after sexual maturity. This may be an adaptation to the scarce food supply in the cave environment. With paedomorphosis, the cave salamander develops its necessary sexual organs without expending energy to develop other less essential adult characteristics.

The skin of the cave salamander (Proteus anguinus) *has lost almost all its pigment, giving the animal a white, pasty appearance. The head lacks eyes and so the salamander is totally blind.*

CAVES AS A NATURAL MUSEUM

The cool dry environment of some deeper caves, and the relatively small number of decomposers and scavengers compared to the surface, results in a very slow rate of decay of organic material in caves. Occasionally, prehistoric animal remains are found in these caves, preserved largely intact for many thousands of years. Species of cave bear, giant sloth, and small rodent have been found, along with their feces, preserved by a natural process of mummification. Scientists believe that these extinct species either used the caves for shelter, or they may have been dragged inside by predators.

A large number of cave-dwelling species do not show adaptations of any kind, and yet they too are strictly cave dwellers. In many species of arthropods, the cave-dwelling forms lack any obvious modification of their antennae or other sensory structures, and maintain the surface pigmentation. For example, the Ground beetle *Trechus micros*, found in Britain, is neither eyeless nor endowed with special long legs or antennae, yet it only lives in caves. As is usually the case, there are often as many exceptions to the rule as those on which the rule is based!

The occasional cave visitor

A large number of organisms use caves during some part of their life. A number of invertebrates take advantage of the protected environment at the cave entrance. The cave opening provides abundant organic material, as well as the moist and temperate conditions preferred by invertebrates for growth and reproduction. The cooler, more protected environment of the cave is also used by insects when they enter diapause (a state similar to hibernation). In Britain, Tissue moths (*Triphosa dubitata*) and Herald moths (*Scoliopteryx libatrix*) are often found at the mouth of caves. The Herald moths move deeper into caves when they are ready to go into deep diapause. Tissue moths prefer the areas closer to the cave opening where they can quickly become awakened.

The cave openings and the areas near the entrances of caves are also used by vertebrates. They provide sites that are sheltered from the weather and are inaccessible to predators. Several species of birds, such as swifts and swallows, nest in cave openings.

Bat colonies

The bat is the vertebrate most associated with cave life. Of the 1000 species of bats in the world, a large proportion are cave-roosting. Some of the most spectacular bat caves occur in New Mexico. Several million Mexican free-tail bats (*Tadarida brasiliensis*) roost in one cave alone. Every evening in the warmer months, this huge bat colony leaves the cave to forage on flying insects such as mosquitoes. This one cave of bats can consume thousands of kilograms of flying insects every night.

Bats rely on the cave for security during the daytime when they are not feeding and during the long winter months when many species hibernate. In the cool recesses of the cave the bat's body temperature can drop to levels close to the temperature of the immediate surroundings, thereby reducing the bat's metabolism and its need for food. It is critical that the cave temperature remains constant during this time, as the bat stores just enough nutrients in its tissues to survive the winter months. Fluctuations in the cave's temperature could result in the bat awakening periodically, which uses up energy. Then the bat might starve in its sleep before the end of the winter.

Bats are well adapted for cave life. They have a highly developed echolocation system to assist in their navigation in the caves (see BATS). Although the eyes are small, the bat, unlike other cave-dwelling species, has reasonably good vision.

The community of cave dwellers

A more simplified set of ecological interactions are at work in the cave than on the surface, partly due to the smaller number of species and the limited resources found in caves. Parasitism is extensive in cave organisms (see PARASITISM). Bats harbor a range of parasites, including wingless bloodsucking flies of the family Nycteribiidae, as well as fleas, ticks, and mites. Some fungi are parasitic on cave-living invertebrates. For example, the fungus *Hirsutella dipterigina* lives on the fly *Heleomyza serrata*, producing a forest of antler-like fruiting bodies.

Many predators live in caves, including omnivorous snails, such as *Oxychilus cellarius* from Europe, which secretes enzymes that allow it to digest the exoskeletons of insects. Although these snails mainly scavenge on dead insects on the cave floor, they are sometimes known to attack living insects, especially moths. Other predators include the larvae of a cave-living fungus gnat from New Zealand (*Arachnocampa luminosa*). These predatory larvae are known as glowworms. They live in groups on cave walls, surrounded by hanging sticky threads. The larvae are luminous and so attract small flying insects, which become trapped in the sticky threads and are promptly eaten.

K. HOSOUME/J. KAUFMANN

See also: ADAPTATION; BIOMES AND HABITATS; VISION.

Further reading:

Chapman, Philip. *Caves and Cave Life*. New York: HarperCollins, 1993.

Southeast Asian birds called Cave swiftlets (Collocalia spp.) show many adaptations for cave life. They have large whiskers around their beaks and large eyes to detect objects in the darkness of the cave. They also use echolocation to navigate in the dark. Cave swiftlets make nests out of saliva and stick them to the roof or walls of the cave, where they are safe from natural predators. These nests are used to make a Chinese delicacy known as bird's-nest soup.

CELLS

Cells are the basic structural and functional units of all living organisms

Just as it may be difficult for us to grasp the enormity of the universe, so the infinitesimal smallness of the cell and its structures challenges our understanding. The basic cell is the building block of all living things. Most cells are too small to be seen with the naked eye. Even the largest of human cells, the ovum, or egg, is barely the size of the period at the end of this sentence. Many cells are too small even to be seen under a light microscope, and the structures within them are tinier still – submicroscopic. So, it is hardly surprising that the cell did not feature in the observations of early biologists, who believed that living things arose by "spontaneous generation," suddenly developing from dead or decomposing matter.

It was only in late 17th-century Europe, with the use of the newly invented light microscope, that cells first came into view. Pioneers in cell biology include two Dutchmen: Jan Swammerdam, a physician and tireless microscopist who, in 1658, became the first person to see a red blood cell; and Anton van Leeuwenhoek, the Delft draper and part-time microscopist who ground his own lenses and reported his observations directly to the Royal Society in London. Then, in the early 1660s, the

CORE FACTS

- Cells vary widely in size: the smallest bacteria measure 0.2 μm across, and the nerve cells of a giraffe may be a yard in length.
- Modern cell theory states that: a) cells are the building blocks of all life; b) all organisms consist of one or more cells; and c) all cells are derived from preexisting cells.
- There are two basic types of cells: eukaryotes and prokaryotes. Eukaryotic cells contain a true membrane-encircled nucleus and membrane-bound organelles; prokaryotic cells have no nucleus or organelles. They posses a single circular strand of DNA.
- Plant, fungal, and prokaryotic cells all posses a cell wall. Animal cells have no cell wall.
- Endocytosis is the process by which molecules enter a cell; exocytosis is the process by which materials leave a cell.
- Every cell has a plasma membrane, which contains the cell components and controls the movement of ions and molecules in and out of the cell.
- Cells first appeared on Earth over 3 billion years ago.
- Mitosis results in two genetically identical diploid daughter cells; meiosis results in four genetically distinct haploid daughter cells, or gametes.

CONNECTIONS

- Cells are essential to life, because they are responsible for the structure and functioning of organisms at the most basic level. As Alfred North Whitehead stated in 1925, "The living cell is to biology what the electron and the proton are to physics."

- The cell is like a tiny chemical processing plant. There is constant activity, with raw materials being moved in and processed through many chemical reactions. New products are packaged and moved to other parts of the cell or transported out through the plasma membrane. The study of these processes is known as **BIOCHEMISTRY.**

- Cells can be isolated from individual tissues of animals and plants, and grown as single cells in the laboratory. These cell cultures have many applications. They might be used in **MICROBIOLOGY** to study the effects of **VIRUSES** on cells. In **CANCER** research they might be used to study the effects of carcinogens on **DNA.**

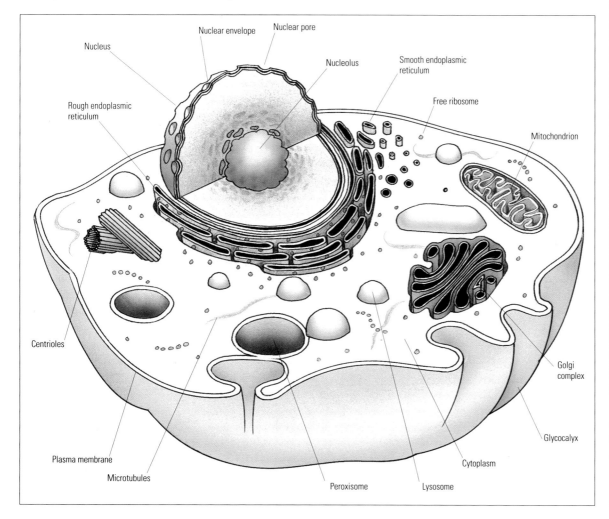

A typical animal cell. The tiny internal structures, or organelles, shown here were first observed in 1932 with the invention of the electron microscope.

Nuclear envelope
Nuclear pore
Nucleus
Nucleolus
Smooth endoplasmic reticulum
Rough endoplasmic reticulum
Free ribosome
Mitochondrion
Centrioles
Golgi complex
Plasma membrane
Glycocalyx
Microtubules
Cytoplasm
Peroxisome
Lysosome

CELL DIFFERENTIATION

Most animals derive from a single cell that divides many times, its daughter cells undergoing progressive changes, or differentiation, as the organism develops. Throughout the process of differentiation, the cells of the embryo take on specialized structures and functions and join with similar cells to form tissues and organs. This is possible because groups of genes express themselves at different stages of development, while others become "switched off" to block further activity (see GENETICS). Genes may be able to signal to other genes to direct cell groups along a particular line of development. In mature organisms, cells may grow, replace themselves, and die, but their specialized traits remain unchanged. Even when they are taken from their normal surroundings, and cultured in a laboratory, they "remember" what kinds of cell they are.

As techniques for analyzing cell structure and function have become more sophisticated, scientists have been able to distinguish many types of cells: for example, ten different human lymphocytes (white blood cells). Cells are classified according to where they are found and what they do. Most organs contain many different tissues – sheets of cells specialized to perform particular functions.

Epithelial cells form tissues lining the internal or external surfaces of many organs, ranging from the lumen (the hollow center) of the intestine and the synovial cavity surrounding joints, to the hair follicles, skin, and the cornea of the eye. Some secrete substances – tears, mucus, tooth enamel, hydrochloric acid – while others, in the intestines and kidneys, are absorptive. Even in a simple invertebrate, such as the hydra (see JELLYFISH, SEA ANEMONES, AND HYDRAS), there are secretory and digestive epithelial cells inside the body cavity, and stinging, sensory, interstitial (connecting), and muscle-like epithelial cells on the outside.

Examples of other vertebrate cell types include neurons (nerve cells), oligodendrocytes (insulating cells), and glial (network) cells in the nervous system. The supporting structure and framework of the body depends on fibroblasts, which secrete the extracellular matrix, osteoblasts which make bone, and chondrocytes, which produce cartilage. Contractile cells make up six different skeletal muscle cell types, various smooth muscles (in arteries, and digestive and urinary tracts), synchronized cardiac muscles that make the heart beat, and muscles that control the iris and exocrine gland secretion. Sensory cells make up the structures in the sense organs – hair cells in the ears, taste buds, olfactory support cells in the nose, and rod cells in the retina.

Not all cells are completely differentiated, even in a mature organism. Some tissues, especially where there is a rapid turnover of cells, retain "embryonic" stem cells. These are capable of reproducing prolifically, continuously yielding a large number of precursor cells, as well as replacing themselves. The most common stem cells are found in the bone marrow, with others involved in the production of skin cells and sperm. Most cells, regardless of speciality or function, have a natural life span, which varies from a few days in the case of blood cells, to 70 years or more for cells in the lens of the eye.

A CLOSER LOOK

English scientist Robert Hooke, one of the founders of the Royal Society, appropriated the word cells (from the Latin, meaning "small rooms") to describe the tiny box-like chambers he observed in a piece of cork. Other microscopists continued to record their observations, but noone had yet questioned the status of the cell in the basic life processes.

The cell theory

More than a century and a half was to pass before another group of investigators, by now armed with more powerful microscopes, began piecing together what is now known as cell theory. Outstanding figures in German scientific circles of the early 19th century were the lawyer-turned-botanist Matthias Schleiden, and the anatomist Theodor Schwann.

In 1838, Schleiden announced his findings that all vegetable matter is made up of cells, the first time this possibility had been spelled out. Inspired by Schleiden, Schwann took the concept farther, insisting that the cell is the basic structural unit of all living matter, animals as well as plants. According to Schwann, "cells are organisms, and entire animals and plants are aggregates of these organisms arranged according to definite rules."

By the mid-19th century, the first two points of the modern cell theory were in place. These are: a) that the cell is the building block of all life forms; and b) that all organisms, whether plants or animals, consist of one or more cells. Finally, in 1855, another German scientist, Rudolf Virchow, revered as the father of cellular pathology, contributed the third point. Virchow concluded that all cells derive from division of preexisting cells, never by the aggregation of cell parts.

At the time that Schleiden, Schwann, and their contemporaries were laying the foundations of modern cell biology, the best lenses available enabled microscopists to distinguish structures only one micrometer apart. Since most internal cell structures measure 1-10 μm, the cell's working parts remained mostly unexplored until the invention of the electron microscope in 1932.

At its simplest, a typical cell is a minute capsule existing either independently or, in multicellular organisms, alongside other cells. Cells are defined by plasma membranes made of proteins and lipids. They are filled with a fluid called cytoplasm and with organelles (meaning "little organs"), which perform specific functions for the cell. Cells come in a remarkable range of shapes; they can be spherical, like the ovum or egg, hexagonal, like those in the liver, rectangular like those lining the intestine, or flattened, like those lining the blood vessels.

Different cells vary enormously in size, from the smallest bacteria measuring 0.2 μm across to the yard-long nerve cells of the giraffe. The total volume of the cell depends on the surface available for the intake of nutrients and excretion of waste products. Some specialist cells, such as those lining the small intestine, have a vastly increased surface area due to finger-like projections called microvilli, which protrude into the hollow center of the organ.

Prokaryotes and eukaryotes

Organisms can be placed in two broad groups on the basis of their cell structure. The prokaryotes, cells with no defined nucleus, comprise bacteria and cyanobacteria (blue-green algae). The eukaryotes, literally meaning "true nucleus," comprise all other life forms, including animals, plants, fungi, and protozoa. The main distinction between the two is that the much larger cells of eukaryotic organisms have a true, membrane-encircled nucleus, whereas the more primitive prokaryotic cells do not.

A distinctive feature of eukaryotic organisms is their internal membranes, which compartmentalize the specific processes occurring in the organelles –

the cell's specialized working parts. Each organelle has its own membrane, similar in structure to others in the cell, but with an individual chemical composition and associated enzymes. Eukaryotic cells also have the ability to exchange materials between these membrane-enclosed compartments and the exterior of the cell. The two cell types also differ in the amount and distribution of their DNA. Prokaryotic DNA is a circular molecule while eukaryotic cells contain dramatically more genetic material packaged into the nucleus.

Plasma membranes

Every cell has a plasma membrane, which is a complex living structure that both encloses the cell to maintain its structure and shape, and allows it to interact with its environment in a controlled fashion. Insoluble in water, the plasma membrane is also selectively permeable so that only certain substances are able to pass through when required. The permeability can be altered to regulate this exchange across the membrane, a capacity that is essential for efficient cell functioning.

An important function of the plasma membrane is communication. Receptors on the extracellular (outside) surface receive chemical messages from distant and adjacent cells and from the surrounding extracellular space. The plasma membrane also provides anchorage for the cytoskeleton, the web-like structure that acts as the cell's "scaffolding."

All membranes have the same basic structure — with variations between prokaryotes and eukaryotes. Under an electron microscope, a membrane looks like a sandwich, with two dark outer layers and a light "filling." What we see is a two-tiered structure made up of phospholipids, fat molecules with a phosphate group at one end. When these phospholipids come together in water, they form a bilayer, with the hydrophilic (water-loving) "heads" in each layer facing outward into the watery fluid. The hydrophobic (water-hating) "tails" face each other in the interior of the membrane. The lipid molecules move independently of each other, as if the bilayer were a fluid. Interspersed among the lipids in the membrane are proteins. Some of these proteins are integral, spanning the bilayer, while some are found on one surface only, usually inside the cell. Those with carbohydrate chains attached are known as glycoproteins. Some proteins are involved in transport, moving substances across the membrane. Others are enzymes, associated with the chemical reactions taking place on the membrane. Yet others are receptors for specific chemical messengers from distant parts of the organism.

Transport across the plasma membrane

Nutrients, ions, water, chemicals, and waste products enter or leave the cell by crossing the plasmamembrane. This transport may be a passive or an active process. Small molecules, such as oxygen and carbon dioxide, can cross the membrane through protein channels by passive diffusion. Larger molecules, such as glucose, rely on a process called facilitated diffusion, in which they are transported into

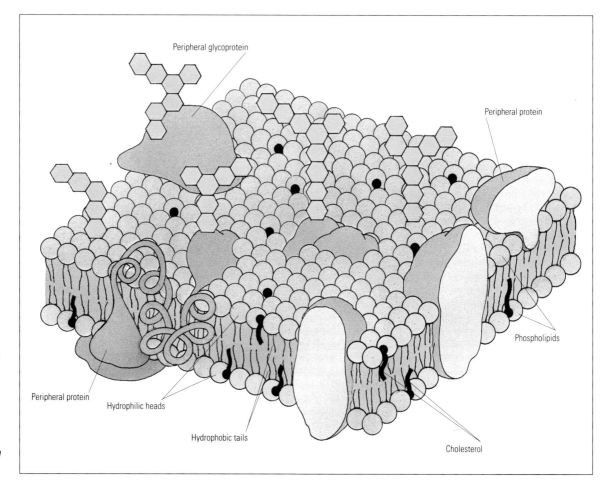

The fluid-mosaic model of plasma membranes was proposed by Jonathan Singer of the University of California and Garth Nicolson of the Salk Institute in 1972. According to this model, plasma membranes consist of two layers of phospholipid molecules with globular proteins embedded among them, arranged in a random mosaic pattern.

Peripheral glycoprotein

Peripheral protein

Phospholipids

Peripheral protein

Hydrophilic heads

Hydrophobic tails

Cholesterol

the cell by carrier proteins. Water is transported passively by means of osmosis. Passive processes depend on the movement of molecules from an area of high concentration (in this case, the extracellular fluid), to one of lower concentration (the cytoplasm).

Unlike passive processes, active ones require an input of energy, as they involve the movement of molecules against the concentration gradient. The energy is used to "pump" substances, such as sodium and potassium, "uphill," from a lower to a higher concentration, across the plasma membrane. Transport pumps make use of a group of integral carrier proteins that span the lipid bilayer.

Another form of active transport, unique to eukaryotes, is endocytosis, where the cell takes in a molecule or particle on its surface. There are two types of endocytosis: phagocytosis and pinocytosis. In phagocytosis, large solid particles, such as bacteria, are engulfed as folds of the plasma membrane extend pseudopodia ("false feet") to surround them. Once the particle is enclosed, the membrane fuses on the point of contact leaving the particle free-floating in a vacuole. This vacuole fuses with lysosomes and the ingested material is broken down. Many protozoa are phagocytic, as are white blood cells such as neutrophils (see BLOOD) in vertebrates. In pinocytosis, the membrane encloses drops of fluid rather than solid particles, and forms a vesicle (fluid-filled sac) inside the cell.

Cell junctions

Cells are linked to their neighbors at junctions, special sites on the extracellular surface. These adaptations to the lipid bilayer evolved when cells gave up self-sufficiency to cooperate and join with others in multicellular organisms. Junctions may strengthen the bond between cells, seal the membranes, or allow easier exchange of information between adjacent cells. In plants, the only junctions in the rigid cell wall are plasmodesmata (singular, plasmodesma), openings in the cell wall through which the plasma membrane runs continuously from cell to cell. In the center of the tube, a cylindrical membrane, a desmotubule, runs between the smooth endoplasmic reticulum in each cell.

Cell walls

Although the plasma membrane forms the boundary between a cell and its environment, many cells also have an external structure. In plants, bacteria, and some fungi, this structure takes the form of a cell wall, which forms a type of scaffolding around the vulnerable plasma membrane. In higher plants it provides protection and rigidity, but allows little movement. When the cell takes in fluid and expands, it exerts a pressure called turgor pressure in reaction to the opposite pressure of the cell wall, making the cell turgid. New plant cells have a more flexible primary cell wall, which allows for change in size and shape. Like the thicker and stronger secondary cell wall, its supporting meshwork is mostly made up of the carbohydrate cellulose (see CELLU-

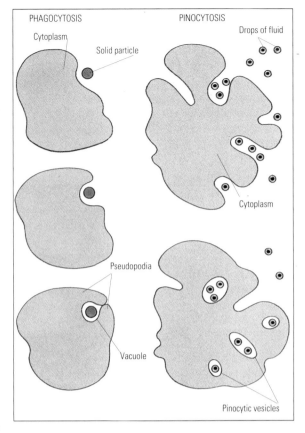

ENDOCYTOSIS. *In phagocytosis (cell eating), large solid particles are enclosed by folds of the plasma membrane (pseudopodia or "false feet"). In pinocytosis (cell drinking), the membrane folds inward, beneath the molecule, enclosing dissolved materials.*

LOSE), combined with other carbohydrates and proteins. A simpler cellulose wall surrounds most algae and some fungi cells, but most fungi have a cell wall made of chitin (also present in insect exoskeletons), and yeast cells have a wall made of complex carbohydrates called glucon and mannan.

Animal cells do not have a cell wall. Instead, they have an outer coating, the glycocalyx, and, external to this, a so-called fuzzy layer. The glycocalyx is a complex sugar coating, which protects the proteins in the plasma membrane. It is adhesive in places, and helps to join cells together. A vital component of the fuzzy layer is a fibrous protein called collagen, which forms up to a third of the total body protein in higher vertebrates. Collagen, secreted in cells known as fibroblasts, is essential to maintain the form of cells in many parts of the body. Fibroblasts occur in connective tissue, such as bone, cartilage, ligaments, and tendons.

Although collagen provides support to many tissues, it does not have the elasticity required by those tissues that are continually changing shape, such as the skin, lungs, and intestines. These incorporate another protein, elastin. The ageing process demonstrates the respective roles of these two proteins: over many years, collagen loses its flexibility – causing stiffening of the joints – and elastin is lost from tissues such as the skin, which then becomes wrinkled.

Flagella and cilia

Not all cells lead a sedentary life. Some have flagella (singular, flagellum) – long whip-like tails, used for movement by both prokaryotes and eukaryotes. Prokaryotic flagella, composed of a protein called flagellin, rotate at variable speeds like propellers. Eukaryotic flagella are composed of tiny microtubules, made from a protein called tubulin, which move with a wave-like motion.

Cilia (singular, cilium), are short and hair-like structures, similar to flagella, which cover most or all of the cell surface in single-celled eukaryotes. Their wave-like movement is used to propel protozoa, such as *Paramecium*. Multicellular organisms also have ciliated cells. Sheets of these cells, which transport substances along on the synchronized waves of the cilia, are found lining the upper airways (to clear debris from the lungs) in mammals.

THE CELL FACTORY

Unlike prokaryotic cells, which generally consist of a single compartment surrounded by a plasma membrane, eukaryotic cells are elaborately divided up into distinct membrane-encircled compartments, each with its own specific function. In some ways, the cell is rather like a miniature factory, with each organelle making its individual contribution to the conversion of "raw materials," such as oxygen, water, and nutrients, into the substances needed by the organism for growth, energy, repair, and reproduction. To fulfill its biochemical contracts, the eukaryotic cell has evolved four major distinguishing features: a plasma membrane, which maintains the shape of the cell and contains its contents; a nucleus, or control center, which incorporates "instructions" in the form of DNA for the efficient running of the cell; the cytoplasm, which comprises the bulk of the cell body; and, within the cytoplasm, a selection of organelles, each carrying out a specific function.

The nucleus

The outstanding feature of the eukaryotic cell is the nucleus, encapsulated in its own double membrane called the nuclear envelope. Numerous small openings in the envelope, known as pores, enable water-soluble molecules to pass to and fro between the nucleus and the cytoplasm. The nucleus contains the genetic material arranged in chromosomes, the numbers of which vary between species (46 in humans). It is from the nuclear control center that the whole process of protein synthesis is directed; and the proteins synthesized here are enzymes, which then dictate and control many of the activities of the cell (see DNA). Also present within the nuclear envelope are the nucleoli (singular, nucleolus). These are small round structures involved in the formation of other cell structures called ribosomes, the sites of protein synthesis. Nucleoli are composed mainly of ribonucleic acid (RNA). The nucleus' semifluid component is called nucleoplasm.

CELL EVOLUTION

The first cell appeared on Earth at least 3.5 billion years ago. Phospholipid molecules and small free-floating RNA molecues, able to synthesize amino acids, had probably already existed independently for hundreds of millions of years. The opportunity for advancement toward higher life forms came with the formation of membranes to contain the early genetic material and its products. Then, as now, phospholipids tended to form a double-layered vesicle, capable of excluding water-soluble molecules. Replicating within its new boundaries, primitive RNA could begin to evolve.

The absence of oxygen in the early atmosphere meant that metabolism had to be anaerobic (occurring without oxygen), and the scarcity of organic (carbon-containing) matter meant that inorganic material was necessary to meet the energy requirements of the cells. The earliest single-celled organisms used sulfides, hydrogen, and ammonia molecules for energy, and carbon from carbon dioxide, bicarbonate, and carbonate for protein synthesis. The capability to harness energy from sunlight – photosynthesis – meant that cells could use first oxidized sulfur (giving off sulphur as a waste product) and then water (with oxygen molecules as waste products) when they became more efficient.

There is fossil evidence of large colonies, called stromatolites, of these early anaerobes, found in Western Australia and dating back 3.4 billion years. They "fed" on carbonate or silica and used sunlight for metabolism, forming extensive layered mats. After these anareobic cyanobacteria (blue-green algae) began to split water, it took around 1.5 billion years for sufficient oxygen to build up in the atmosphere for aerobic metabolism.

Nearly three billion years after Earth was formed, primitive prokaryotes metabolized and reproduced in a nutrient-rich primordial soup, surrounded by an atmosphere containing 21 percent oxygen. Aerobic metabolism and the availability of organic compounds for biosynthesis fueled the evolutionary leap forward to more complex life forms: the eukaryotic cells. Of course, not all anaerobic prokaryotes followed this evolutionary pathway. Scientists have discovered bacteria living today in the most extreme, inhospitable environments on Earth – places that are boiling hot, devoid of organic nutrients and sunlight, with excess sulfur or salt.

Researchers have also suggested that some prokaryotes found themselves privileged and protected habitats: inside eukaryotic cells. According to the endosymbiotic theory, mitochondria evolved from prokaryotes, which colonized more energy-efficient eukaryotes around 1.5 billion years ago, before the separation of plants and animals (chloroplasts seem to have been a later development). The evidence includes the fact that mitochondria have their own DNA (but no nuclear envelope), and that they synthesize some of their own ribosomes and enzymes. Their inner membrane also differs from other intracellular membranes, a relationship that is thought to have developed from parasitism (for the benefit of the guest), through an endosymbiont relationship (mutually beneficial to both guest and host), and finally total dependence.

Other membrane-bound structures, including the nucleus, evolved in a different way. According to the autogenous hypothesis, the DNA of ancient prokaryotes was anchored to a specialized region of the plasma membrane, adjacent to the ribosomes. The chromosomes were first partially surrounded by the infolding of the plasma membrane (the mesosome) and then completely encircled to make the nucleus – a phenomenon seen in some present-day bacteria.

EVOLUTION

The cytoskeleton

Surrounding the cell nucleus, the nutrient-rich sea of cytoplasm is currently being reevaluated using advanced techniques, including high-voltage electron microscopy. Once thought of as an uninteresting clear gel, the cytoplasm has gained interest with the discovery of a complex meshwork of three distinct but interconnected systems, forming what is now known as the cytoskeleton.

The three main components of the cytoskeleton, each made up of its own characteristic protein units, are: the microtubules, each about 25 nm in diameter and made of the protein tubulin; microfilaments, 7 nm in diameter and made of the protein actin; and intermediate filaments, ranging from 8 to 12 nm in diameter and composed of any of several related proteins. Each of these three structures also has a number of accessory proteins associated with it, which give the cytoskeletal systems their versatility and flexibility. The cytoskeleton helps to maintain the shape of the cell and is also involved in cell movement and division. Microfilaments, for example, are important components of muscle cells. They are involved in intracellular movements; for example, the contractile movement of heart muscle cells. Microtubules are key components of cilia and flagella.

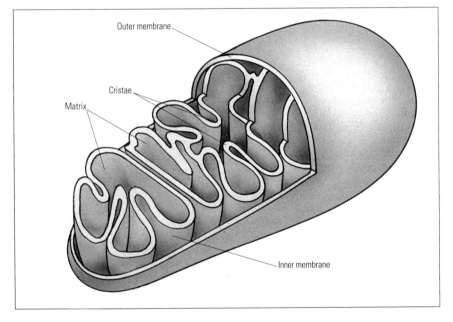

Structure of a mitochondrion. The permeability of the outer membrane effectively makes the space between the two mitochondrial membranes continuous with the cytoplasm.

Mitochondria

Within the cytoplasm are the mitochondria (singular, mitochondrion), the "powerhouses" of the cell. Mitochondria are small, oval-shaped structures, enclosed by a double membrane. The outer membrane is smooth and easily permeable to molecules, such as glucose, needed as "fuel." The inner membrane, is highly folded and impermeable to most solutes. Its infoldings are called cristae (singular, crista) which extend the membrane's surface area, enhancing its functioning. The mitochondrion's function is to extract energy from sugars and other molecules, conserving as much of it as possible as an energy store, in the form of a molecule called

adenosine triphosphate, or ATP (see ENERGY; CITRIC ACID CYCLE). Each mitochondrion is roughly the size of an entire bacterial cell (around 1 μm wide and up to 8 μm long).

Mitochondria are present in the hundreds in most eukaryotic cells, particularly those such as muscle or sperm cell tails, which are very active and require a large amount of energy. Like chloroplasts, which fulfill a similar function in plant cells, mitochondria possess their own circular DNA, and can reproduce independently of the main cell. The DNA, together with the ribosomes that give the mitochondrion the capacity to synthesize some of its own proteins, is contained in the semifluid substance that fills the inside of the organelle. The existance of separate DNA molecules in mitochondria, and also in chloroplasts suggest that both mitochondria and chloroplasts may have evolved from prokaryotes that originally lived symbiotically inside larger cells (see the box on page 273). This theory gains weight from the discovery that the protein-synthesizing ribosomes found in the mitochondria of eukaryotic cells are very different from those found in the cytoplasm. However, they are intriguingly similar to the ribosomes found in the more primitive prokaryotic cells.

Chloroplasts

Larger than mitochondria, chloroplasts occur only in plants, where they are the sites of photosynthesis, the process by which sugars are manufactured in the presence of light (see PHOTOSYNTHESIS). Chloroplasts are enclosed by a double membrane and contain a gel-like fluid called a matrix. A third membrane system consists of stacked disks called grana (singular, granum) where chlorophyll, the pigment responsible for the green coloration of most plants, is stored. The chloroplast belongs to a group of organelles known as plastids, which carry out a range of functions in plants. Others in the group include leucoplasts, which store proteins, fats, and carbohydrates; amyloplasts, which store starch; and pigment-containing chromoplasts, which are responsible for the coloration of fruits, flowers, and other plant parts.

The rough with the smooth

The endoplasmic reticulum (ER) is a winding, tubular structure that extends throughout the cytoplasm and can be described as the cell's "assembly line." The endoplasmic reticulum consists of tubular membranes continuous with the outer membrane of the nuclear envelope, and flattened sacs called cisternae, enclosing an internal space, or lumen. Because of the continuity of the nucleus and endoplasmic reticulum, the space between the nuclear membranes is in fact part of the same compartment as the ER lumen.

Endoplasmic reticulum is described as rough or smooth depending on its appearance under the electron microscope. Rough ER has ribosomes clinging to the side of its membrane, facing into the cytoplasm. Ribosomes are the sites where proteins are synthesized and are present in the cytoplasm in numbers ranging from hundreds to hundreds of thousands. The smooth endoplasmic reticulum, however, has no ribosomes. It is concerned with the packaging of secretory proteins and with the synthesis of lipids (fats) and steroids. The smooth ER is also responsible for the "detoxification" of various compounds, such as drugs, which might damage the cell.

Ribosomes

The ribosome is the "workbench" of the cell factory, the actual site of protein synthesis. More numerous than most other cell structures, ribosomes are not true organelles in that they are not encircled by a membrane. They are found in both eukaryotic and prokaryotic cells attached to the ER. Compared to organelles, ribosomes are tiny: about 20 x 30 nm in eukaryotic cells, tinier still in prokaryotes. There are thousands of ribosomes in the cytoplasm of prokaryotic cells and hundreds of thousands in eukaryotic cells.

Each ribosome consists of one large and one small subunit: these structures differ between prokaryotic and eukaryotic cells, not only in size, but also in makeup. The two subunits come together when they attach to messenger RNA and begin to synthesize a protein (see DNA; PROTEINS). Prokaryotic ribosomes have their own distinct protein and RNA molecules.

The Golgi complex

Close by the smooth ER, and associated with it, is the cell factory's "export department," the Golgi complex, or Golgi apparatus. One of the few intracellular structures to come to light before the arrival of the electron microscope, it was discovered in 1896 by the Italian neurohistologist Camillo Golgi, who is renowned for his work on the nervous system. The Golgi complex comprises a mass of tightly enfolded membranes and flattened sacs layered one atop another.

The Golgi complex continues the processing and packaging of cell secretory proteins that begins in the ER. It takes in materials (mostly proteins) contained in small, fluid-filled sacs called vesicles, which bud off the endoplasmic reticulum. After processing, the "finished products" are forwarded to the plasma membrane by means of secretory vesicles (which in turn bud off the Golgi complex). The contents of the vesicles are discharged to the exterior of the cell by exocytosis. The Golgi complex also synthesizes complex carbohydrates for the cells.

Lysosomes

Enzymes are also synthesized on the rough endoplasmic reticulum and transferred to the Golgi complex. The Golgi complex packages the enzymes into self-contained bundles, bound by a single membrane, which bud away from the Golgi apparatus and become lysosomes.

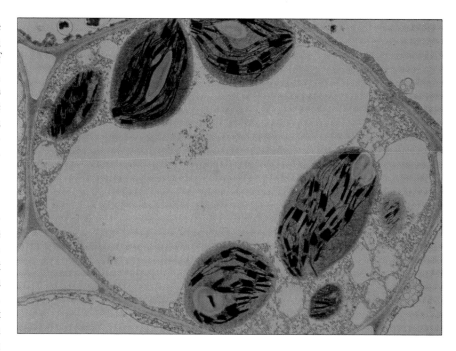

Lysosomes are important to the cell economy as providers of powerful enzymes called hydrolases, which can digest nutrient molecules such as proteins, carbohydrates, and fats; the breakdown products of this digestive process can then be put to work by the cell, recycled, or discarded. But these enzymes are so voracious that they must be carefully contained in order to prevent them devouring everything in their path.

In its predigestive phase, one of these organelles is known as a primary lysosome. To begin digestion, a primary lysosome must first meet and fuse with a membrane-encircled vacuole containing nutrient particles – a kind of cellular food storage bin. After fusion, the vacuole is known as a secondary lysosome, and the enzymes it has taken aboard are able to digest its contents, breaking them down into smaller and smaller particles. After some time, these breakdown products are small enough to pass out through the lysosomes's single membrane into the cytoplasm, so they can be recycled.

Vacuoles

In animal cells, there are many vacuoles, organelles that may be used for storage or transport. Protozoa and some white blood cells, for example, practice phagocytosis, or "cell eating," a type of endocytosis in which a section of the plasma membrane envelopes a food particle on the outside of the cell, cutting it off from the extracellular environment. The hijacked particle is then internalized as a vacuole which fuses with lysosomes to allow digestion of the contents, as described above.

The major responsibility of the large central vacuole that is a feature of most mature plant cells is in maintaining the cells' turgor pressure – and thus the crispness of the entire plant. If the central vacuole malfunctions, the whole plant wilts. Vacuoles in plants may also play some part in storage and digestion within the cell.

A typical plant cell (from a grass leaf) seen under the electron microscope. The cell wall, cell membrane, chloroplasts, and central vacuole are clearly visible.

The peroxisome

The peroxisome is an organelle similar to the lysosome. They are similar in size and each is bound by a single membrane. Found in plant and animal cells, peroxisomes are able to both generate and degrade hydrogen peroxide (H_2O_2), a waste-product resulting from various metabolic processes. Hydrogen peroxide is a highly toxic molecule, but it can be broken down into water and oxygen by the enzyme catalase.

CELL DIVISION

Cells divide into new, genetically identical daughter cells in a process called the cell cycle, which includes mitosis. This process involves each cell dividing into two cells, each of which then divide into two more cells, and so on. Cells involved in sexual reproduction divide by another process, called meiosis, to produce four reproductive cells with half the amount of genetic material.

The cell cycle

The cell cycle takes place in two stages: interphase, the period of growth and replication of cell contents, and M phase, which includes mitosis (division of the chromosomes) and cytokinesis (division of the cell membrane and contents). Each turn of this cycle culminates in two separate cells.

Throughout the longer period of interphase, the cell increases in size. DNA in the nucleus directs various cellular activities, including synthesis of cell components, and the nucleus prepares for the next cell division. There are three phases to interphase: G1 (G for gap), S (synthesis) phase, and G2.

The G1 phase is the first gap, the time between the end of the previous M phase and the beginning of the S phase. G1 is the phase of growth during which cells carry out their specialized functions. Toward the end there is an increase in activity of the enzymes needed for DNA synthesis. The G1 phase is usually the longest phase of the cell cycle although the length depends on the cell type. Some cells, such as intestinal lining cells, have a short gap before beginning to divide again, whereas liver cells divide more slowly, and nerve cells rarely divide at all. Cells that do not divide are said to enter G0 phase. Growth is so rapid in the early embryo that there is no gap at all. When an organism is growing, or during repair after an injury, new cells are produced at a faster than normal rate.

The S phase is the period of DNA replication. The DNA, in the form of chromosomes, replicates itself exactly. Each chromosome is now composed of two strands of chromatin (consisting of DNA and proteins) held together by a centromere. Each chromatin strand is called a chromatid, and the two identical strands are referred to as a chromatid pair or sister chromatids. The timing of S phase depends on factors such as the cell reaching an adequate size.

The G2 phase is the cell's second gap phase. Increased protein synthesis takes place as the cell completes its preparation for division.

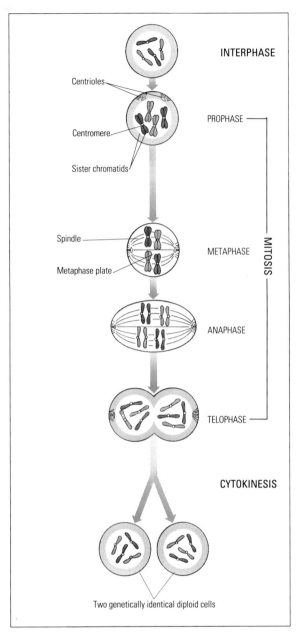

THE CELL CYCLE. DNA is duplicated by chromosome replication during interphase. In prophase the nuclear membrane breaks down and the spindle appears. The replicated chromosomes are separated during metaphase, anaphase, and telophase to produce two identical new cells at cytokinesis.

Labels on figure: INTERPHASE; Centrioles; Centromere; PROPHASE; Sister chromatids; Spindle; METAPHASE; Metaphase plate; MITOSIS; ANAPHASE; TELOPHASE; CYTOKINESIS; Two genetically identical diploid cells

Mitosis

Now the M phase begins. There are four stages of of mitosis: prophase, metaphase, anaphase, and telophase.

In prophase, the chromosome sets condense. The sister chromatids, joined at the centromere, are now visible under a microscope, and the nucleolus disperses. A structure known as the centriole replicates and a new structure, the microtubular mitotic spindle, forms alongside the chromosomes. The spindle links the two centrioles, which migrate to opposite poles of the cell. The nuclear envelope breaks up into vesicles, and the spindle spans the middle of the cell.

At the beginning of metaphase, the chromosomes line up along the equator of the spindle attached by their centromeres. Once all the pairs are in position, a process that may take an hour or longer, the sister chromatids split apart at the centromere. During anaphase, each chromatid migrates rapidly to opposite poles, pulled by the spindle microtubules. Within minutes, the chromosomes

MEIOSIS. At prophase I, duplicated chromosomes exchange genetic material within homologous pairs. Division I produces two new cells containing the full (haploid) complement of chromosomes. In division II there is no duplication of DNA. The stages are repeated with sister chromatids separating to produce four distinct haploid daughter cells.

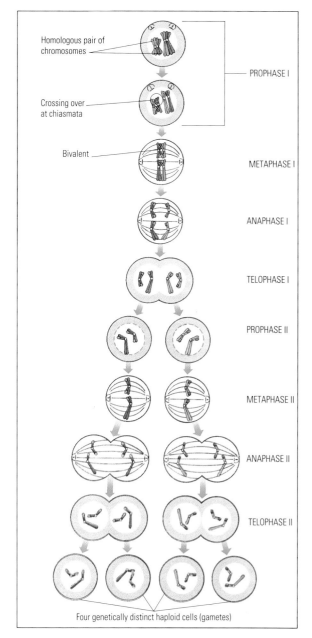

Homologous pair of chromosomes

PROPHASE I

Crossing over at chiasmata

Bivalent

METAPHASE I

ANAPHASE I

TELOPHASE I

PROPHASE II

METAPHASE II

ANAPHASE II

TELOPHASE II

Four genetically distinct haploid cells (gametes)

mals. This is known as anastral mitosis. Because of the rigid cell wall, cleavage of the cell during cytokinesis is impossible. Instead a new cell wall has to be created between the daughter cells. This begins at the equator, where small membrane vesicles, derived from the Golgi apparatus, line up and eventually fuse to make a membrane-bound cell plate. The vesicles contain cell wall precursors, which make up the primary, noncellulose part of the wall. The cell plate incorporates new plasmodesmata for communication between cells. It expands to reach the original cell wall, and the membrane fuses with the inner plasma membrane.

Meiosis

Meiosis is the specialized form of cell division by which cells produce four reproductive cells (gametes), each containing half the number of chromosomes of the parent cells. There is also often an exchange of genetic material, which helps to encourage genetic diversity within groups of organisms. In any organism, meiosis only occurs to produce reproductive cells. In humans, these gametes are the sperm in males, and ova in females. During reproduction, gametes from a male and a female, will fuse to combine their genetic material, restoring the original number of chromosomes.

Cells are normally diploid, containing pairs of homologous chromosomes in which each chromosome carries identical DNA. They undergo meiosis to yield haploid reproductive cells, a reduction process requiring two separate cell divisions, with DNA replicating itself only once. There are eight stages of meiosis: prophase I, metaphase I, anaphase I, telophase I, prophase II, metaphase II, anaphase II, and telophase II.

As the cell enters prophase I, the longest stage of meiosis, sister chromatids are tightly joined at the centromere. Each pair also has its equivalent (one inherited from the mother and one from the father), known as homologous chromosomes.

A process known as crossing over may now take place. The homologous pairs exchange genetic material through a process of breakage and rejoining at sites called chiasmata (singular, chiasma). This exchange of genetic material occurs at random along the length of the chromosomes and assures a new mix of genetic information.

Events similar to prophase in the cell cycle also take place with the formation of a spindle, the duplication of centrioles in animal cells, and the disappearance of the nuclear envelope.

At metaphase I the chromatids are aligned along the equator of the spindle. When the cell enters anaphase I, the chiasmata break down, allowing the homologues to move to opposite poles, while the sister chromatids remain close together. Meiotic division I ends with telophase I, in which new nuclear envelopes and cell membranes form. Meiotic division II follows a brief rest at interphase, but this time there is no intervening replication of DNA. The stages of division are repeated.

reach the centrosomes (the areas containing the centrioles). The cell begins to elongate by lengthening of the spindle microtubules, and the cell enters telophase (from the Greek *telos*, end). In telophase, the nuclear membrane reforms around each group of chromosomes and the cell elongates further.

Cytokinesis

The second event in M phase, cytokinesis, begins as the chromatid pairs are drawn toward opposite poles. Cleavage, the division of the cell membrane, takes place at the equator, perpendicular to the mitotic spindle. Each new cell will get precisely half the chromosomes, a copy of each identical pair. A contractile ring of the proteins actin and myosin draws the cell membrane inward.

Plant cells

Mitosis in plant cells differs in several important ways. Plant cells lack centrioles, so the mitotic spindles do not meet at each pole to form the characteristic star or astral array seen in mitosis in ani-

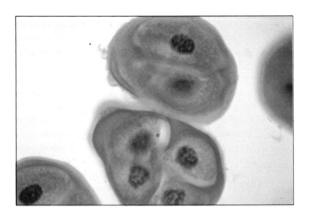

Telophase II in crocus.

However, at prophase II there is no pairing of homologous chromosomes (only one chromosome of each pair is present) and no crossing over. At anaphase II, the sister chromatids are finally separated and drawn to opposite poles. The process ends with four genetically distinct haploid cells.

PROKARYOTIC CELLS

Prokaryotes (bacteria and blue-green algae) are generally single-celled organisms, though some form colonies or filaments containing specialized cells. Prokaryotic cells are tiny (1-10 μm), much smaller than eukaryotic cells, around ten times their size.

Prokaryotes have cell walls which provide a framework to support and protect the plasma membrane and cytoplasm, and prevent the cell from bursting due to osmotic pressure. These cell walls differ from plant cell walls. A typical bacterial cell wall is 5-10 nm thick and is composed of very large carbohydrate and protein chains called peptidoglycan polymers. Some bacteria, known as Gram positive bacteria because of the way they stain (see BACTERIA), have walls made only of a single layer of peptidoglycans. Others, such as *Escherichia coli,* which are Gram negative, have a second outer layer of lipopolysaccharides (lipids containing polysaccharides). The difference in cell wall structure is significant in the treatment of bacterial diseases: Gram negative bacteria are much more resistant to antibiotics than Gram positive bacteria. Some bacteria have an extra mucus-like coating surrounding the cell wall, known as the capsule, which protects the bacteria from attack by a host organism's immune system. These bacteria are particularly infectious.

Bacteria such as *E. coli* that live in digestive tracts also have another outer structure made of hundreds of tiny projections called pili (hairs in Latin). Pili are composed of a protein called pilin and help the bacteria to stick to surfaces inside a host cell.

The prokaryotic plasma membrane below the cell wall fulfills the same functions as a eukaryotic membrane but lacks cholesterol, giving it different fluidity properties. The membrane encloses dense cytoplasm that contains ribosomes and storage granules holding glycogen, lipid, or phosphate compounds. Prokaryotic cells do not have the cytoskeletal support system found in eukaryotic cells.

The prokaryotic cell has a single long circular chromosome in a dense area in the cytoplasm known as the nucleoid. A convoluted, whorled membranous structure called the mesosome projects into the cell from the plasma membrane. It may be a source of new membrane during cell division or act as a crude mitochondrian. Not all prokaryotic cells can propel themselves, but some have flagella that are different in structure from eukaryotic flagella and also move differently (see BACTERIA).

The numbers game

Bacteria divide by a process called binary fission. This begins when the cell becomes elongated and the DNA replicates. Each chromosome is attached to a special part of the plasma membrane instead of migrating to either end. An indentation forms in the cell wall and membrane, between the two regions holding the DNA. The deepening furrow creates two cytoplasmic compartments, eventually enclosed by cell walls. This is repeated for as long as the environment can support the population. In ideal conditions, bacteria can divide every 20 minutes, reaching 5 billion cells in less than half a day. This rapid reproduction also means that bacteria can evolve quickly to adapt to new living conditions.

E. SAREWITZ

See also: BACTERIA; CHROMOSOMES; CYTOLOGY; DNA; ENERGY; GENETICS; METABOLISM; MUTATION; PHOTOSYNTHESIS; REPRODUCTION.

Further reading:

Alberts, B., Bray, D., Lewis, J., Raff, M., Roberts, K., and Watson, J.D. *Molecular Biology of the Cell.* 3rd edition. New York: Garland Publishing, Inc., 1994.
Becker, W.M. and Deanero, D.W. *The World of the Cell.* 2nd edition. Redwood City, California: Benjamin/Cummins, 1991.
Perspectives on Cellular Regulation: from Bacteria to Cancer. Edited by J. Campisi et al. New York: Wiley-Liss, 1991.
Welch, W.J. "How Cells Respond to Stress", *Scientific American,* **268**, pp.56-64, May 1993.

LOSING CONTROL

Cell division is controlled by signals received from the cell's environment. The origin of these signals may be distant (via hormones and other chemical messengers) or adjacent (from neighboring cells). It also depends on directions from the cell's own genes. Normally, growth factors (hormones produced by other cells) stimulate cell division, either for cell growth or for repair and replenishment. On the other side of the genetic coin, suppressor genes act by "switching off" the chain of events that leads to cell division.

However, a cell may begin to divide independently of external stimuli if the regulatory gene becomes permanently "switched on." This rogue gene is called an oncogene, and the breakdown of control over its activity leads to cancer.

A CLOSER LOOK

CELLULOSE

Cellulose is a complex carbohydrate and the main structural component of plant cell walls

Cellulose, a complex carbohydrate, is the most abundant organic molecule on Earth. It is the main building material of plant cell walls and gives plants their structure. It also has important industrial uses. The paper in this book is made largely of cellulose. The clothes you are wearing probably contain cellulose.

The structure of cellulose

Carbohydrates are made up of sugar units. They can be monosaccharides (made up of one sugar unit), disaccharides (two units), or polysaccharides (many units). Cellulose is a polysaccharide with between 8000 and 15,000 glucose units. It is made in the plant from glucose formed by photosynthesis.

Glucose has two main forms: α-glucose and ß-glucose. The difference between these forms is due to the positions of the hydrogen atom (H) and hydroxyl group (OH) on the carbon atom in position 1 in the ring of carbon atoms shown below.

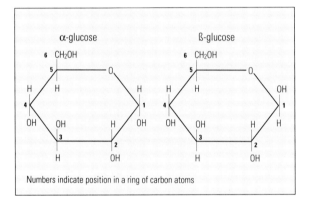

Numbers indicate position in a ring of carbon atoms

Cellulose is made up of ß-glucose units, whereas starch, another complex carbohydrate, is composed of α-glucose.

The glucose units that form cellulose are linked together in a long, straight, unbranching chain. These chains lie parallel to each other. The molecules are crosslinked by bonds between the chains. This bonding produces bundles of about 40 to 70 cellulose molecules, known as microfibrils, which can be seen under an electron microscope. Microfibrils are themselves bound together into larger bundles called macrofibrils, which are large

enough to be seen under an optical microscope. This arrangement gives cellulose a high tensile strength.

The role of cellulose in plant cell walls

Plant cells are surrounded by a strong supporting wall, which consists mainly of cellulose. The cell walls provide structural support for the plant. The rigidity of any part of a plant is related to the thickness of its cell walls.

Within the cell wall, the long bundles of cellulose are embedded in a matrix of other polysaccharides. The cell wall is similar to reinforced concrete, where the cellulose fibers are the steel rods and the matrix material around them is the concrete. The cellulose bundles cannot stretch, so the way they are arranged determines the shape and rigidity of the plant cell.

As the cell grows, new layers of cellulose are deposited on the cell wall. Each new layer is laid down inside the last layer so that the oldest material is on the outside. When a cell first forms, its wall is thin and composed mainly of cellulose. This is called the cell's primary wall. In the primary cell wall the cellulose bundles are sparse. They are arranged in a criss-cross pattern so that the growing cell can expand.

After reaching full size, some cells form a secondary cell wall on the inner surface of the primary wall. In the secondary cell wall the cellulose bundles are laid down in a more dense and organized way. The cellulose bundles in each layer are parallel, and the orientation often changes in successive layers.

As the secondary wall develops, other materials may be incorporated into the cell wall. In the

CORE FACTS

■ Cellulose is made up of between 8000 and 15,000 glucose units.

■ Cellulose is a major component of plant cell walls and gives plants their structure.

■ Cellulose is used to make paper, material, and the chemical nitrocellulose.

■ Cellulose is the most abundant organic molecule on Earth.

Cellulose fibrils magnified x 30,000. The long straight cellulose molecules are crosslinked by bonds to form tough fibers. It is this arrangement that gives cellulose its strength.

woody parts of a plant, the cell walls contain a large amount of the complex molecule lignin, which makes the wall stronger. Fatty or waxy substances are often present in cell walls to reduce water loss.

Digestion of cellulose

Humans and many other animals cannot digest cellulose. They lack the enzymes, known as cellulases, that break down the cellulose chains. Cellulose is important in the diet, however. It acts as bulk fiber, which stimulates the intestine and helps to expel intestinal waste.

Many microorganisms, including certain bacteria and protozoa, produce cellulases and are able to digest cellulose. In some animals, these microorganisms live in the alimentary tract. Ruminants, such as cattle and goats, can digest grass because microorganisms in their digestive tract break down the cellulose into glucose units, which the animals can absorb and use.

Fungi secrete cellulases that break down cellulose into soluble carbohydrates, which the fungal cells can absorb. Fungi play an important role in the decomposition of wood and other plant material.

Molecules similar to cellulose

Starch and cellulose are the most abundant polysaccharides in plants. Whereas cellulose is the main structural material, starch is the plant's food store. The bonds joining the α-glucose units in the starch molecule can be broken by enzymes called amylases. In this way, starch is broken down into its component glucose units when these are needed to provide energy.

Chitin is another polysaccharide with a structure and function very similar to cellulose. Like cellulose, the sugar units in chitin form a long, straight chain. Chitin is the main component of the hard exoskeleton of many arthropods and mollusks. Most fungi have a chitin-like polysaccharide, rather than cellulose, in their cell walls.

M. MAHALIK/K. McCALLUM

See also: CARBOHYDRATES; CELLS; DIGESTIVE SYSTEMS; FUNGI KINGDOM; PLANT KINGDOM.

Further reading:

Raven, P., Evert, F., and Eichhorn, S. *Biology of Plants,* 5th edition. New York: Worth Pub., 1992.

INDUSTRIAL USES OF CELLULOSE

Cellulose is the essential component of paper and many industrial fibers. Plastics, photographic film, rayon, and explosives are all formed from chemically modified cellulose. Its long straight chain structure gives cellulose its economic importance. The major sources of cellulose are plant fibers (cotton, hemp, flax, and jute) and wood.

Papermaking

Paper is made from wood, which is composed of about 50 percent cellulose. The cellulose is removed from the wood by a pulping process, which may be mechanical (where the woodchips are ground up under a flow of water) or chemical. The resulting pulp is then washed and often bleached. In the papermaking machine the pulp is pumped over a vibrating mesh. Initially, all the fibers in the pulp lie in the direction of the flow, but as the mesh vibrates, the fibers move around and form an interlocking web. As the water drains out of the pulp, it leaves a web of fibers, which is then pressed, smoothed, and dried to make paper.

Cotton and other fibers

Plant fibers are long, thin cells with a thick wall. They can be obtained from several plant species, but their most important source is cotton (*Gossypium* spp.). In cotton, the fiber cells are found on the surface of the cotton seed. Each seed bears many thousands of these fibers, which can be as long as 2¾ in (7 cm). As the cotton pod ripens, the fiber cells die. The dead fiber cells are 90 percent cellulose. They are very strong, and can be twisted to form thread or yarn, most of which is used to weave cloth.

Jute (*Corchorus* spp.) is another important source of plant fibers. Jute is coarser than cotton and not as strong. The fiber cells occur as bundles in the stems and are 75 percent cellulose. To remove the fibers, the plant stems are tied together and placed in ponds, where bacteria and fungi decompose the surrounding tissues. The

remaining fibers are then dried and spun into yarn, which is mainly used for industrial products such as the backing for carpets.

Rayon

Most rayon is made from wood pulp using the viscose process, which was developed in 1892. To make rayon, cellulose is chemically treated to convert it into a liquid, and then treated again to turn it back into fibers. The wood pulp is treated with sodium hydroxide and then carbon disulfide to form a compound called cellulose xanthate. When this compound is treated with more sodium hydroxide, it forms a sticky substance, known as viscose. The viscose is squeezed through a group of spinnerets (fine nozzles) into an acid bath. The resulting strands are twisted into a thread. The rayon thread is then washed, bleached, and dried. If the viscose is passed through a narrow slit, rather than through spinnerets, a sheet of transparent film, commonly known as cellophane, is produced.

Cellulose nitrate and celluloid

Cellulose nitrate, commonly called nitrocellulose, is a highly flammable, fluffy white substance that is made by treating cotton with nitric acid. This substance was used to make the first ever synthetic plastic.

In 1869 the American inventor, John W. Hyatt, mixed nitrocellulose with camphor to produce a plastic known as celluloid. Celluloid was first developed as a cheaper subsitute for ivory. It was used to make toothbrushes, combs, dentures, and photographic film. Early motion pictures were made using celluloid film. However, the flammability of the celluloid was a serious problem, causing several fires in movie houses. Because of its flammability, celluloid has been largely replaced by newer plastics for most uses.

Many of the products that were originally made from cellulose are now being manufactured more cheaply and easily by the petrochemical industry.

SCIENCE AND SOCIETY

CENTIPEDES AND MILLIPEDES

Centipedes and millipedes are many-legged creatures from the phylum Arthropoda. Despite the popular belief, however, they do not have 100 and 1000 pairs of legs. Depending on the species, centipedes have between 15 and 177 pairs of legs, with one pair for each segment of the body. Millipedes usually have from 20 to 80 pairs of legs, although there is a tropical African species with up to 375 pairs.

It is fairly easy to tell centipedes from millipedes. Centipedes have one pair of legs attached to each body segment. In millipedes, on the other hand, each of the trunk segments is actually two body segments fused together. These fused sections are called diplosegments. Each diplosegment has two pairs of legs. This is an important difference between the two types of animal.

Centipedes and millipedes belong in separate classes: centipedes in the Chilopoda and millipedes in the Diplopoda. These two classes are part of the superclass Myriapoda (meaning "many feet") and are collectively known as myriapods. Like other arthropods, such as insects and crustaceans, centipedes and millipedes have a segmented body and a hardened exoskeleton (body covering).

CENTIPEDES

The class Chilopoda contains about 3000 species, which are divided into four orders. These are the Geophilomorpha, the Scolopendromorpha, the Lithobiomorpha, and the Scutigeromorpha.

All centipedes have a head with a segmented body. The head has mouthparts and a pair of antennae. The last few body segments do not bear legs.

Centipedes are found throughout the world, from north of the Arctic Circle to the equatorial tropics, and in every major biome, including tundra and deserts. Vegetation strongly influences the distribution of centipedes; some are grassland inhabitants, others live in woodlands and on forest floors. One species is commonly found in buildings.

Centipedes and millipedes are many-legged arthropods belonging to the superclass Myriapoda

Centipedes need a damp environment. Their exoskeleton lacks the waxy layers found in the cuticle of insects. This puts centipedes at risk of drying out unless they stay in humid places: grassland, tundra, and desert species live under stones and fallen plant material.

Centipedes excrete their metabolic nitrogen-containing waste in the form of toxic ammonia (insects mainly excrete a nontoxic uric acid). The ammonia has to be diluted many times before excretion, otherwise the animal would poison itself. This requires an abundant supply of water, which the centipede must obtain from its environment.

Centipedes are mainly nocturnal creatures, though some tropical forms are active during daylight hours. The animals are less likely to dry out if they are active at night.

The Geophilomorpha are long and worm-like, with between 31 and 177 pairs of legs. Most geophilomorphs are solitary, but some species occasionally feed in groups.

The Scolopendromorpha include large tropical species with 21 to 23 pairs of legs. The largest members of this group can reach lengths of over 10 in (25 cm). Members of the Scolopendromorpha are solitary and display a ritualistic fighting reaction when they encounter each other. These "fights"

A centipede (Scolopendra cingulata) *eating prey. Centipedes are active carnivores. They have long legs for running, and poisonous claws for subduing prey.*

are in fact meeting rituals. They prevent the centipedes from biting one another, which could be fatal. When two male *Scolopendra cingulata* meet, each tries to grab the hind end of the other with its back legs. The animals may lock together for over an hour.

The Lithobiomorpha are soft-bodied animals with 15 pairs of legs. Lithobiomorphs are widely distributed, being found throughout temperate regions in houses and other buildings, leaf litter, logs, and deep burrows.

The Scutigeromorpha have 15 pairs of very long legs, some of which are almost as long as the animal's body (1⅕ in or 30 mm). The natural distribution of Scutigeromorpha is restricted to the tropics and subtropics, although some members of this group have become established outside these regions. Commonly called house centipedes, they are found in many states in the United States. They are a fastidious group: many species spend up to 20 minutes at a time cleaning their antennae and other appendages.

Movement
Centipedes are generally faster runners than millipedes. The geophilomorphs have relatively short legs: these animals are built for burrowing rather than running. By contrast, the scolopendromorphs are long-legged and do not burrow. They achieve high speeds with their long legs and by moving their limbs quickly.

The Lithobiomorpha and the Scutigeromorpha are the fastest of the centipedes. They generally possess very long limbs, which give the animals a long stride. In the Scutigeromorpha, the fastest of the myriapods, speeds of up to 16½ in per second (420 mm per second) have been recorded for a specimen ⅘ in (22 mm) long. The sensation must be dramatic. It is equivalent to a human running at speeds of over 74½ mph (120 km/h)!

To help in running, the Scutigeromorpha have spines on their feet that grip the earth. They are the only centipedes to have large compound eyes, which may give these fast runners a wide field of vision. The Scutigeromorpha also possess special spiracles (openings that allow gas exchange; see GILLS AND SPIRACLES) along their back to increase the rate of gas exchange to the muscles.

Diet
Centipedes are largely carnivorous, and some species are active hunters. In drier areas, they hunt for prey at night when the cooler temperatures and higher humidity reduce water loss through their exoskeleton. Other species are sedentary hunters (also known as "sit-and-wait" predators). These species wait for food to come to them.

Centipedes have fang-tipped appendages (called maxillipeds) under the head, which are attached to poison sacs. Some species have powerful poisons that can be painful to humans. The toxin of many species contains serotonin, an important pain-producing substance. The presence of serotonin suggests that the poison is mainly used for defense, although it can also be used to subdue prey.

The different orders of centipede have different diets. Geophilomorphs feed on a variety of annelid worms (such as earthworms), snails, and other arthropods. Scolopendromorphs eat larger prey, including small mice, small toads, lizards, small snakes, and frogs, as well as other arthropods. Some species can capture flying insects in midair: the centipede rears up and snatches the insect in its poison fangs. Scolopendromorphs will also eat fruit and other types of plant material.

The Lithobiomorpha feed mostly on soft-bodied invertebrates, such as slugs, worms, and insect larvae, and may eat plant material on occasions. Some researchers have noted a strong tendency to cannibalism in this order. Cannibalism is most common when centipede densities are at their highest. This suggests that it functions as a way of controlling the population.

The Scutigeromorpha eat a wide variety of invertebrates. The centipede first bites its victim, then waits until all movement has ended before it begins to feast on its prey. These animals have very long poison fangs, which allow them to tackle prey that is too big for other centipedes of a similar size.

Reproduction
Following a courtship ritual, which may last hours, the male spins a web over the opening of the female's burrow and deposits a package of sperm (called a spermatophore) in the web. The female later detects the sperm with her antennae, then maneuvers her body over it, and swings back and forth until the sperm has been picked up by her genitals. The female lays between three and 75 eggs, depending on the species. The eggs are laid

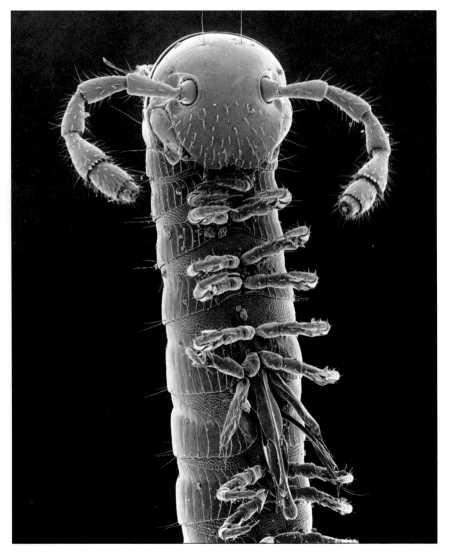

The head end of a millipede magnified x 60. Apart from the first three, each of the leg-bearing body segments is a fused diplosegment. Each diplosegment has two pairs of legs.

under bark or stones, in burrows, or directly in the soil. In some species the female remains with her eggs to guard them.

Some species of centipede include parthenogenetic females, which can reproduce without the sperm of a male. In this form of reproduction all the offspring are exact genetic replicas of their female parent.

The embryonic development of the centipede follows two general pathways. In the geophilomorphs and the scolopendromorphs, the young hatch with all or most of their legs. The young of these groups are often brooded by the female until they are large enough to catch their own prey.

In the Lithobiomorpha and the Scutigeromorpha the eggs are laid singly and are not brooded by the female. The young are born without all their legs, and additional legs grow as the centipede molts. Adult centipedes take around 30 to 40 minutes to molt. At this time, the animal is very vulnerable to attack. The head capsule splits first, and the animal pulls itself out of the old exoskeleton with a series of jerks. It takes about 48 hours for the new exoskeleton to harden.

MILLIPEDES

The class Diplopoda comprises 10,000 species of arthropods divided into two subclasses. Millipedes range from $\frac{1}{16}$ in (2 mm) to over 1 ft (30 cm) in length. The subclass Penicillata (also known as the Pselaphognatha) is a small group of very minute millipedes sometimes referred to as "bristly" millipedes. The bodies of these bark-dwelling millipedes are covered with numerous hair-like serrated setae (projections of the exoskeleton), which give them a bristled appearance.

The majority of millipedes are members of the subclass Chilognatha. The chilognathans have a calcified cuticle, and are generally long and thin with numerous legs. These millipedes are found in or near the surface of soil.

Millipedes have three main body parts: head, body, and telson. The head possesses mouthparts and a number of sensory structures, including the antennae and the eyes (although some species are blind and lack eyes). The head capsule is usually heavily calcified to ram through soil and leaf litter. The body is long and cylindrical in shape. The telson consists of a pre-anal ring, which aids defecation.

The cuticle consists of three layers, which together make up the exoskeleton. Millipedes must absorb the calcium they need for their exoskeletons from their food. They play an important role in cycling calcium through the ecosystem. The calcified cuticle is permeable to water, so millipedes must stay in humid areas. To cut down water loss in drier conditions, some species incorporate a layer of waterproofing. In desert millipedes, this waterproofing is in the form of a thin layer of wax over the cuticle, which dramatically reduces water loss.

Most millipedes are dull in color. Cave-dwelling forms are white, having lost most or all of their pig-

---

MILLIPEDE SELF-DEFENSE

Being slow-moving animals, millipedes cannot escape attackers by running away and must rely on other ways of protecting themselves. Most millipedes depend on their ability to roll up into a tight ball. This protects the softer parts of the body and also cuts down water loss. The exoskeleton offers some protection from small predators, but is no match for larger enemies. Some millipedes have glands running along the length of the body, which produce defensive secretions. In one group of millipedes, the defensive secretion is chemically similar to the sedatives known as quaaludes. This secretion sedates the millipede's predator.

A CLOSER LOOK

---

ment. There are, however, some very brightly colored tropical species, with brilliant patterns of red, yellow, and black. These bright colors probably act as a warning to potential attackers.

Movement

Millipedes have a hard calcified head capsule. With their strong legs and sturdy head, millipedes can plough through soils and force their way between roots, using microhabitats possibly inaccessible to other arthropods.

Having diplosegments also helps them burrow. The force with which a millipede can push comes from its legs. The more legs that are in contact with the ground at any one time, the more force can be exerted.

Millipedes have relatively short legs compared to centipedes. Walking is a highly coordinated activity, involving wavelike movements of groups of legs on either side of the body. Millipedes are not fast movers: they are built more for burrowing than for running. Millipede body shape depends on the animal's habits and lifestyle. There are bulldozers, borers, rollers, and bark-dwellers.

Bulldozers have long cylindrical bodies, which they use to ram through debris and soil. These are probably the most familiar millipedes in appearance. Borers have an articulating (flexible) exoskeleton in each ring of the body, which allows the body to widen and open up a crevice or burrow. Rollers can roll up into a tight ball as a means of defense. This also cuts down water loss by reducing the exposed surface area. Bark dwellers are not good

---

MILLIPEDE SWARMING

Unlike the more solitary centipedes, millipedes have been known to gather in large numbers. There are reports of millipedes gathering in farm fields in such numbers that cattle would not graze. There are even reports of millipedes preventing trains from moving as thousands of crushed millipede bodies made the tracks too slippery. These outbreaks seem to happen every seven to eight years and involve mostly adult animals, suggesting excess reproduction as a cause. Other suggested causes include rainfall patterns and variations in the food supply. The millipedes are unlikely to be migrating, as most of the swarms do not seem to be moving in a particular direction.

Most millipedes are herbivores, burrowing through soil and dead leaves. Their diet of dead plant material makes them important nutrient recyclers.

burrowers, but are sufficiently small and flat to fit into small crevices underneath bark.

Diet

Most millipedes feed on plant material, though a few species are known to be carnivorous, and others scavenge dead animals. Most prefer to eat dead plant material, which gives them an important ecological role as nutrient recyclers in woodlands. They use their stout jaws to chew on partly decomposed leaves. By breaking up leaves and other plant parts, millipedes facilitate the action of smaller soil decomposers, such as bacteria.

Reproduction

The male millipede produces a packet of sperm, which in some species is deposited in a web. In others, sperm transfer is direct from male to female. These males have gonopods, modified legs near the head, which they use to transfer the sperm.

Some millipedes, such as *Polyxenus lagurus*, perform a complex courtship ritual. The male spins a mesh of threads in a zigzag manner over a small crevice. He places his spermatophores onto the web and then extends a thick double thread downward from the crevice. A passing female follows the thread back to the crevice, where she takes up the sperm packets.

For the millipede *Cylindroiulus punctatus*, the mating ritual is even more elaborate. The male runs along the back of the female, then rotates until the lower sides of their bodies are together. The male strokes the female until she is receptive, at which point he inserts sperm packets directly into the female's spermatheca (a small sac-like structure used to receive and store sperm). There are also cases of parthenogenesis in millipedes.

Millipedes reproduce by laying eggs. Many millipedes build a nest for their eggs. Some millipedes make a protective coating for the eggs by eating earth and mixing the fecal material with a secretion produced by the rectal glands.

Millipedes grow to adult size by passing through a series of molts. In some species molting is very frequent, with over 10 percent of the animal's life being spent in a molt. Adult animals also molt periodically. Adult molts are often timed to coincide with certain climatic conditions, such as a dry period, as this seems to help the molting process. Millipedes hide before molting, because at this time the animal is particularly vulnerable to attack.

K. HOSOUME/J. KAUFMANN

See also: ARTHROPODS.

Further reading:
Cymborowski, Bronislaw. *Insect Endocrinology*. New York: Elsevier Science Pub. Co., 1992.
Insect Potpourri: Adventures in Entomology. Edited by Jean Adams. Gainesville, Florida: Sandhill Crane Press, 1992.
Preston-Mafham, Ken. *Discovering Centipedes and Millipedes*. New York: Bookwright Press, 1990.

EVOLUTION OF THE MYRIAPODS

Little is known about the evolution of the myriapods, as few fossils have been found. Some researchers believe that centipedes and millipedes evolved separately from a primitive group of myriapods. Other experts think that millipedes are more closely related to insects than to centipedes.

The oldest fossil that has been found is of a centipede-type animal from the Upper Silurian Period, over 400 million years ago. The oldest millipede-like animal is called *Kampecaris tuberculata*, also from the Silurian. During the Carboniferous Period, over 300 million years ago, myriapods diversified greatly.

The largest myriapod fossil is of the giant *Arthropleura*, dating from the Devonian Period approximately 345 to 405 million years ago. This enormous animal was over 6 ft (1.8 m) long and almost 1½ ft (0.5 m) across.

After the Carboniferous Period, the number of myriapod fossils declines and there is a large gap until the Oligocene Epoch, approximately 23 to 36 million years ago. Fossils from this time have been found embedded in amber. By this time, the myriapods already looked very like those of today.

EVOLUTION

CHAPARRAL BIOME

The chaparral biome is a widespread vegetation community found in California in the United States

Chaparral is a widespread vegetation community found in California in the United States. It is composed mainly of evergreen woody shrubs that are adapted to drought and fire and can survive endless cycles of burn and regrowth. Similar vegetation communities are also found in the Mediterranean, the African Cape, central Chile, and southwestern Australia. Although the species of plants in these widespread communities are very different, they all share adaptations to survive drought and fire. However, chaparral typically refers only to the vegetation community found in California and northern Baja California, Mexico.

Although it is of little commercial value, chaparral has a major role in the watershed cover of California, as it is found along the hills and lower mountain slopes throughout the state. Animals as well as plants help define the chaparral. Many species of wildlife have their own adaptations to drought and fire.

The climate of the chaparral region consists of mild winter temperatures with limited rainfall (12 to 24 in or 30 to 60 cm per year), which falls during a few intense winter storms. The summers are hot and accompanied by prolonged drought. From May to November there is usually no measurable rainfall other than a few scattered thunderstorms. It is during this period that brush fires – caused by humans or by natural factors – occur. This climate pattern is known as a Mediterranean-type, as it is similar to that found in the coastal areas surrounding the Mediterranean Sea.

These Mule deer (Odocoileus hemionus), typical chaparral animals, are moving along trails through the shrubby vegetation.

tosynthesis continues on a limited scale. Dormancy reduces the plant's need for water, a critical ingredient for photosynthesis and other metabolic processes. Dormancy also reduces the rate of gas exchange, cutting down the amount of water lost by evaporation.

The evergreen nature of the chaparral shrubs is an adaptation that allows the plants to take advantage of rainwater whenever it falls. Deciduous plants, in contrast, need to grow new leaves in the spring in order to take advantage of rainwater for active growth and photosynthesis. Despite the effectiveness of dormancy as a means of surviving drought, chaparral plants die back considerably during long periods of sustained drought. However, even if only one or two branches remain on a chaparral plant, it can recover when winter rains arrive.

To aid in the capture of water when it does fall, most chaparral shrubs have two sets of roots. One root system consists of a long tap root, which can absorb water from deep in the ground. The sec-

CORE FACTS

- The chaparral is a vegetation community found in California in the United States.
- The chaparral has mild winters and hot, dry summers, which are sometimes accompanied by periods of drought.
- Periodic brush fires rage through the chaparral.
- The chaparral vegetation and wildlife are adapted to cope with the drought and the fires.

CONNECTIONS

● Chaparral plants show many similarities to **DESERT** species. Both have adapted to cope with periods of drought.

● In **DORMANCY**, plant **METABOLISM** slows to the minimum needed to sustain life.

Adaptations to drought

The most distinctive characteristic of chaparral vegetation is the leaf. The leaves of chaparral plants are typically small and evergreen with a thick, waxy cuticle. This type of leaf is referred to as sclerophyllous. The small size reduces the amount of water that is lost from the leaf by evaporation. The waxy cuticle is another barrier against water loss. It also provides an effective defense against insects and other herbivores.

Most chaparral plants become dormant during the dry summer months (see DORMANCY). During this time, metabolic processes slow down, but pho-

THE ORIGIN OF THE TERM CHAPARRAL

The term chaparral comes from the Spanish word chaparro, which originally referred to a thicket of shrubby evergreen oaks. Later, the term was applied to dense thickets of brushland in general. In fact, a cowboy's chaparajos, or chaps, are the leather pant coverings worn when riding through shrub thickets such as chaparral. The term chaparral is also applied to the foothill vegetation of the Rocky Mountains in west central North America. This vegetation community should not be confused with Mediterranean-type chaparral, as the Rocky Mountain chaparral is summer growing and winter deciduous, whereas the more typical chaparral is evergreen, winter growing, and summer dormant.

ond root system has lateral roots, which run just under the surface of the soil. They capture rainwater before it can percolate down to the deeper soil layers.

Chaparral fires

Chaparral is often referred to as a "fire community" because of the fires that sweep through the chaparral every 10 to 40 years. The fast-burning fires can reach temperatures as high as 1290°F (700°C), burning up all the plant material on the surface.

Strange as it may seem, these periodic fires are beneficial to the chaparral. Fire removes dead plant material that has built up during the years of drought, converting the material into soil-building ash and releasing the minerals within it. Fire also opens up the vegetation, letting light reach the ground so that new growth can take place. Beneficial soil bacteria are far more abundant after a fire. Chaparral shrubs can resprout from the base following fire. In some species, where the seeds have tough coats, germination is stimulated by fire. Recurrent fires prevent the growth of large trees and so maintain the shrubby vegetation.

Chaparral animals

The chaparral also supports its own collection of wildlife. Large animals, such as Mule deer (*Odocoileus hemionus*) and coyotes (*Canis latrans*), move through the thick brush along trails. For small species, such as rodents, rabbits, and reptiles, the chaparral provides an effective cover against predators including the Red-tailed hawk (*Buteo jamaicensis*) and the Barn owl (*Tyto alba*).

Reptiles, such as coastal horned lizards (*Phrynosoma* spp.), alligator lizards (*Gerrhonotus* spp.), and Pacific rattlesnakes (*Crotalus* spp.), are very common. They are particularly abundant in open areas within the shrubbery, where they can bask in the sun and thermoregulate. (Reptiles rely on the temperature of the environment to keep their bodies at a constant temperature; see REPTILES). Snakes are an effective predator on rodents, able to move easily through the dense brush.

A number of bird species are found almost exclusively in the chaparral; examples are the wrentit (*Chamaea fasciata*), thrasher (*Toxosloma redivivum*), and the Vocal scrub jay (*Aphelocoma californica*). Most birds remain in the upper branches of the vegetation, but towhees (*Pipilo* spp.) and quails (*Callipepla* spp.) spend much of their time on the ground foraging for food. The more abundant mammals include Deer mice (*Peromyscus* spp.) and the Dusky-footed wood rats (*Neotoma* spp.). These rats build large and complex nests, which are often used by other smaller wildlife.

The wildlife of the chaparral is as much adapted to drought as is the vegetation. Many species can go without water for long periods. To avoid water loss and the intense summer heat of midday, most of the wildlife is only active at night, or in the early mornings and the late afternoons.

HUMANS IN THE CHAPARRAL

The chaparral has become a favorite place to build new homes and other developments, particularly in Southern California. Attracted by the gentle slopes, pretty views, and relatively inexpensive cost, entirely new communities have spread through the chaparral in just a few years.

The combination of chaparral and surburban homes has proved to be disastrous. The chaparral requires periodic fires to renew the soil and remove dead plant material. However, fire is a serious threat to homeowners, and all attempts are made to extinguish fires in neighboring chaparral when they flare up. Because the fires are extinguished and prevented from running their full course, thicker vegetation builds up. When a large fire does go out of control, the accumulation of dry material results in an extremely hot and fast-moving fire that can consume homes and entire communities in a matter of minutes.

In the last ten years, thousands of homes have been lost to raging fires in the chaparral in Southern California. Another unfortunate consequence of these hot fires is the destruction of chaparral plants, so that they cannot resprout from the remaining stumps, and the killing of the seeds within the soil. When the seasonal rains do come, mud slides are frequent, as the vegetation is no longer present to hold the soil in place. These mud slides provide an additional threat to homeowners and further hinder the recovery of the chaparral. More and more people are questioning the wisdom of building sizeable communities within the chaparral.

AT RISK

Chaparral animals are even adapted to survive fire. The smaller animals take refuge in underground burrows. Larger species, such as deer, can move quickly out of an area threatened by fire. After a fire, wildlife activities concentrate around newly opened areas, where the fast sprouting vegetation provides an abundant food supply.

K. HOSOUME/J. KAUFMANN

See also: BIOMES AND HABITATS.

Further reading:

World Wildlife Habitats. New York: Marshall Cavendish, 1992.

Chaparral vegetation is dominated by evergreen shrubs but in spring and early summer, when water is available, herbaceous species, such as this Monkey flower (Mimulus cardinalis), can be found. Other characteristic species include mariposas (Calochortus spp.), tidytips (Laya platyglossa), and shooting stars (Dodecatheon spp.).

CHEMOTHERAPY

Chemotherapy is the treatment of disease by chemicals or drugs, specifically the treatment of cancer

There are many popular concepts of chemotherapy. It has been seen as a sophisticated system of "magic bullets" that target cancer cells and obliterate them from the body, and as a very toxic sytem of poisons that make patients bald, weak, and nauseated. Both these ideas have some truth in them. While chemotherapy usually refers to the treatment of cancer by drugs, in its broadest sense it also refers to treatment of other diseases, particularly infections by bacteria, viruses, and parasites. However, the discussion that follows will focus on cancer chemotherapy. Antibiotics are covered in a separate entry (see ANTIBIOTICS).

Early chemotherapy

The first cancer drug, or chemotherapeutic agent, was discovered by accident following an explosion of mustard gas in Naples, Italy, during World War II. Soldiers exposed to the gas died when their lymph glands wasted away and the blood cells formed in the bone marrow disappeared. Researchers then decided to try a similar chemical, nitrogen mustard, to treat cancer of the lymphatic system. The first treatment took place at Yale University in 1943.

During the 1940s, American cancer researcher Charles Brenton Huggins discovered that hormones influence the growth of malignant tumors. His early research focused on the role of male sex hormones in prostate cancer. He recommended surgical removal of the hormone-producing glands (castration) along with administration of female sex hormones. Huggins later pioneered the use of diethylstilbestrol (DES), one of the first synthetic sex hormones, or steroids. DES was used as an alternative to castration in men suffering from prostate cancer. The drug was also used from the 1940s through the 1960s to prevent miscarriage, but was banned for that use after it was linked to vaginal cancer in patients' daughters. For demonstrating the link between hormones and cancer, Huggins was awarded the Nobel Prize for Physiology or Medicine in 1966.

Today, the development of chemotherapeutic agents focuses on understanding how cancer cells develop and how the drugs act on them.

CORE FACTS

- Chemotherapy usually refers to the treatment of cancer by drugs. However, it also encompasses the treatment of other diseases, such as bacterial and viral infections, and includes drugs such as antibiotics.
- Most chemotherapy drugs affect DNA or cell division.
- Chemotherapy drugs are often used in combination to avoid side effects and drug resistance.

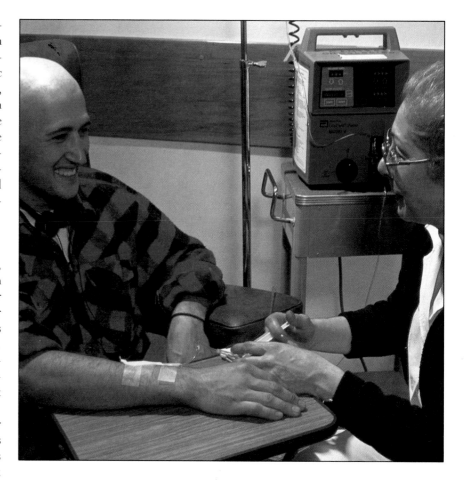

A cancer patient receiving chemotherapy. Drugs can be injected directly into arteries leading to a tumor. This allows high doses of chemotherapy to be given, while reducing the effects on normal tissues.

Tumor growth

Cancers usually develop from a single cell or a small group of cells in which the mechanisms for regulating growth are no longer working properly. As these "malignant" cells divide and increase in number, they generally form a small mass or tumor, which continues to grow as the cells divide. The amount of time it takes for each doubling in size is called the doubling time. Even in cancers that do not form tumors (such as leukemia), the number of malignant cells will increase progressively. However, in most cancers that are big enough to be detected, fewer than half of the cells are dividing.

Most chemotherapy drugs affect either DNA (deoxyribonucleic acid) synthesis or cell division (see DNA; CELLS). This makes them most effective against cells that are dividing since this is the only time that cells synthesize DNA. In some parts of the adult body, such as the ovaries and testes, bone marrow, and the hair follicles, the normal cells actively divide and may naturally divide more frequently than tumor cells in these locations. These

CONNECTIONS

- The study of the action of chemical substances, particularly drugs, on humans and animals is known as **PHARMACOLOGY**.

- Some cancer patients are able to reduce some of the side effects that chemotherapy can cause by using various types of **ALTERNATIVE MEDICINE**.

- Not only human diseases are treated by drugs. Chemotherapy, including antibiotics, can also be used to treat many **DISEASES OF ANIMALS**.

normal cells and cancer cells can die in two ways. First, a cell may undergo necrosis, in which loss of nutrients and oxygen simply causes it to "shut-down" the processes that keep it alive. Second, cells can undergo apoptosis, in which the cell actively synthesizes enzymes that destroy the cell's nucleus – the cell actually commits suicide. This happens as part of the normal development of the embryo as well as in the immune system of adults.

Apoptosis also takes place when the immune system attacks abnormal cells, such as cancer cells, as well as when some drugs are used to kill cancer cells.

Mechanisms of chemotherapy drugs

Chemotherapy drugs work by interfering with DNA synthesis and cell division at various different levels.

The synthesis of DNA can be blocked by drugs that inhibit the action of DNA polymerase, an enzyme that synthesizes new DNA strands. Other enzymes that may be inactivated are the topoisomerases, which affect the way the DNA helix twists. The DNA helix can also be inactivated by the drug cyclophosphamide, which may cause the two strands of the double helix to join together. Another drug, bleomycin, breaks DNA strands. Other drugs can block the synthesis of the purines and pyramidines, which are the building blocks of DNA and RNA. Mitosis, part of the process of cell division, can be blocked by drugs that interfere with the assembly of the microtubules that form the spindle (see CELLS).

Conversely, some tumors may rely on steroid hormones in the body to keep them alive and growing. In these cases, synthetic hormones can halt the growth of malignant tumors by attaching to hormone receptors in the cancer cells. A particularly effective drug in these circumstances is tamoxifen, which is similar to the female hormone estrogen. Tamoxifen seems to inhibit the growth of hormone-dependent breast cancer.

Combination therapy and new strategies

More than one drug is often used to kill tumors, and to avoid some of the problems of drug resistance that are sometimes a problem in cancer chemotherapy (see box above). Combination chemotherapy is so successful in the treatment of some tumors that the majority of patients with Hodgkin's disease (cancer of the lymphatic tissues in the lymph nodes and spleen) and some other lymphomas, certain leukemias, and cancer of the testis, now have a high cure rate.

Another way of using chemotherapy is to treat tumors first by surgery or radiation, and use chemotherapy afterwards, either to shrink the tumor further, or to prevent the cancer from spreading through the body (metastasis). This approach has been used with many types of cancer, and has been particularly successful in treating breast cancer.

DRUG RESISTANCE

One of the major problems in the chemotherapy of cancers is that the cells may become resistant to these drugs. Our understanding of the mechanisms of this resistance has improved and, as a result, is leading to improved treatment.

Gene amplification is one way in which tumor cells can become resistant to drugs. Extra copies of genes are produced and the protein products of these genes protect the cell from the effects of chemotherapy. For example, the drug methotrexate inhibits the enzyme that ultimately interferes with the ability of the cell to synthesize thymine (one of the nucleic acids that make up DNA). In cells that are resistant to methotrexate, many copies of the gene for this enzyme may be reproduced, so increasing the amount of the enzyme produced and overcoming the effects of the drug. Changes in the structure of the enzyme may also occur, so that it is no longer inhibited by methotrexate.

A CLOSER LOOK

One of the reasons why very high doses of chemotherapy drugs are so dangerous is that they can kill the cells in the bone marrow that produce blood cells. This often causes anemia, reduced numbers of white blood cells (responsible for immunity; see IMMUNE SYSTEMS) and damages the platelets (responsible for blood clotting; see BLOOD), usually leading to severe infections and bleeding. One strategy to avoid these problems is to give very high doses of chemotherapy, killing both the cancer cells and the bone marrow cells. Since this would, of course, be lethal to the patient, the treatment is followed by a bone marrow transplant. However, this remains a dangerous option that doctors consider very carefully before they using.

Although not drugs, antibodies are also used as a form of chemotherapy. Antibodies are proteins that the immune system produces in response to the presence of a foreign substance or marker (antigen) (see ANTIBODIES). Antibodies that are able to neutralize antigens on tumor cells can, in some cases, destroy the tumor cells. These antibodies can be produced in a test tube and then injected into the patient, or they can be produced by the patient's own immune system after injection with a preparation of the tumor antigens (tumor vaccine). This approach has been used in treating colon cancer and skin cancer.

The challenge for the future is to find a way to treat the many cancers that still show little or no response to chemotherapy. Unfortunately, these make up the great majority of cancers. At the same time, scientists continue to search for drugs that cause less damage to the noncancerous tissues of the body.

D. JACOBY

See also: ANTIBIOTICS; CANCER; CELLS; GENETICS; IMMUNE SYSTEMS.

Further reading:

Chemotherapy: What It Is: How It Helps. Atlanta, Georgia: American Cancer Society, 1993.